CREOLE GENTLEMEN

New World in the Atlantic World

Jack P. Greene and Amy Turner Bushnell, Series Editors

Tropical Versailles: Empire, Monarchy, and the Portuguese Royal Court in Rio de Janiero, 1808–1821
By Kirsten Schultz

Creole Gentlemen: The Maryland Elite, 1691–1776
By Trevor Burnard

CREOLE Gentlemen

THE MARYLAND ELITE, 1691–1776

TREVOR BURNARD

ROUTLEDGE

New York and London

Published in 2002 by
Routledge
29 West 35th Street
New York, NY 10001

Published in Great Britain in 2002 by
Routledge
11 New Fetter Lane
London EC4P 4EE

Routledge is an imprint of the Taylor & Francis Group

Printed in the United States of America on acid-free paper
Design and typography: Jack Donner

Library of Congress Cataloging-in-Publication Data

Burnard, Trevor G. (Trevor Graeme), 1961–
      Creole gentlemen : the Maryland elite, 1691–1776 / Trevor Burnard.
         p. cm.
      Includes bibliographical references and index.
      ISBN 0-415-93173-8 — ISBN 0-415-93174-6 (pbk.)
         1. Maryland—History—Colonial period, ca. 1600–1775. 2. Elite
(Social sciences)—Maryland—History—18th century. 3. Upper class—
Maryland—History—18th century. 4. Upper class—Maryland—Social
Conditions—18th century. 5. Upper class—Maryland—Economic
conditions—18th century. 6. Maryland—History—Social Conditions—
18th century. 7. Maryland—History—Economic conditions—18th century.
I. Title.
F184 .B89 2002
975.2'02—dc21   2001034992

CONTENTS

List of Abbreviations   vi

Acknowledgments   vii

1. *Problems and Perspectives*   1
   A Picture of the Maryland Elite

2. *A Gentleman's Competence*   21
   The Economic Ambitions of the Maryland Elite

3. *"A Species of Capital Attached*   61
   to Certain Mercantile Houses"
   Elite Debts and the Significance of Credit

4. *Patriarchy and Affection*   103
   The Demography and Character of Elite Families

5. *Arrows over Time*   139
   Elite Inheritance Practices

6. *The Rule of Gentlemen*   167
   Elite Political Involvement

7. *The Development of Provincial Consciousness*   205
   The Formation of Elite Identity

8. *Conclusion*   237
   Toward a History of Elites
   in the Eighteenth-Century British Empire

Appendix   265
   The Creation of the Elite Sample of Wealthy Marylanders

Index   271

LIST OF ABBREVIATIONS

AHR	American Historical Review
AM	Archives of Maryland (Baltimore, 1882–)
EcHR	Economic History Review
JAH	Journal of American History
JEH	Journal of Economic History
JIH	Journal of Interdisciplinary History
JSocH	Journal of Social History
JSH	Journal of Southern History
MdHM	Maryland Historical Magazine
MHR	Maryland Hall of Records
MHS	Maryland Historical Society
SLJ	Southern Literary Journal
TEV	Total Estate Value
VMHB	Virginia Magazine of History and Biography
WMQ	William and Mary Quarterly

ACKNOWLEDGMENTS

Creole Gentlemen has been a long time in the making. It began soon after I arrived in September 1983 from Dunedin, in the south of New Zealand, to take up doctoral studies at The Johns Hopkins University. Eventually, a version of *Creole Gentlemen*, much different to that presented here, was completed as a doctoral dissertation in early 1988, midway through my first year in my first permanent academic position at the University of the West Indies at Mona in Kingston, Jamaica. Revisions were begun and sporadically continued when I returned to New Zealand in 1989 to take up positions at the University of Waikato and at the University of Canterbury. The final version was completed in England at my current post at Brunel University in the autumn and winter of 2000–2001. My peregrinations between imperial centers and postcolonial peripheries has, I hope, given me a greater appreciation of what it meant to be a provincial citizen of an imperial state in the eighteenth century. My detours into seventeenth- and eighteenth-century Caribbean history have also given me a better insight into what was typical and unusual about the lives of moderately well off gentlemen at the edges of the Atlantic plantation world.

It gives me great pleasure at journey's end to thank the people who assisted me on this circuitous and often disrupted voyage. First, I wish to thank Jack Greene, who served as the advisor for the doctorate on which this book is loosely based. I could not have hoped for a better guide to colonial British America or a better dissertation advisor. He has continued to be enormously helpful—personally, professionally, and intellectually—in all of my travails since graduation. It is a great pleasure to be able to publish this work in his and Amy Bushnell's series with Routledge. Bill Freehling and John Pocock were also very helpful at The Johns Hopkins University in sharpening my arguments. The research for this book was mainly carried out at the Maryland Historical Society and, in particular, at the Maryland Hall of Records. It could not have been accomplished without the generous assistance of Lois Green Carr, who allowed me to use some of the research that she and others have generated and who allowed me to share some of her vast knowledge about Chesapeake history. Jean Russo was also extremely helpful and generous in providing me with access to her researches. Just as generous was Ed Papenfuse, with whom I commuted to Annapolis for most of a year, and who helped me in numerous ways both materially and intellectually. I also wish to thank the archivists at the Hall of Records for their assistance, especially Richard Richardson and Phoebe Jacobson. Much of the first draft of this book was completed in the pleasant environs of the Philadelphia Center for Early American Studies, where I benefited from the counsel of Richard Dunn, Mike Zuckerman, Ric Northrup, Donna Rilling, and Susan Manckiewicz. In Philadelphia, Alison Games not only forced me to improve my argument and especially my writing but also was of great material assistance at a crucial time.

My colleagues in Jamaica, New Zealand, and England have been very supportive of this project and understanding about its delays as I worked on projects on early Jamaica. My friends in the Australia and New Zealand American Studies Association have eased the difficulties of working on early American topics in the Antipodes by providing important fora where I could present and refine my work. Rhys Isaac, Shane White, John Salmond, and Peter Coleman have been especially helpful. Ken Morgan, Peter Cain, Huw Bowen, Peter Mancall, and Mike McDonnell have saved me from some errors through careful readings of part of the finished manuscript. I owe a particular debt of thanks to Christine Daniels, whose encouragement of this project has been constant and invaluable and whose detailed commentary on my work has given it whatever shape and cogency it has. Chris, more than anyone, deserves my thanks for enabling me to push this book to completion. I am also grateful to my editors at Routledge, New

York, Brendan O'Malley and Stefanie Forster, for their expeditious help in eliminating infelicities in the transformation of manuscript into published book.

As usual, my greatest thanks are to my family. My wife, Deborah, has lived with this book ever since we first met, at a wet and windy Wellington barbecue in 1989. Sensibly, she has been interested in more important things than rich white dead men in colonial America but without her it is difficult to see how this book could have been completed. I hope that she is pleased with the result, and that our children, Nicholas and Eleanor, may also, one day, find what their father did when he was not looking after them of some interest. Tommaso Astarita is not family but has been as close as a family member ever since we first met as incoming graduate students in the autumn of 1983 and ever supportive of this book and its author. I only wish that he finds this book as interesting as I have found his books on early modern southern Italy. The book is dedicated to my parents, Dorothy and Ray Burnard. Sadly, my father did not live to see this book finished, but without his and my mother's financial and emotional support over many miles and many years this book and this author would be much the poorer.

CHAPTER I

Problems and Perspectives
A Picture of the Maryland Elite

If only because of their importance in the American Revolution, their role in providing the ideology that shaped the Constitution, and their significance as the first leaders of the new nation, wealthy merchants and planters in the Chesapeake have never lacked admirers, critics, and chroniclers. Elite gentlemen dominated the economy and polity of the most prosperous region in the mainland British colonies, introduced slavery into North America, benefited from the emergent slave system, and bequeathed to posterity an image of high living, cultivation, and power. As the groups that commanded most influence and that gave tone and definition to their communities, elites were very important in colonial society.[1] Yet we still do not know all that much about them. Quite rightly, in the past two decades scholars writing on the colonial period have concentrated upon those members of society previously overlooked in traditional histories: servants, slaves, women, and poor planters.[2] Because of recent interest, much of the underlying social and economic structure of the region is now known. We need to look afresh at elites in the region in light of new knowledge regarding patterns of economic development, political life, family organization, population growth, and settlement.[3]

My aim in this study is to provide a portrait of wealthy men in one important area of the Chesapeake, Maryland, from the late seventeenth century, when a distinctive provincial elite began to emerge, to the third quarter of the eighteenth century, immediately before the American Revolution, when the elite was at the height of its power. To capture larger issues of economic, political, ideological, and demographic development, I have examined the composition of the elite, its social and economic attributes, and how these changed over time. A prosopographical analysis of 461 wealthy Marylanders provides the necessary database for such an analysis.

By analyzing the elite's economic activities, we can see how the elite moved away from occupational diversification toward increased specialization and toward increased commitment to planting. In addition, we can explore the degree to which members of the elite were enmeshed in credit-debt relationships both in the Chesapeake and in the transatlantic world, and the significance of those relationships. Through an examination of elite family relationships and inheritance practices, we can see how exclusive the elite was, can examine the character of elite relationships both in the family and outside the family, and can assess the extent to which wealthy men were able to separate themselves from other groups in society. An account of the elite in the public arena enables us to appreciate the extent and nature of wealthy Marylanders' involvement in political affairs and the success of these men in defining what it meant to be a colonial Marylander. How, for example, were elite conceptions of their role in the province received, and what problems did members of the elite face in their attempts to control the destiny of the colony and their fellow colonists? Moreover, how significant was elite consciousness of their position as wealthy provincials for the creation of a discernible colonial Maryland identity?

Explicit in the last chapter and conclusion and implicit in the whole work is the conviction that the Maryland elite needs to be understood in a transatlantic context. The Maryland elite defined itself not only in relationship to others in colonial society but also in relationship to the metropolis of Britain. Such self-definition was hardly surprising for native-born provincials within a large and growing empire. In this respect, wealthy Marylanders were similar to Creole elites in other parts of the British Empire and to provincial Britons and Irishmen. The fundamental differences between regions in British America were lessened by a growing awareness by elites that they defined what it meant to be a resident of a cultural province of Britain. This process was integrative in two respects. Each elite desired to replicate British society in the New World and was increasingly preoccupied with its British heritage. This preoccupation advanced as the New World was drawn more and more into the economic and social orbit of transatlantic relationships. Affluent and talented colonials eagerly defined themselves as English gentlemen. They aped English manners, were anxious to receive the latest fashions of London, and endeavored to enjoy the benefits of high society in provincial centers. This mimetic impulse among colonial elites created a general standardization of procedures, tastes, and assumptions as early American society became anglicized.[4]

The inherent tensions within this anglicizing process and the inability of individual members of the Maryland elite to become completely anglicized united the Maryland elite. This process was not peculiar to them. Creole elites in the eighteenth century did not transform themselves into English gentlemen. In their attitudes to wealth, their inheritance practices, their life-styles, and especially in their participation in a social system based on slavery that had no precise counterpart in Britain, wealthy colonials differed from their counterparts in Britain. British Americans were well aware of these differences and of their provincial status, which by definition made them inferior to gentry in metropolitan Britain. At first they endeavored to lessen the contradictions and ambivalences that were attached to provincialism. Gradually, they came to accept and even applaud provincialism. Eventually, the elite developed a provincial consciousness: shared social, economic, and political characteristics and a commitment to these characteristics and to their native land. Although this analysis does not extend to the Revolution, the Chesapeake elite's prominent role in that conflict can be understood only by examining the growth of provincial consciousness within the elite from the late seventeenth to the mid-eighteenth century.[5]

Increasing settlement in tidewater Maryland during the colonial period led to alterations but not complete transformations of the Chesapeake landscape. Trees and water dominated the landscape as much in 1724 when Hugh Jones described the Chesapeake as "a perfect Forest, except where the woods are cleared for Plantations" as they did when the earliest settlers first ventured into the region.[6] These tidewater lands were low and level. Large tidal rivers deep enough to accommodate any vessel of the day punctuated the landscape. Rich lands, abundant rainfall, and a climate favorable to the growing of agricultural crops were accompanied by large rivers ideal for transportation.[7] Consequently, early settlers concentrated on the production of a staple crop, tobacco, which they exported to Europe. The colony was soon pulled into the orbit of Atlantic trade and prospered.[8]

Beneath the underlying continuity of the physical landscape in colonial Maryland there were, of course, regional variations and changes over time. Further inland and north of the prime tobacco land of the western shore were the rolling hills and lush valleys of the piedmont, to which large numbers of settlers moved, from older regions of the Chesapeake, from Britain, from Pennsylvania and Delaware, and, increasingly, from Germany. As settlement expanded, some areas of the Chesapeake, notably the piedmont and northern regions of the Eastern Shore, moved from solely producing tobacco to a more diversified agricultural economy including grain as well as tobacco. Further, as the population grew from 26,200 in 1690, 43,000 in 1710, 141,000 in 1755, and to 248,000 in 1780, large areas of land were cleared and cultivated and small towns emerged. Until the 1770s the most prominent small town was Annapolis, when Baltimore overtook it in size if not altogether in importance.

Changes in landscape and the growth of settlement were exceeded by changes in social and economic organization. For the first half-century of its existence, Maryland was populated largely by single, white, male immigrants from Britain. Many of these immigrants were indentured servants who hoped to survive their terms of servitude to tobacco planters and themselves obtain land and a living, precarious as it often was, from the growing of the "stinking Weede." Maryland was a rough, rude frontier community, characterized by a relative equality of wealth, rudimentary standards of living, and considerable economic opportunity. If not the best country for a poor man, it certainly was a remarkably egalitarian society compared to Britain. Small planters as a consequence were dominant economically and politically.[9]

Two developments beginning in the late seventeenth century destroyed small planter dominance, leading to the rule of wealthy merchant-planters. Increased settlement, a decline in servant immigration, and the workings of time led to a largely native-born white population. Native-born Creoles, many of whom had greater access to land and wealth than immigrants and recently freed servants, soon came to monopolize political power. They quickly separated themselves economically and socially from the mass of small planters. This process was facilitated and accelerated by the transition from a labor system based on white servants to one primarily reliant on imported African slaves. Native-born children with substantial inheritances were more easily able to acquire slaves (who were considerably more expensive than servants) than were poor whites. Slavery soon became very profitable. Very quickly, a planter who owned slaves could repay his initial investment, increase the profits of his estate, and provide a handsome inheritance for his children.[10]

The Maryland elite was the beneficiary of these intertwined developments. From the abundant public records in the Maryland Hall of Records, I have isolated all those men who left over £650 (with pounds held constant at 1700 values) in personal assets in the inventories of four representative counties, Anne Arundel and Baltimore on the Western Shore and Talbot and Somerset on the Eastern Shore. The reasons for choosing wealth as the primary determinant for elite status and the reasons for stipulating £650 as a minimal qualification for elite entry are discussed in the Appendix. Readers interested in the methodological assumptions undergirding this work should look at this section first. It helps to explain what to many will be an odd choice, favoring wealth (and, in the context of colonial Maryland, considerable wealth at that) as the sine qua non qualification for entry into the elite rather than achievement of high political office or ownership of substantial numbers of slaves.

The four counties chosen provide a good cross section of the social and economic diversity of colonial Maryland. Anne Arundel was the wealthiest county in the region with a reputation for producing abundant yields of the highest quality tobacco, a reputation that still held into the nineteenth century.[11] It was a classic tobacco county with a numerous and wealthy elite and a large slave population. Moreover, with the capital of Maryland, Annapolis, within its boundaries, it was the seat of government, the locus of colonial culture, and the major center of commerce in the province until the rise of Baltimore in the last half of the eighteenth century.[12] Its neighbor, Baltimore County, was settled later and was more economically diverse than Anne Arundel, with less tobacco, more wheat and corn, and, after 1750, a considerable number of iron manufacturing industries and a growing urban area in which mercantile activity was directed less toward tidewater Maryland than toward the rich backcountry and Philadelphia.[13]

Talbot County on the Eastern Shore shared with Anne Arundel easy access to the water routes that facilitated both settlement and the production of tobacco. Initial dependence on tobacco lessened over time, especially after 1750, when grain farming became important. Planters in Talbot County, however, never abandoned tobacco entirely. Grain farming complemented the production of tobacco leading to a diversified market economy. Although there were fewer wealthy people in Talbot County than in Baltimore and Anne Arundel, the county was the home of some of the most prominent families in the whole province. These families were remarkably cohesive and controlled the affairs of the county to a greater extent than any other elite in Maryland. Urban development was limited, and the county remained rural, homogeneous, and oligarchal well into the nineteenth century.[14]

Somerset County was even less touched by urban sophistication than Talbot County. Somerset formed a counterpoint to the other three counties because it remained a rural backwater, only marginally drawn into the Atlantic trade network. Full of swampy, poor quality land, Somerset was one of the poorest areas in the whole Chesapeake tidewater. Like all other areas in the seventeenth-century Chesapeake it concentrated on tobacco as its main crop, although it supplemented tobacco with shipping lumber and livestock to the West Indies. In the eighteenth century it diversified further, moving into the production of corn. Yet it remained poor, with a larger percentage of its population dying poor and a smaller proportion attaining elite status than elsewhere in Maryland.[15]

Thus, the four counties provide a wide cross section of colonial Maryland society, enabling us to examine the elite in a variety of settings, from wealthy Anne Arundel to backward Somerset, and in a variety of economies from the mercantile milieu of Baltimore and Annapolis to the tobacco regions of Anne Arundel and the grain areas of Baltimore and the Eastern Shore. Nevertheless, this study does not capture all of the diversity of colonial Maryland. Certainly, the inclusion of a southern Western Shore county with a sizable and wealthy Catholic population such as St Mary's County or the late settled Frederick County with its large German component would probably have altered some of this study's conclusions, perhaps deemphasizing the ethnic and cultural homogeneity of the Maryland elite. It is unlikely, however, that the inclusion of another county would alter substantially the major arguments presented here. Very few people in the backcountry acquired the amount of wealth necessary for inclusion in this study, and studies of the lower Western Shore by Lois Green Carr, Lorena Walsh, and Bayly Marks suggest that religion was less important than the establishment of a flourishing tobacco economy in determining social patterns in that region (Tables 1.1–1.3).[16]

From a total of 6,410 people who went through probate between 1691 and 1776, 461 men left personal estates over £650. The majority of Marylanders who left inventories were poor: 54 percent of decedents left inventoried wealth below £100 and a further 20 percent had estates worth between £101 and £225. Some of this group may have owned land or labor but seldom would

Table 1.1   Wealth Distribution in Maryland Inventories (Four Counties), 1691–1776[a]

TEV (£)	1 (N)	2 (%)	3 (%)	4 (%)	5 (%)
1–50	2399	37	37	4	4
51–100	1236	19	57	6	9
101–225	1301	20	77	13	22
226–400	649	10	87	12	35
401–649	364	6	93	12	47
650+	461	7	100	54	100

[a] 1 number of probated estates; 2 percentage of total inventories; 3 cumulative percentage of total inventories; 4 percentage of total wealth; 5 cumulative percentage of total wealth.

Source: Inventories and Accounts, Inventories, *MHR*.

Table 1.2 Changes in Wealth Distribution over Time:
Percentage of Total Inventories by Wealth Level

TEV (£)	Pre-1708	1709–25	1726–42	1743–59	1760+
1–50	48	49	36	32	29
51–100	20	20	20	20	18
101–225	18	18	20	22	22
226–400	7	6	11	12	13
401–649	4	3	6	7	8
650+	4	5	7	8	10

Source: Inventories and Accounts, Inventories, *MHR*.

Table 1.3 Changes in Wealth Distribution over Time:
Percentage of Total Wealth Held by Wealth Level

TEV	Pre-1708	1709–25	1726–42	1743–59	1760+
1–50	8	7	3	3	2
51–100	10	9	5	5	4
101–225	19	17	11	13	11
226–400	15	12	12	14	12
401–649	14	7	11	16	13
650+	36	48	58	50	58

Source: Inventories and Accounts, Inventories, *MHR*.

have owned much of either and would certainly have found it
impossible to do much more than eke out a marginal and precarious existence as laborers or tenant farmers. Certainly they would
have been unable to accumulate substantial assets that they could
pass to their heirs. As Maryland became more prosperous in the
eighteenth century, however, the proportion of the population that
was poor declined and the proportion that was affluent increased.
Whereas two-thirds of inventories probated between 1691 and
1708 were below £100 and 85 percent were below £225, the
respective percentages declined to 47 percent and 69 percent for
inventories probated between 1760 and 1776. Mean estate value
also more than doubled in that period, rising from £151 to £333.

Consequently, the numbers of rich men and their proportion within the total population increased notably over time. Very few men died in the seventeenth century with estates worth more than £650. Only 37 estates between 1691 and 1708 qualified for membership in this sample. Nearly five times as many estates could be classified as elite between 1760 and 1776, and the proportion of elite estates in the total inventoried population more than doubled to nearly 10 percent. The number of wealthy Marylanders continually increased over the course of the eighteenth century. This rise in white per capita wealth was the result of the improvement of tidewater lands; price increases in agricultural commodities, especially for tobacco after 1750; and higher productivity arising out of the replacement of an African-born slave population with one that was native-born. Rises in white per capita wealth were particularly evident at higher wealth levels and resulted in heightened if not excessive wealth inequality.[17]

Although the numbers of rich men increased over time, individual elite worth did not increase. After rising to a high of £2,257 for elite members dying between 1726 and 1742, the average elite estate declined to below £2,000 for wealthy Marylanders dying after 1742. Median elite wealth followed the same pattern. After increasing from £1,036 for elite members dying before 1708 to £1,314 for those dying between 1726 and 1742, median elite wealth declined to £1,124 for decedents after 1760. Moreover, the number of large estates (over £2,500 in personal property) did not increase at the same pace as the growth of the elite as a whole. There were 36 estates worth over £2,500 before 1743 and 46 estates worth that much in a larger elite population dying after 1742. These figures suggest relatively open entry into the elite. In a society moving from a frontier to a settled existence, the wealth of well-established inheritors should have increased dramatically from generation to generation.

Nevertheless, even though the ranks of the very rich did not increase as much as might have been expected in the general prosperity of the late colonial period, wealth in Maryland did become more concentrated over time. What this shows, however, is that the wealthy became more numerous and prosperity become more widespread rather than the ocurrence of fundamental changes in wealth distribution. Before 1708, estates valued at over £650 accounted for just over one-third of total probated wealth. By 1760–1776 58 percent of inventoried wealth was concentrated in the hands of the 10 percent of the population that left estates worth over £650. Although wealth inequality did increase, the growth in the number of Marylanders who attained a comfortable sufficiency was more important. Between 1760 and 1776 over 30 percent of decedents left inventories worth over £225—a level of wealth some steps removed from poverty, indicating the ownership of both land and labor.[18] At the same time, the percentage of very poor estates, those under £50, shrank to below 30 percent, a dramatic reversal from the late seventeenth century, when nearly half the estates probated were of very poor people (Table 1.2).

As wealth levels in Maryland rose, so too did the likelihood that the wealthiest Marylanders would be native born. In the eighteenth century, few immigrants became wealthy unless they had arrived with substantial capital or family connections.[19] In the

Table 1.4 Principal Characteristics of Maryland Elite over Time

	Pre-1708	1709–25	1726–42	1743–59	1760+	Total
Generational status (%)						
Immigrant	69	39	28	25	9	25
Native born	31	61	72	76	92	75
Elite father	64	81	64	56	55	58
Ethnic origin (%)						
English/Welsh	89	94	92	91	91	91
Scottish	4	2	4	6	6	5
Irish	4	4	3	4	3	3
Other	4	0	1	0	1	1
Religion (%)						
Anglican	63	69	72	75	84	77
Quaker	31	21	26	19	10	18
Presbyterian	3	6	0	6	5	3
Catholic	3	4	2	1	1	2

Source: Probate Records, *MHR*; Edward C. Papenfuse et al., *Biographical Dictionary of Maryland Legislators, 1635–1789*, 2 Vols. (Baltimore and London, 1979 and 1985); various genealogical works.

seventeenth century, many of the early elite, as one would expect in a frontier society, were immigrants. Over half of the sample dying before 1726 and two-thirds of those dying before 1708 were immigrants. But native-born Marylanders soon came to predominate, and the percentage of wealthy Marylanders who were immigrants declined to less than 9 percent after 1759. In the late seventeenth century, it was still possible for an indentured servant long resident in Maryland to gain sufficient wealth to rise into the ranks of the rich and powerful. Nicholas Gassaway, for example, arrived as a servant in 1649 or 1650, rapidly acquired land and wealth, and ended his life as a legislator with a total estate value (TEV) of £1,459. By the eighteenth century, immigrants who achieved elite status tended to have high status on arrival. Increasingly, immigrants who became elite were men like Samuel Chamberlaine, a Liverpool merchant of high status who married almost immediately into a wealthy family on reaching Maryland and who was appointed a justice of the peace (J.P.) in Talbot County in 1723, two years after his arrival in the country.

The native born soon came to outnumber immigrants within the elite, as in society as a whole. By 1760 over 90 percent of the elite were native born, with two-thirds being at least the third generation of their family in the colony. It is possible to determine the backgrounds of a majority of the native-born elite. A sizable but hardly overwhelming proportion replicated their father's positions in society: 189 men were the sons of elite fathers, with 72 being the sons of legislators. If we combine these 189 men with the 48 immigrants who had high status on arrival in Maryland, and the 17 decedents who did not have elite fathers but who did have elite grandfathers, then 55 percent of the elite came from high status backgrounds.[20]

These figures do not mean that elite members who were not from elite backgrounds were originally poor. Nearly a third of wealthy Marylanders whose fathers' wealth is known came from the middling ranks of Maryland society. The fathers of these men left between £225 and £400 at death, a wealth level implying the ownership of several slaves and a moderate-sized plantation. It is not surprising that a percentage of men from economically respectable if not wealthy backgrounds would become wealthy: growing prosperity would inevitably propel some men of moderate

wealth into the ranks of the genuinely well-off. Equally not surprising, only a small number of the very rich were native-born men
whose fathers left estates below £225. Over time the proportion
of the elite from lowly backgrounds declined from 22 percent in
the late seventeenth and early eighteenth centuries to 14 percent
immediately before the Revolution. Entry into the elite became
more difficult over time for men without inherited wealth. For men
from middling wealth (fathers leaving between £225 and £650) no
decline in opportunity occurred. In fact, their numbers in the elite
increased over time. Even if a recognizable native-born gentry class
had emerged in Maryland by the middle of the eighteenth century,
that gentry class remained, as Charles Steffen has pointed out,
characterized by "a remarkable degree of openness, fluidity and
impermanence."21

Whether they were native born or immigrants to the colony,
most elite members shared one common characteristic. The Mary-
land elite was overwhelmingly English in ethnic background. Of
389 men whose paternal heritage can be ascertained, 352 were of
English descent, 19 were Scots, 12 were Irishmen, and 3 were
Welshmen. Just three men were not British: Mareen Duvall, a
French Huguenot; Christian Geist, who was Dutch; and Barnet
Holtzinger, who was German. Culturally homogeneous, the elite
also shared similar religious orientations. Despite the fact that
Maryland had been founded as a Catholic refuge, the vast majority of the elite in these four counties were Protestant with a substantial portion being Anglican.22 Just six elite members were
Catholic, four of whom died before 1726. Quakers—18 percent
of the elite—were the only significant religious minority. Over
time, Anglican predominance increased so that 84 percent of
wealthy Marylanders who died between 1760 and 1776 and
whose religion is known were Anglicans. Undoubtedly the percentage was higher because it is likely that most of those whose
religion is unknown also belonged to the Church of England.
Quakers declined appreciably after mid-century. After 1760, the
percentage of elite members who were Quakers declined to under
10 percent. Nevertheless, some of the oldest and wealthiest families in Maryland, such as the Chews, the Dickinsons, and the Galloways, stayed Quakers. To a degree, Quakers differed from the
broad body of the elite, most obviously in the fact that their
refusal to swear oaths denied them political office after 1689, but

also by the usual Quaker practice of marrying within their own community. In most respects, however, Quakers were indistinguishable from other elite members. Thus, except in politics, from which Catholics and Quakers were excluded, the impact of religion as a factor in determining elite behavior was slight. Indeed, as ministers complained, the elite's principal religious problem was not related to what type of religion they practiced but was their general weakness of commitment to religion.

Readers should be aware of what this book does not cover, as well as what it does cover. It does not deal with the role of the elite in hastening the American Revolution or concern itself with its fate during that conflict. Such issues are well covered elsewhere.[23] The gentlemen whose lives are studied all died as subjects of the British Crown and, as far as can be discerned, as loyal members of the British Empire. Although it is difficult not to anticipate the great conflict that was to come, I want to examine the elite purely as a colonial elite, part of a growing transatlantic empire where elite comparisons were made directly with Britain and other plantation colonies. Second, the important question of the relationship of wealthy Marylanders with their slaves will be touched on only tangentially rather than directly. Slavery touched every aspect of wealthy gentlemen's lives: slaves were the basis of their wealth, the source of much of their power, and the objects of their desires and greatest fears. The significance of slavery should be apparent throughout the following discussion, even when not directly addressed. The nature of master/slave interactions deserves a treatment by itself. Fortunately, recent work on the Chesapeake has explicitly concerned itself with these topics. I would not wish to duplicate such scholarship here.[24] Finally, although this a work explicitly concerned with gender—the title indicates that concern—it is one-sided in its concern. It concentrates on the activities of men and the development of a male public culture. Women are not absent from this story—they can hardly be when maleness is so often defined as a contrast to femaleness, and talking about family and inheritance without discussing the role of women is clearly nonsense—but they do not play the lead roles. I hope, however, that people interested in women in the colonial Chesapeake will be able to use some of the evidence marshaled here about their menfolk to flesh out insights derived from the recent flowering of

interest in women and gender history in British-American plantation societies.[25] Understanding what it meant to be a Creole and
what it meant to be a gentleman in a provincial society on the edge
of the Atlantic Ocean in the late seventeenth and the eighteenth
century may be useful in exploring other topics and questions in
colonial British-American history.

The elite that emerges from this study is distinctive in several
respects. First, it was a colonial elite as much as a Creole elite, tied
into the increasingly integrated Atlantic world of the late seventeenth and eighteenth centuries. Nevertheless, its social and economic position reflected the intermediate status that Maryland—a
true Middle Colony—had within the Atlantic system and especially within British-American New World plantation societies.
Wealthy Marylanders were part of the plantation system and
indeed one of principal contentions in this study is that they
increasingly redefined themselves as a planter class during the
eighteenth century. But they were marginal players in the Atlantic
world compared with the great planters who dominated societies
farther south and in the British West Indies. The Maryland elite
should not be taken as altogether typical of planter elites in the
New World. They were not especially wealthy—the £650 required
here for entry into the top 5–10 percent of wealth holders in
Maryland would have been insufficient to attain even average
wealth in lowcountry South Carolina or Jamaica. Nor were they
as committed to slavery or to plantation agriculture as were elites
farther south. Relatively few wealthy Marylanders owned substantial slave labor forces of 50 or more slaves. More importantly,
they combined slave ownership with a multitude of other labor
arrangements, such as indentured servitude, free wage labor, hired
slave labor, and convict labor, that marked them as closer to
wealthy farmers in northern colonies than to planters in southern
and West Indian planter colonies. They resembled northern farmers also in the type of crops that they grew, increasingly combining
the staple production of tobacco with the production of cereals.
By the Revolution, Maryland was as oriented toward the urban
and grain-growing states of Delaware and Pennsylvania as it was
to the rural, staple-producing states of Virginia and the Carolinas.
Maryland came to resemble its northern neighbors even more
following the Revolution as Baltimore grew to become a major

seaboard city, reflecting the economic penetration of Maryland by Philadelphia's merchants and an enlarging of the Middle Colonies region. Moreover, Marylanders, especially in Baltimore, reexamined their devotion to slavery without abandoning their devotion to slavery as an institution. The state was being transformed from a slave society into a society with slaves and with a notably large free black population.[26]

Yet if Maryland became less and less southern, it did not become entirely northern either. In particular, wealthy Marylanders seldom displayed the full devotion to industrial capitalism and entrepreneurship evinced by northern merchants. Throughout the eighteenth century, wealthy Marylanders moved from being nascent entrepreneurs, devoted to profit and willing to make money in a variety of ways, to becoming a cautious, risk-averse planter class, burdened by little debt and more eager for a "competency" than for great fortunes. As will be discussed in Chapters 2 and 3, wealthy Marylanders eschewed risk in favor of becoming efficient managers of fixed resources and became increasingly ambivalent about their relation to capitalism. In abandoning trade and avoiding risk, wealthy Marylanders were responding to changes in the organization of Atlantic trade that increasingly excluded them from active participation and were demonstrating through their actions that maintaining gentility was more important than maximizing profit. Such policies made perfect sense given their economic circumstances, but had a profound impact on Maryland's social and economic development.

Achieving genteel status was one of the primary forces driving elite culture in the eighteenth century. Gentility, as defined in the Chesapeake, was less a matter of birth (though that was not unimportant) than of behavior—something closer to what historians have termed respectability, the assertion of a person's moral worth as an individual seen through genteel behavior, than to traditional British notions, where gentility was more closely linked with birth and status.[27] Wealthy Marylanders sought to be recognized as genteel in order to demonstrate to themselves and to others that they were cultivated men, deserving of their elevated position within Maryland society and equally deserving of the attention of metropolitan arbiters of fashion. Adopting gentility as a value worked better in securing the former approbation than the latter. Within

Maryland, gentility served a particularly important purpose in providing the elite with a justification for their superiority over common people. It encompassed traditional British upper-class values such as politeness, liberality, sociability, hospitality, and stewardship. It also embraced new concepts such as wit, joviality, taste, and fraternity. Gentility was useful also in providing a means whereby the elite could regulate entry into their ranks. It provided a mode of behavior that separated gentlemen from ordinary folk but that was not resented by the ambitious newly affluent who also aspired to gentility. If a person could demonstrate gentility through wealth, status, and especially behavior, then that person—even an outsider or a newcomer—could be easily incorporated into elite society. Adherence to gentility as a primary value enabled Maryland gentlemen to steer a careful course between the Scylla of undue openness to arrivistes, who might diminish the prestige and authority of the elite, and the Charybdis of excessive exclusiveness, which would breed resentment among those excluded and exacerbate distances between social classes. Contrary to other accounts of the Chesapeake gentry's associational behavior, I argue that wealthy gentlemen in Maryland neither retreated into domesticity nor formed themselves into exclusive clans. Their ranks were always accessible to people of talent and breeding and the elite was generally outward looking, expansive, and inclusive.[28]

Gentility helps us to a certain extent to explain the enduring power of elite authority in a society in which authority was always fragile, deference was incomplete, and obedience to established rule was always conditional. The almost exclusive dominance of the elite over political power was seldom challenged from below during the period under study, despite the fact that associational patterns were largely horizontal rather than vertical. The separate social strata—the genteel, the common, the propertyless, and the enslaved—did not often mix together. The elite, in particular, were far from being socially inclusive and were seldom concerned with developing extensive patronage links between themselves and other social strata. They sought out people like themselves, both to marry and also to socialize with and do business. Society was far from being homogeneous, organically unified, and consensual. Each group stuck mainly to its own kind.

Nevertheless, small freeholders, who were the majority of the electorate, acquiesced to elite rule rather than asserting their own power. They did so not so much because the elite skillfully employed patronage or because the elite exploited whites' fears of blacks, but because small freeholders tacitly accepted deference as a normal condition in politics and agreed with most elite policies. Gentility aided this process, as it was generally agreed that government should be reserved for enlightened and capable men, in short gentlemen "of Ability and Fortune" set off from their fellows by superior education and clear and refined ideas and conduct, and who successfully adhered to genteel values such as moderation, humility, integrity, and generosity.[29] But freeholders did not abstain from political involvement altogether or give the elite *carte blanche* to rule as they pleased. When they disagreed with large planters, as they did in the 1730s and 1740s over the issue of tobacco regulation, they made their displeasure known and did not hesitate to use their political power. Thus, allegiance, even in a deferential society, was conditional on the continued agreement between the elite and freeholders about established goals. Even within this consensus, however, tensions existed. Poor whites by no means always acquiesced to elite authority and proved to be persistent irritants to the elite-dominated order. Elite members were keenly aware that these tensions existed and that vigilant and responsible government was necessary to prevent considerable social disorder. Responsible government meant a responsible and genteel elite. Colonial leaders and defenders of established hierarchical social relations were always concerned with preventing elite delinquencies in the performance of their duties. Unfortunately, the often self-indulgent Chesapeake elite was frequently irresponsible, sometimes to the extent of breaching elite cohesion. Thus, not only were there definite limits to the acceptance of elite rule but the elite was neither as monolithic nor as united in the preservation of its own power as one might expect in a genuinely oligarchical and deferential society.

NOTES

1. Jack P. Greene and J.R. Pole, "Reconstructing British-American Colonial history: An Introduction," in Jack P. Greene and J.R. Pole (eds.), *Colonial British America* (Baltimore: Johns Hopkins University Press, 1984), 15.
2. Surveys of the now vast literature on the colonial Chesapeake include Thad W. Tate, "The Seventeenth-Century Chesapeake and Its Modern Historians," in Thad W. Tate and David L. Ammerman (eds.), *The Chesapeake in*

the Seventeenth Century: Essays on Anglo-American Society (Chapel Hill: University of North Carolina Press, 1979), 3–50; Allan Kulikoff, "The Colonial Chesapeake: Seedbed of Antebellum Culture?," *JSH*, XLV (1979), 513–40; Anita H. Rutman, "Still Planting the Seeds of Hope: The Recent Literature of the Early Chesapeake Region," *VMHB*, 95 (1987), 1–24; and Lois Green Carr, Philip D. Morgan, and Jean B. Russo, "Introduction," in Lois Green Carr, Philip D. Morgan, and Jean B. Russo (eds.), *Colonial Chesapeake Society* (Chapel Hill: University of North Carolina Press, 1988), 1–46.

3. For recent works on the Chesapeake elite, see Albert H. Tillson, Jr., *Gentry and Common Folk: Political Culture on a Virginia Frontier, 1740–1789* (Lexington: University Press of Kentucky, 1991); Kathleen M. Brown, *Good Wives, Nasty Wenches, and Anxious Patriarchs: Gender, Race, and Power in Colonial Virginia* (Chapel Hill: University of North Carolina Press, 1996); Kenneth Lockridge, "Colonial Self-Fashioning: Paradoxes and Pathologies in the Construction of Genteel Identity in Eighteenth-Century America," in Ronald Hoffman, Mechal Sobel, and Frederika J. Teute (eds.), *Through a Glass Darkly: Reflections on Personal Identity in Early America* (Chapel Hill: University of North Carolina Press, 1997), 274–339; and Michal J. Rozbicki, *The Complete Colonial Gentleman: Cultural Legitimacy in Plantation America* (Charlottesville: University of Virginia Press, 1998).

4. Jack P. Greene, *Pursuits of Happiness: The Social Development of Early Modern British Colonies and the Formation of American Culture* (Chapel Hill: University of North Carolina Press, 1988), 93–100; and T.H. Breen, "An Empire of Goods: The Anglicization of Colonial America, 1690–1776," *Journal of British Studies*, XXV (1986), 467–99.

5. For a similar interpretation, see Michal J. Rozbicki, "The Curse of Provincialism: Negative Perceptions of the Colonial American Gentry," *JSH*, LXIII (1997), 727–52.

6. Hugh Jones, *The Present State of Virginia from whence is Inferred a Short View of Maryland and North Carolina* (1724), Richard L. Morton (ed.) (Chapel Hill: University of North Carolina Press, 1956), 75. For alterations in the early Chesapeake landscape, see James Horn, *Adapting to a New World: English Society in the Seventeenth-Century Chesapeake* (Chapel Hill: University of North Carolina Press, 1994), 121–200.

7. Arthur P. Middleton, *Tobacco Coast: A Maritime History of the Chesapeake* (Newport News, Va.: Mariners' Museum, 1953). For the ecology of the American South, see Timothy H. Silver, *A New Face on the Countryside: Indians, Colonists, and Slaves in South Atlantic Forests, 1500–1800* (Cambridge: Cambridge University Press, 1990).

8. Paul G.E. Clemens, *The Atlantic Economy and Colonial Maryland's Eastern Shore: From Tobacco to Grain* (Ithaca, NY: Cornell University Press, 1980).

9. Tate and Ammerman (eds.), *The Chesapeake in the Seventeenth Century*; Gloria L. Main, *Tobacco Colony: Life in Early America, 1650–1720* (Princeton, NJ: Princeton University Press, 1982); and Lois Green Carr, Lorena S. Walsh, and Russell R. Menard, *Robert Cole's World: Agriculture and Society in Early Maryland* (Chapel Hill: University of North Carolina Press, 1991).

10. David W. Jordan, *Foundations of Representative Government in Maryland 1632–1715* (Cambridge: Cambridge University Press, 1987), 141–82; Clemens, *Atlantic Economy*, 29–40; Bernard Bailyn, "Politics and Social Structure in Virginia," in James M. Smith (ed.), *Seventeenth Century America: Essays in Colonial History* (Chapel Hill: University of North Carolina

Press, 1959), 90–115; Edmund Morgan, *American Slavery-American Freedom: The Ordeal of Colonial Virginia* (New York: W. W. Norton, 1975), Chapters 14–17; Russell R. Menard, "From Servants to Slaves: The Transformation of the Chesapeake Labor System," *Southern Studies*, XVI (1977), 315–90; and Allan Kulikoff, *Tobacco and Slaves: The Development of Southern Cultures in the Chesapeake, 1680–1800* (Chapel Hill: University of North Carolina Press, 1986), 37–43. The Maryland labor system never became as reliant on slavery as did plantation societies further south and in the Caribbean. For discussions of the continuing importance of tenancy and wage labor in Maryland, see, inter alia, Christine Daniels, "'Getting his [or her] Livelihood': Free Workers in Slave Anglo-America, 1675–1810," *Agricultural History*, 71 (1997), 125–61; and Steven Sarson, "Landlessness and Tenancy in Early National Prince George's County, Maryland," *WMQ*, LVII (2000), 569–98.

11. J.T. Ducatel, "Outlines of the Physical Geography of Maryland, Embracing Its Prominent Geographical Features," *Transactions of the Maryland Academy of Sciences and Literature*, I (1837), 33. An important survey of the economies of the various tobacco-raising regions of the Chesapeake is Lorena S. Walsh, "Summing the Parts: Implications for Estimating Chesapeake Output and Income Subregionally," *WMQ*, LVI (1999), 53–94.

12. Carville V. Earle, *The Evolution of a Tidewater Settlement System: All Hallow's Parish, Maryland, 1650–1783* (Chicago: University of Chicago Press, 1975); Edward C. Papenfuse, Jr., *In Pursuit of Profit: The Annapolis Merchants in the Era of the American Revolution* (Baltimore: Johns Hopkins University Press, 1975); and Nancy Baker, "Annapolis, Maryland, 1695–1730," *MdHM*, 81, (1986), 191–209.

13. Clarence P. Gould, "The Economic Causes of the Rise of Baltimore: Johns Hopkins University Press," in *Essays Presented to Charles McLean Andrews by his Students* (New Haven: Yale University Press, 1931), 225–51; and Charles Steffen, "Gentry and Bourgeois: Patterns of Merchant Investment in Baltimore County, Maryland, 1658–1776," *JSH*, 20 (1987), 531–48.

14. Clemens, *Atlantic Economy*; Jean Burrell Russo, "Free Workers in a Plantation Economy: Talbot County, Maryland, 1690–1759" (unpublished Ph.D., Johns Hopkins University, 1983); and Keith Mason, "A Region in Revolt: The Eastern Shore of Maryland, 1740–1790," (unpublished Ph.D., Johns Hopkins University, 1985).

15. Lois Green Carr, "Diversification in the Colonial Chesapeake: Somerset County, Maryland, in Comparative Perspective," in Carr, Morgan, and Russo (eds.), *Colonial Chesapeake Society*, 342–82.

16. See Ronald Hoffman, "'Marylando-Hibernus': Charles Carroll the Settler, 1660–1720," *WMQ*, 3d. Ser., XLV (1988), 207–36. For an analysis of economic performance in St. Mary's County see Lois Green Carr and Russell R. Menard, "Wealth and Welfare in Early Maryland: Evidence from St. Mary's County," *WMQ*, LVI (1999), 95–120; and Bayly Ellen Marks, "Economics and Society in a Staple Plantation System, St Mary's County, Maryland, 1790–1840" (unpublished Ph.D., University of Maryland, 1979). For Maryland's backcountry, see Elizabeth A. Kessel, "Germans in the Making of Frederick County, Maryland," in Robert D. Mitchell (ed.), *Appalachian Frontiers: Settlement, Society, and Development in the Pre-Industrial Era* (Lexington: University Press of Kentucky, 1991), 87–104. For Catholics, see Beatrix Betancourt Hardy, "Papists in a Protestant Age: The Catholic Gentry and Community in Colonial Maryland, 1689–1776" (unpublished Ph.D., University of Maryland, 1993).

17. See Allan Kulikoff, "The Economic Growth of the Eighteenth Century Chesapeake Colonies," *JEH*, 39 (1979), 275–88.
18. Carr and Menard, "Wealth and Welfare."
19. Jordan, *Foundations of Representative Government*, 141–82.
20. This presumes, unreasonably, that none of the 85 men whose father's status cannot be determined was from elite backgrounds.
21. Charles Steffen, *From Gentlemen to Townsmen: The Gentry of Baltimore County, Maryland, 1660–1776* (Lexington: University Press of Kentucky, 1993), 27, 42.
22. There were, however, a number of counties, such as Charles County in southern Maryland, in which Catholic gentry were still plentiful. Jean B. Lee, *The Price of Nationhood: The American Revolution in Charles County* (New York: W. W. Norton, 1994); Hardy, "Papists in a Protestant Age."
23. See Ronald Hoffman, *A Spirit of Dissension: Economics, Politics, and the Revolution in Maryland* (Baltimore: Johns Hopkins University Press, 1973); Rhys Isaac, *The Transformation of Virginia, 1740–1790* (Chapel Hill: University of North Carolina Press, 1982); T. H. Breen, *Tobacco Culture: The Mentality of the Great Tidewater Planters on the Eve of Revolution* (Princeton, NJ: Princeton University Press); and Woody Holton, *Forced Founders: Indians, Debtors, Slaves, and the Making of the American Revolution in Virginia* (Chapel Hill: University of North Carolina Press).
24. See, in particular, Philip D. Morgan, *Slave Counterpoint: Black Culture in the Eighteenth-Century Chesapeake & Lowcountry* (Chapel Hill: University of North Carolina Press, 1998); Lorena S. Walsh, *From Calabar to Carter's Grove: A History of a Virginia Slave Community* (Charlottesville: University of Virginia Press, 1997); Kulikoff, *Tobacco and Slaves*, 317–420; and Ira Berlin, *Many Thousands Gone: The First Two Centuries of Slavery in North America* (Cambridge: Cambridge University Press, 1998), 29–46, 109–41, 256–89.
25. See Brown, *Good Wives, Nasty Wenches, & Anxious Patriarchs*; Mary Beth Norton, *Founding Mothers and Fathers: Gendered Power and the Formation of American Society* (New York: Alfred A. Knopf, 1996); and Cynthia A. Kierner, *Beyond the Household: Women's Place in the Early South, 1700–1845* (Ithaca, NY: Cornell University Press, 1998), 9–68.
26. John J. McCusker and Russell R. Menard, *The Economy of British America 1607–1789* (Chapel Hill: University of North Carolina Press, 1985), 190; and T. Stephen Whitman, *The Price of Freedom: Slavery and Manumission in Baltimore and Early National Maryland* (Lexington: University Press of Kentucky, 1997).
27. For the distinction between respectability and gentility, see Woodruff D. Smith, "Complications of the Commonplace; Tea, Sugar, and Imperialism," *JIH*, XXIII (1992), 275–77.
28. For rival interpretations, see Kulikoff, *Tobacco and Slaves*, 7–10, 259–60; Daniel Blake Smith, *Inside the Great House: Planter Family Life in Eighteenth-Century Chesapeake Society* (Ithaca, NY: Cornell University Press, 1980); Jan Lewis, *The Pursuit of Happiness: Family and Values in Jefferson's Virginia* (Cambridge: Cambridge University Press, 1983); and Trevor Burnard, "A Tangled Cousinry? Associational Networks of the Maryland Elite, 1691–1776," *JSH*, LXI (1995), 17–44.
29. Jack P. Greene, *Negotiated Authorities: Essays in Colonial Political and Constitutional History* (Charlottesville: University of Virginia Press, 1994), 267, 270, 273.

CHAPTER 2

A Gentleman's Competence

The Economic Ambitions of the Maryland Elite

The distinguishing characteristic of the Maryland elite was that it was wealthy. Its wealth enabled them to live appreciably better in the eighteenth century than did their seventeenth-century ancestors and than the majority of the population.[1] A personal estate of more than £650, plus real estate, allowed elite Marylanders to buy slaves, purchase luxury goods, build fine houses attached to large acreages, and cut fine figures in their local communities. Part of this chapter details the extent of elite wealth and the composition of such wealth and changes in both over time. The major aim of this chapter, however, is more elusive: how do we explain a trend toward increased specialization in the eighteenth century away from the occupational versatility that characterized the wealthiest Marylanders until the first third of the eighteenth century? How do we account for wealthy Marylanders' tendency to diversify their agricultural activities beyond the simple production of tobacco to growing a wider variety of crops? Most importantly, what did wealthy Marylanders feel about the undeniable advance in the eighteenth century of market relations, the spread of a commercial mentality, and the beginnings of an extensive consumer culture?

On the one hand, wealthy Marylanders were eager participants in the economic transformations of the Chesapeake in the eighteenth century. They were careful capitalists who attempted to increase the value of their estates through assiduous attention to proper management. Yet they were conservators rather than speculators, unwilling to gamble freely in the marketplace if such gambles would place their properties at risk and thus abuse their duties to descendants.[2] One reason for this strategy of conservation was that structural changes in the Chesapeake economy over the eighteenth century made it increasingly difficult for all but the very wealthiest to compete in a competitive transatlantic marketplace. But, just as important, although difficult to elucidate from the abundant but uncommunicative records about wealth holding, were changes in wealthy native-born Marylanders' attitudes toward commerce. Aggressive merchant-planter entrepreneurs in the seventeenth and early eighteenth centuries, most wealthy Marylanders became less entrepreneurial and more managerial in their outlook in the second half of the eighteenth century as they concentrated on becoming good planters. Their actions were pragmatic responses to changing economic realities and were undertaken with a due appreciation of the values of the marketplace.

Yet the collective result of many individual decisions by wealthy men to specialize in agriculture rather than combine commerce with planting altered the social and economic trajectory of their province and the planter class. The transformation of an occupationally diverse Maryland elite into a planting class by the end of the colonial period was logical and economically rational given the changing nature of the Atlantic economy. This transformation, however, meant that planters after the Revolution were relatively uninvolved in the most dynamic areas of the Maryland economy, especially manufacturing and commerce in the booming town of Baltimore. The descendants of wealthy planters tended to stick to what they knew—planting—with deleterious consequences for their economic and social standing. As profits from planting declined in the last decades of the eighteenth century, the planter descendants of this elite sample faced relative social and economic decline.

In a number of insightful articles written in the mid 1960s, Aubrey Land presented a model of the economic bases of the Chesapeake eighteenth-century elite that has proved remarkably durable. Land characterized the Chesapeake elite as "merchant-planters," and noted that "as entrepreneurs they gave the Chesapeake economy both organization and direction." Their entrepreneurial orientation was evident in the numerous activities in which they engaged. Merchant-planters were involved not only in planting and merchandising but were also moneylenders, land speculators, lawyers, and officeholders. Trading was as important as the profits obtained from tobacco production.[3] Gloria Main agrees: "Occupational versatility, not specialization in the tobacco culture, marked the careers of Maryland's richest men." As Paul Clemens succinctly notes: "What established the power of the merchant-planters and most clearly set them apart from elites in other colonies was the diversity of their activities . . . the merchant-planters . . . made their money in as many ways as they possibly could."[4]

What is surprising, given historians' insistence on the dynamic and entrepreneurial nature of the colonial Chesapeake elite, is that we do not talk about the descendants of these entrepreneurs, the antebellum southern planters, in quite the same way. Historians acknowledge that antebellum planters were businessmen, were undoubtedly capitalists, and sometimes showed considerable entrepreneurial expertise, even if there is enormous controversy over the extent and nature of planters' capitalist orientation. Yet even those historians who most ardently insist that planters were profoundly affected by the market economy and who argue that planters were guided by profits more than paternalism see antebellum planters as managers rather than entrepreneurs. James Oakes, for instance, equates antebellum planters' "prevailing entrepreneurial ethos" with the development of the ideal plantation. This plantation was to be a model of efficiency. Efficiency he defines as the establishment of a rationalized bureaucracy. Within this bureaucracy, profits could be maximized. Significantly, however, Oakes assumes that the maximization of profits entailed the reduction rather than the expansion of risk. The idealized planter, therefore, was less Land's acquisitive and innovative entrepreneur, dabbling in a variety of ever-expanding fields, than a rational and efficient manager of fixed resources. Most importantly, his activities were predicated upon reducing rather than welcoming risk.[5]

Thus, when historians describe both eighteenth-century merchant–planters and nineteenth-century planters as entrepreneurs, they employ two different definitions of entrepreneurship.

Land and Clemens adopt a Schumpeterian model of entrepreneurship. For Schumpeter, the key constitutive entrepreneurial functions are innovation and the acceptance of risk. An entrepreneur, therefore, is an agent of change, not concerned merely with the perpetuation of the existing allocation of resources but with improving upon them.[6] It is difficult to see antebellum planters as entrepreneurs in this Schumpeterian sense. Southern planters were notoriously risk averse, even if safety-first behavior was eminently reasonable and prudent if a planter wished to retain his independent decision-making capacity.[7] If antebellum planters were entrepreneurial, they could only be so using a Weberian interpretation of entrepreneurship. Weber emphasizes the importance of efficient managerial techniques, stressing that the key to competitive success for the entrepreneurial businessman is not so much innovation as the thoroughgoing rationalization of every aspect of his enterprise. Yet for Weber innovation is central to an entrepreneurial ethos, even if this innovation may be less bold than the transforming innovations essential to Schumpeter. Even in a Weberian schema, however, antebellum planters are only the most marginal type of entrepreneurs.

Wealthy Marylanders in the mid-eighteenth century differed considerably from their forebears in their economic orientations and attitudes. In the late seventeenth and early eighteenth centuries wealthy Marylanders were occupationally versatile. Some wealthy Marylanders, especially the richest men in the province, continued to enjoy a diversity of sources of income throughout the colonial period. But most elite Marylanders reduced their occupational versatility over the course of the eighteenth century. They changed for the following reasons: increasing occupational specialization, the gradual elimination of merchandising as a source of elite income, a general reluctance to undertake risky projects, and a burgeoning interest in gentility, often at the expense of possible profit maximization. Most important were structural changes in the early modern Atlantic economy, changes that marginalized planters in what was a plantation system on the margins of the plantation world.

The easiest way to survey the changes that occurred in the Maryland elite over the course of the eighteenth century is to compare wealthy Marylanders in the late seventeenth century to their descendants. By the middle decades of the eighteenth century, the most significant determinant of economic behavior was whether an elite member was a migrant—migrants who became elite tended to be merchants whereas native-born wealthy Marylanders tended to be planters. Differences between migrants and the native born were less important in the seventeenth century. A large number of Marylanders were migrants. Several managed to attain elite status. They did so because they pursued diverse occupations. John Hammond I, for example, was a migrant who became a very prominent officeholder and the progenitor of one of colonial Maryland's most powerful families. Over the course of his life, he acquired through purchase and patent 2,609 acres and personal property to the value of £1,920. Hammond was a classic merchant-planter, active in the transatlantic trade. He left merchandise to the value of £478, making him a sizable trader. But he did not specialize in trading alone. He bought land and slaves, owning 21 slaves at his death, which accounted for 24 percent of his total estate value (TEV) and produced a tobacco crop worth at least £119. In addition, Hammond augmented his income by lending out money, with debtors owing him £301 at his death. Despite his wealth, however, Hammond lived spartanly. His inventory shows that he owned no china, no jewelry, no elaborate furniture, and not even a chamber pot. The only luxury goods he had were a few books and a small amount of silver plate that was probably as much investment as indulgence. Clearly, Hammond ploughed what surplus capital he had into the purchase of additional inputs of slaves and land and into building his estate in order to provide for his four sons and two daughters.[8]

One might expect native-born elite members to concern themselves less with establishing themselves than with cultivating more comfortable circumstances for the enjoyment of their inheritances. But they appear to have behaved in the same way as ambitious migrants. They avoided luxury, avidly acquired land and slaves for future benefit, and busily gained income from a variety of sources. John Chew, a third-generation elite member, for example, left a large estate of £1,540. Like Hammond, Chew was a merchant-planter, willing to undertake the risks of trade despite the cushion of a large inheritance. A part owner of a ship engaged in the tobacco trade, he tied up much of his wealth in merchandise with £146 as his share of the ship and £175 in merchandise. Overall, therefore, one-fifth of his TEV was devoted to trading. At the same time, however, Chew purchased slaves. At his death, he owned 23 slaves. Again, like Hammond, he lent money out on loan. The differences between the migrant Hammond and the native-born Chew were imperceptible.[9]

By the latter half of the eighteenth century native-born and migrant elite members were no longer occupationally similar. Native-born men, inheriting sizable quantities of both land and slaves, both of which were increasing in value, concentrated on planting. They stopped their involvement in trade. Migrants were able to move into these potentially lucrative if risky areas. Wealthy native-born Marylanders' shift away from trading can be illustrated by examining the economic activities of the Dorsey family. The Dorseys were a large and prominent family from Anne Arundel and Baltimore Counties. There were seventeen Dorseys who qualified for this elite sample, far and away the most for any family. The Dorseys, led by John and Edward Dorsey, second-generation Marylanders and provincial councilors, were substantial merchant-planters in the late seventeenth century and early eighteenth century. The next generation, the third generation of Dorseys in Maryland, led by Caleb Dorsey, Joshua Dorsey, and John Dorsey, continued involvement in both trade and planting, even though Joshua Dorsey drastically curtailed his mercantile operations near the end of his life. Their children, however, threw off most of these mercantile interests. Of the thirteen fourth- and fifth-generation Dorseys who attained elite status, just two continued to be traders. Only one Dorsey, Edward Dorsey, derived a substantial income from merchandise. All the others, such as John Dorsey, specialized as planters.

John Dorsey was the son of the merchant-planter, Caleb Dorsey. He never engaged in trade himself. After his father deeded to him well over 1,000 acres in 1732, when John was 24, he concentrated all his attentions on planting. At his death in 1765 he left to his three sons and four daughters approximately 1,800 acres and 33 slaves.[10] Significantly, his estate of £1,195 was an appreciably lower estate than the estate of any of his five brothers, all of whom did not concentrate quite as singlemindedly on planting. His estate was especially small compared to his most successful brother,

Edward, who left £12,231 at his death, derived from a number of different occupations, including trading. Yet John Dorsey was hardly destitute. He left minimal debts, was able to provide his children with comfortable inheritances, and by the end of his life had attained a sufficiency of available consumer goods, including a riding chaise. He may have been able to emulate his brother's success through trading but by so doing he could just as conceivably have endangered his comfortable elite position.

Changes in economic organization in the Chesapeake from the second quarter of the eighteenth century onward also worked against native-born wealthy Marylanders entering into trade. Whether the decline in wealthy native-born Marylanders entering trade was caused by the sons of merchant-planters opting to avoid the perils of trade for the pleasures and relative safety of planting or whether changes in transatlantic trading patterns forced native-born scions out of lucrative merchant careers is difficult to ascertain. My belief is that the abandonment of trade by a significant portion of the native-born elite was a deliberate choice, made for rational reasons, which coincided with the growing exclusiveness of British Atlantic international trade. The majority of native-born Marylanders with inherited wealth in land and slaves decided to settle for a comfortable sufficiency as planters rather than bear the considerable risks that the quest for a much larger fortune derived from trade might bring.[11]

Nevertheless, developments in transatlantic trade also brought disadvantages for local native-born merchants that may have encouraged many to stick to agriculture. Major structural modifications in the organization of Chesapeake trade occurred in the eighteenth century. Especially important were changes in the consignment system, in which independent local merchants were displaced by resident factors originally from Britain. In the eighteenth century, mercantilist restrictions and a marketing system focused on Britain kept the supply of shipping and commercial services firmly in metropolitan hands. To succeed in commerce in the eighteenth-century Chesapeake required more attention to trade than seventeenth-century planter-merchants were accustomed to exert. It was best carried on by men with close links to London commercial factors. Changes in business scale also operated to reduce opportunities for native-born merchant-planters. As Jacob Price has shown, there was a revolutionary change in scale of British firms trading to America that led to a much higher concentration of business in fewer but larger firms. The principals of these firms preferred to use friends and relatives as factors rather than colonials whom London merchants did not know. Few native-born Marylanders could offer British merchants the wide range of skills and services that they increasingly required, and those that did needed to be fully involved in trade as specialized merchants. The first decades of the eighteenth century saw the emergence of functionally specialized merchants, almost all of whom began as factors of large London commercial houses. These men, Maryland's first professional merchant group, became increasingly important in the decades immediately before the Revolution.[12]

Price argues that "the growth of the independent indigenous merchant was the most dynamic feature in the Chesapeake economy" in this period. Charles Steffen has provided a good account of how indigenous merchants became established in Baltimore County. The merchant-planters who dominated trade in the seventeenth century were replaced in the early eighteenth century by agents of large London firms who in turn were supplanted by a small group of specialized native-born and migrant merchants. The investment strategies of eighteenth-century merchants increasingly diverged from those of the planter elite. Some Marylanders were drawn to specialize in trade by the prospect of great gain. Yet most became traders because other alternatives, notably planting, were denied them. The native-born merchant class tended to be younger sons whose fathers could not establish them on land or immigrants without sufficient capital to establish viable landed estates. Native-born merchants emanated from the ranks of property owners immediately below this elite sample: the average TEV of the fathers of mid-eighteenth-century native-born Baltimore merchants was £378. Elder sons or younger sons of wealthier fathers were still able to achieve prosperity through planting rather than undertake a more risky career as a specialized merchant. It left the field open to others.[13]

Thus, the wealthy native born moved away from merchandising. Migrants, however, continued to find trade attractive. Ambitious migrants, such as David McCulloch, became specialized merchants rather than planters. McCulloch immigrated to Maryland around mid-century, made an advantageous marriage with the daughter of the wealthy merchant James Dick, and by his death had accumulated a considerable fortune. Unlike earlier migrants, however, McCulloch did not invest his growing profits into establishing his own plantation. He owned just 240 acres, mostly near Annapolis. He probably bought this land in the hopes of profiting from urban expansion—he had also bought three urban lots. Significantly, his will specified that his land be sold to pay his debts, which were considerable. Of his TEV of £3,364, 10 percent was in the form of merchandise and nearly three-quarters was money lent out on loan.[14] John Dorsey would have been impressed by the size of McCulloch's fortune and by his wide array of consumer goods. But he would have been disturbed by McCulloch's large debts and by his lack of commitment either to landholding or to slaveholding—McCulloch owned only eight slaves.

Unlike Hammond and Chew in the early eighteenth century, Dorsey and McCulloch moved in significantly different worlds. Merchants and planters had evolved into distinct groups that had less and less contact with each other. This distance between merchants and planters grew as Baltimore—oriented toward the Philadelphia market—increasingly became the center of Maryland commerce. In the latter part of the eighteenth century a native-born merchant class developed in Baltimore. But newcomers with capital, skills, and contacts found it far easier to become merchants than to become planters. Migrants dominated the merchant community from the mid-eighteenth century.[15]

Migrants were wise to concentrate on trade. By the late eighteenth century the previously flourishing rural planting economy was under severe strain. The children of elite planters did well if they could maintain the wealth necessary to confirm their elite status.[16] As planters' economic power declined so too did their political importance. Baltimore merchants became as important politically as they were in Maryland's economic life.[17] The Dorseys, having chosen to concentrate on planting, retained their privileged place within Maryland society, being comfortably well-off slave owners and planters, connected by marriage with other families of similar status. Yet few Dorseys distinguished themselves after the colonial period. Of thirty-three fifth-generation males, only one, Edward Dorsey (1758–1799), was seriously rich. Only three Dorseys became legislators. None was a marked political success. By contrast, David McCulloch's son, James, like his father a merchant, made a fortune as the Collector of the Port of Baltimore. He became one of the most powerful men in Baltimore. The differing fortunes of the Dorseys and the McCullochs in the early national period reflect the differing fortunes of merchants and planters in the late eighteenth century.

A more telling comparison is with the Ridgely family, a family of status in the colonial period similar to the Dorseys and with whom the Dorseys extensively intermarried. The Ridgelys, however, chose trade over planting. By the late eighteenth century they had outstripped the Dorseys in terms of wealth and influence. Several Ridgelys were accounted among the very wealthiest of Marylanders. The prominence of the family was acknowledged by the election of Charles Ridgely of Hampton as Maryland's governor in 1816. Trading was the way to fortune, if also sometimes a pathway to disaster. Most of the largest fortunes accumulated in Maryland after the Revolution came from trade, or, in the case of the already wealthy Carrolls, from large-scale money lending. But few native-born descendants of the colonial elite (and by the middle of the eighteenth century the overwhelming proportion of the elite were native born) chose to enter the most dynamic sector of the postrevolutionary Maryland economy.[18]

The economic makeup of the Maryland elite, therefore, altered considerably over time. The elite adopted a planter ethos that made the efficient management of fixed resources and the cultivation of particular planter values a priority. They adopted risk-averse, conservationist strategies, seeing profit maximization as secondary to the maintenance of a comfortable sufficiency. From an economic standpoint, these changing choices may have been less than rational but only if we insist that the elite ought to have sought profit maximization as their primary goal. On the contrary, in the particular context of the eighteenth-century Chesapeake, the drift of wealthy native-born Marylanders toward planting and away from trade made economic and social sense. As we shall see, wealthy Marylanders were motivated very strongly by a quest for gentility, and this quest overrode ambitions for mere moneymaking.

Tables 2.1, 2.2, and 2.3 summarize the changes in the composition of elite wealth over time. They demonstrate the movement of native-born wealthy Marylanders away from trade and show the extent to which they began to specialize as planters. In Tables 2.1 and 2.2, elite Marylanders are divided according to how they obtained the majority of their wealth. The number of men who were merchant-planters declined significantly. Over half of the elite dying before 1726 were equally planters and merchants. But just 22 percent of elite Marylanders dying after 1760 combined planting with trade. The percentage of wealthy Marylanders dying after 1760 who were solely planters increased to 61 percent. Over time trade became an ever-diminishing component of the wealth of native-born elite Marylanders, as Table 2.3 details. Less than 10 percent of the elite who died after 1760 owned trade goods that made up 10 percent or more of their personal estate.

Table 2.1 Derivation of Elite Wealth

Occupation	Pre–1726 (N=97)	1726–42 (N=87)	1743–59 (N=102)	1760+ (N=175)	Total (N=461)
Mainly planting (%)	27	45	50	61	48
Mainly merchandise (%)	4	9	12	9	9
Merchandise/planting (%)	56	37	23	22	32
Professions (%)	13	9	13	7	10
Public office (%)	1	1	3	2	5

Source: Inventories and Accounts, Inventories, *MHR.*

Table 2.2 Derivation of Elite Wealth:
Comparison between Native-Born and Immigrants

| | Native Born | | Immigrants | |
Occupation	Pre–1742 (N=105)	1742+ (N=221)	Pre–1742 (N=71)	1742+ (N=37)
Mainly planting (%)	49	65	5	3
Mainly merchandise (%)	1	4	14	43
Merchandise/planting (%)	42	24	50	24
Professions (%)	5	5	21	27
Public office (%)	4	3	10	4

Source: Inventories and Accounts, Inventories, *MHR.*

Table 2.3 Merchandise in Elite Inventories over Time

Pre–1708	1709–25	1726–42	1743–59	1760+	Total
		With merchandise (%)			
81	85	74	54	34	56
		With merchandise >10% (%)			
44	48	29	16	10	22

Source: Inventories and Accounts, Inventories, *MHR.*

By the middle of the eighteenth century, most wealthy Marylanders were solely planters. Wealthy men who were merchants were few. Significantly, these men could be differentiated from planters in ways impossible earlier in the century. Only nine native-born elite Marylanders dying after 1726 were specialized merchants. Only eleven were professional men. Migrants who became wealthy, on the other hand, were frequently merchants. A substantial minority were professionals. They were seldom solely planters. By the middle of the eighteenth century, the occupational differences between migrants and native-born elite members had become pronounced. Only just over a quarter of migrants were involved with planting. Over 90 percent of the native-born elite were planters. Half of the migrants who achieved elite status obtained their wealth solely as merchants, and a few became wealthy on the profits of legal or medical practices. None became rich through planting alone. Migrants and native-born members had thus become occupationally separate. One formed a merchant class and the other became a planting order.

Nevertheless, because migrants became a progressively smaller proportion of the Maryland elite over time, the overall pattern was that the elite as a whole became increasingly a planter elite. Why did trade become less appealing to native-born Marylanders? Why did they choose to devote most of their attention to planting? First, becoming a merchant entailed considerable risk. As Thomas Doerflinger has shown in his study of colonial Philadelphia merchants, trading was a fraught business. Capital requirements were lower than were needed to begin planting from scratch. But the capital requirements to become a trader were still considerable. Labor costs were high, export markets were far distant and easily glutted, wars were frequent, foreign exchange markets were volatile, and ships were easily lost at sea.[19] Commercial fortunes could be made but the risks of commerce were probably too high for established planters, especially when they could live comfortably and relatively risk free on income derived from agriculture.

The profits possible from trading were larger than for most other types of activity—15 to 20 percent annually from retail goods for local sale. Migrants who had sufficient capital to invest in a coastal vessel and to buy goods on credit and who would have been forced to outlay much larger sums of money to purchase land and slaves for lesser returns than in merchandizing were attracted to trade.[20] But few merchants invested large sums in trading. If we assume that merchants made as much as 20 percent profit on the merchandise listed in their inventories (the more likely profit rate being 15 percent), one-third of merchants earned more than £100 per annum from mercantile operations alone and 10 percent earned as much as £200 per annum. Amos Garrett and Nicholas Rogers II, both of whom probably earned, in a good year, between £500 and £700 per annum from merchandise, were the only two elite members to gain substantial fortunes from trading.

Native-born elite members with moderate estates were more likely to become solely planters than were very rich Marylanders. Daniel Dulany, Sr., Richard Snowden III, and Edward Lloyd III, all of whom died after 1750, each owning more than 50 slaves, continued to build fortunes through trade as well as through agriculture. These very rich men remained merchant-planters, their fortunes allowing them to undertake the risks of commerce without fear of bankruptcy. But even the very richest Marylanders moved increasingly away from trade. Edward Lloyd IV, for example, following his inheritance in 1770 of one of the greatest estates in colonial Maryland, proceeded to contract the scope of his activities. He was much less of a merchant-planter than his father and grandfather, concentrating instead on maximizing profit from his extensive plantations. By the early nineteenth century, the Lloyds, once prominent merchant-planters, had become solely planters—efficient managers of abundant resources rather than ambitious, risk-taking entrepreneurs.[21]

One reason why large planters moved away from trade was that the profits possible from planting became more substantial in the prosperous years after the mid-eighteenth century. Land prices, in particular, increased significantly after mid-century. Following an imperceptible rise before 1750, the price of improved land nearly tripled in settled tidewater counties in Maryland between 1750 and 1776. Rising prices for land and labor made entry into large-scale planting more difficult for newcomers and accentuated the value of an inheritance. A native-born Marylander, inheriting both land and a number of slaves, could earn a comfortable living within the relatively certain economy of planting, especially as tobacco and grain prices rose and the demand for agricultural commodities expanded.[22] Inheritances and gifts of land became increasingly important as the available supply of land dwindled and as buying land became prohibitive for newcomers. In the seventeenth century, land was relatively abundant. Most free men who survived any length of time were able to purchase more than enough land to satisfy both their own needs and also the needs of their children.[23] The children of these seventeenth-century purchasers faced considerable advantages over migrants in becoming planters because they already owned sufficient land. Aquilla Paca II, for example, purchased 1,068 acres in his lifetime but inherited the majority of his large holdings from his father (2,472 acres) and upon his marriage (1,616 acres). Few migrants could afford to buy such large landholdings as land prices increased.[24]

As Charles Steffen argues in his study of Baltimore merchants' involvement in the land market, wealthy Marylanders were buyers rather than sellers of land.[25] Between 1709 and 1717, for example, elite member Gerard Hopkins was involved in numerous land transactions, spending £600.20 on 2,703 acres and selling 43 acres for £25.80. Joseph Cowman, in his land dealings between 1730 and 1753, emulated and bettered Hopkins, buying 1,091 acres while selling none. Wealthy men also acquired land in other ways. Darby Lux, for instance, increased his holdings by 397 acres through defaulted mortgages. Charles Carroll the Settler acquired 12,249 acres by foreclosure and 3,507 acres by marriage and inheritance, as well as 33,481 acres through patent or purchase.[26] Elite members continually built on their initial landed inheritances. They seldom attempted to make a quick profit by rapidly turning over newly purchased land.[27]

Such policies made good economic sense and had serious social consequences. As the value of land increased gradually until the 1760s and then rose dramatically, wealthy Marylanders' estates became ever more valuable without them expending any effort. The gap between large landholders and the landless widened. The importance of inheritance was magnified. Moreover, land became increasingly concentrated even if landownership continued to be well spread. Landless tenants and ex-servants found it increasingly difficult to purchase land in tidewater areas. They moved to less settled regions (where wealthy tidewater elite members often owned land). The extent and importance of inequality in tidewater Maryland and its relationship to the overall economic growth and general prosperity of the region in the decades immediately preceding the Revolution are beyond the scope of this study, but the point to make here is that wealthy Marylanders benefited greatly from development and settlement in Maryland while retaining sufficient landholdings to maintain and improve elite life-styles (Table 2.4).[28]

The average landholding of the Maryland elite member was 2,193 acres.[29] The elite held a disproportionate share of available land, a share that increased with population growth and with a decline in the quantity of unclaimed land.[30] Most land was rural. By mid-century, however, some men, such as John Raitt and Robert Johnson, invested solely in increasingly valuable urban property. These men were migrants who had acquired wealth through commerce or from the professions. Given soil exhaustion rates in the settled parts of the Chesapeake, large planters needed at least 350 acres to maintain a work force of over ten slaves.[31] Only 17 men who were primarily planters had less than this acreage.

Table 2.4 Changes in Elite Landownership over Time

	Average Acres	Under 351 acres (%)	Over 1,500 acres (%)
Pre–1726	2739	7	62
1726–1742	2100	6	49
1743–1759	1733	7	40
1760+	1825[a]	13	41
Total	2077	8	43

[a]This figure excludes the 43,000 acres of Edward Lloyd III (1711–1770).
Source: Land Records, *MHR;* Papenfuse et al., *Biographical Dictionary.*

All were native born and all but two died after 1759, when the pressure of population upon land first became an issue, albeit a minor one, in the tidewater. The children of these land-poor planters found it difficult to replicate their father's wealth and status—11 land-poor planters had no children who were wealthy enough to be elite members. Most wealthy Marylanders, however, inherited or purchased sizable parcels of land. The average land-holding declined over time, but not drastically. Men dying before 1726 owned on average 2,739 acres. Wealthy Marylanders dying after 1760 owned on average 1,825 acres.[32] These landholdings were increasingly valuable as land prices rose rapidly after 1760. In Talbot County, for example, elite members dying after 1759 owned on average nearly 300 acres less land than the cohort dying between 1726 and 1742 (1,543 acres rather than 1,831 acres), but the average value of such holdings almost doubled from £641 to £1,250.

Land needed labor, and in Maryland that meant in the first instance slave labor. Wealthy merchants and planters initiated the introduction of African slaves to the Chesapeake. They were the people who mainly benefited from its introduction, especially with the upturn in the plantation economies of the Upper South from the early 1740s. Wealthy Marylanders from the late seventeenth century onward were slave owners. Slaveholding was almost universal, with 444 elite members owning slaves. The numbers of slaves varied widely from one or two slaves to the 185 slaves of Daniel Dulany, but wealthy Marylanders shared a common identity and a common interest as slaveholders committed to upholding the system of slavery. The average wealthy Marylander owned 23 slaves, of whom 14 were prime hands—males and females aged over 12 who were not superannuated. Over time, the average slaveholding increased from 18 slaves per elite member dying before 1726 to 24 slaves for those dying after 1760. Just over a third of wealthy Marylanders owned between 11 and 20 slaves. But over 40 percent owned 20 or more slaves, 20 percent had at least 30 slaves, and 5 percent owned 50 or more slaves.

The system of slavery that operated in Maryland, however, changed dramatically and continually throughout the colonial period. The emergence of large, economically integrated plantations and the triumph of the planter class around 1680 in Virginia and around 1700 in Maryland was accompanied by a transformation of black life in the region. In the first half-century of life in colonial Maryland, African slaves were few in number and lived in societies in which race relations were more pliable than they were later to become. Blacks and whites lived and worked closely together in a world dominated by small-scale farms. Black slaves were not the majority of the work force—white indentured servants filled that role. Both groups fraternized together on terms of surprising equality. The gap between Africans and their masters was larger but was never immense until the late seventeenth century.

As the plantation system became dominant, racial mores hardened and relationships between blacks and whites became more rigid and less close. Societies with slaves were transformed into slave societies. The lot of blacks deteriorated as planters' domination grew. Greater exploitation of blacks was accompanied by the replacement of what Ira Berlin calls an Atlantic Creole culture with a comprehensive Africanization of slave life. Planters' demand for slaves fueled a more expansive slave trade, mostly in Virginia, but to a lesser extent in Maryland as well. Between 1700 and 1740, British slavers brought 54,000 blacks, mostly from Senegambia and the Bight of Biafra, into the Chesapeake. Maryland received at least 6,639 of these slaves.

The slave population not only increased, it became heavily African and became dominated by Africans in their twenties and thirties. Indentured servitude declined, with Africans replacing English migrants as the principal workers in the fields. This period marked the nadir of race relations in the Chesapeake. Slaves suffered worse working conditions, enjoyed less chance for an autonomous social life, and were oppressed by a nakedly exploitative and resurgent planter elite determined to keep slaves cowed using whatever forms of coercion they deemed necessary. This new regime, however, changed again from mid-century, when the demographic character of Chesapeake slave populations was significantly transformed. Within a very short period of time—often less than a decade—a mainly African slave population that needed to be continually replenished became a self-reproducing Creole population that replenished itself. The flourishing slave trade fell away almost entirely in the tidewater and planters could begin to rely on their slave populations growing naturally. In particular, the proportion of children within the slave population increased dramatically, sex ratios evened out, and slaves became able to form lasting family units.

Planters were able to transfer most of the cost of reproducing their work forces onto the slaves themselves. They reorganized plantation management to take into account the considerable advantages that could be derived from skillfully managing the demographic performance of their slave labor forces. Partly as a consequence of the demographic and cultural transformations of the Chesapeake slave population in the mid-eighteenth century and partly as a result of long-term social transformations in society as a whole, planters adopted a less nakedly exploitative attitude to managing their bondspeople and followed a more ameliorative system of slave management, a system that Philip Morgan has characterized as emerging paternalism (Tables 2.5 and 2.6).[33]

Wealthy Marylanders' relationship to slavery underwent considerable change over the course of the eighteenth century. The average merchant-planter in the late seventeenth and early eighteenth centuries needed to invest in both slaves *and* merchandise to earn a living, rather than gamble all of his wealth on purchasing slaves who could easily die without recouping through labor the cost of purchase. Merchant-planters, nevertheless, appreciated the

Table 2.5 Size of Elite Slaveholdings over Time

	Pre–1726	1726–42	1743–59	1760+	Total
Average number of slaves	18	25	22	25	23
No slaves (%)	2.1	1.2	2.9	5.7	3.7
1–5 slaves (%)	12.5	8.1	8.8	7.4	8.9
6–10 slaves (%)	14.6	13.8	5.9	8.9	10.2
11–20 slaves (%)	43.8	34.5	36.3	32.0	35.9
21–30 slaves (%)	13.5	18.4	29.4	22.9	21.5
31–50 slaves (%)	10.4	14.9	15.7	16.6	14.8
50+ slaves (%)	3.1	9.2	1.0	6.7	5.2

Source: Inventories and Accounts, Inventories, *MHR.*

Table 2.6 Composition of Elite Slave Forces over Time[a]

	Pre–1726	1726–42	1743–59	1760+	Total
Total number of slaves	1727	2141	2218	4167	10253
Working males (%)	44	36	35	33	36
Working females (%)	26	24	24	25	25
Productive hands (%)	70	60	59	58	61
Old people (%)	6	9	7	7	8
Children (%)	25	31	34	35	32
Men/women ratio	1.84	1.59	1.40	1.32	1.48
Male/female ratio[b]	1.69	1.52	1.31	1.31	1.42

[a]Boys and girls aged between 10 and 15 are included as working hands.
[b]Male/female ratio excludes children
Source: Inventories and Accounts, Inventories, *MHR.*

value of buying slaves for their long-term potential. If a slave survived the seasoning process, he or she could pay off the cost of purchase and not only start making profits for the purchaser but also increase the value of the purchase many times over by having children. Slaves were also ideal for including in children's inheritances, especially in daughters' dowries. Because most women moved onto their husband's land at marriage, wealthy men constructed their dowries so that they could add to family wealth by bringing movables such as slaves to their marriages.[34]

Thus, when a wealthy man had surplus capital available, at least until the early eighteenth century, he invested it in buying more slaves, the most cost-effective form of labor available. The initial outlay was great but, depreciated over a working life, the rate of return was higher than for any other form of labor. Annual rates of return varied. Paul Clemens thinks that a tobacco planter would be lucky to clear five pounds per annum for each of his male field hands, meaning that it took seven to nine years for a slave to repay the cost of purchase, and implying an annual rate of return of between 5 and 10 percent. Some planters did much better. John Gresham of Kent County received a rate of return of over 16 percent for an adult male slave in 1738. Of course, this rate of return is predicated on an adult slave working full time, at a time when harvests were plentiful. An underemployed slave (or one who was sick, very young, or elderly) would return less, especially if combined with a downturn in trade.[35] Because profits from planting remained low until the 1730s, however, merchant-planters invested in slaves not so much for their immediate return as for their long-term potential and in the absence of other areas of investment that offered attractive returns. In effect, early merchant-planters were betting on the future prosperity of the region, gambling that their slaves would survive and reproduce and that they would be able to clear, improve, and cultivate increasingly larger percentages of their landholdings.

By mid-century, the situation was different. Many of the elite were solely planters who needed slaves to work already improved land. Most owned enough land to support a labor force of up to 30 slaves. At a certain point, however, additional investment in slaves was counterproductive. This seems to have occurred in the northern Chesapeake when slave forces reached around 30 slaves.[36] Lorena Walsh notes that most overseers could efficiently manage only 10 to 15 working hands in making crops of tobacco and corn and that the total number of field hands on any farm was usually limited to a maximum of about 25.[37] Elite members without huge landholdings or great wealth would not have had enough improved land to utilize properly a labor force of over 30 slaves and may have found it desirable to divest slaves after their slaveholdings passed the 40-slave mark. Although average slaveholdings increased, there was no dramatic growth in the number of very large slaveholdings, with the cohort dying between 1726 and 1742 having the highest proportion of slaveholders with more than 50 slaves. Maryland planters actively managed their slave forces, selling off excess slaves when they could, and combined slave labor with other forms of labor.[38]

Owners of very large numbers of slaves were different from other elite members. They were seldom solely planters. Whereas 85 percent of elite members dying after 1760 owning between 21 and 30 slaves were principally planters, owners of larger numbers of slaves remained merchant-planters. Edward Dorsey, for example, owned 86 slaves. He was a planter, attorney and legislator, merchant, moneylender, and ironmaster. Slaves accounted for

15 percent of his TEV. Despite having one of the largest slave forces in the province, Dorsey did not invest every bit of spare capital into buying slaves. On the contrary, Dorsey had much more of his wealth tied up in loans. Likewise, Nehemiah King, from Somerset County, who died owning 94 slaves, had 63 percent of his TEV out on loan. Slaves made up one-fifth of his TEV. Owners of large numbers of slaves probably acquired many of their slaves virtually by accident, either through natural increase or when loans or mortgages defaulted. Both at high and moderate elite wealth levels, lending money probably offered at least as great and much surer rate of return than further investments in slaves.

It made sense for elite members to concentrate on the management and rationalization of their labor forces rather than on growing those labor forces.[39] Natural population growth changed the composition of elite labor forces, increasing the number of unproductive hands—children and old or disabled slaves—that planters owned. Before 1726, an elite member could expect to have nearly 70 percent of his labor force as productive hands. By 1760 this proportion had declined to under 60 percent. By New World terms, eighteenth-century Chesapeake planters owned remarkably low numbers of productive slaves. In York County, Virginia, in the 1750s, less than 40 percent of slaves were prime hands—men and women aged between 16 and 50. By comparison, slave forces detailed in mid-eighteenth-century Jamaican inventories show that the percentage of slaves who were adult men and women aged between 16 and 44 ranged from between 75 and 85 percent. This decline in productive hands was through the achievement of more equal slave sex ratios, an achievement that also distinguished Chesapeake slave populations from other New World slave populations.[40]

Planters welcomed natural increase because it obviated the need to buy slaves and because it augmented slaveholders' slave investment. But there were economic consequences for wealthy planters that resulted from the rise of Creole slave predominance in the second quarter of the eighteenth century. Too many children and unproductive hands lessened planters' net income from agriculture. On the other hand, increasing slave forces allowed profits to be made from the sale of slaves, usually children and adolescents. A planter had to balance the future advantages to be obtained from larger numbers of slave children against the cost of main-taining those slaves. Wealthy Marylanders probably kept more slaves than they needed for maximum productivity in order to provide slaves as gifts to children on marriage or as an inheri-tance.[41] But slave numbers could eventually reach a level at which owners found it economically productive to sell slaves to stabilize their labor force.[42]

By the mid-eighteenth century, wealthy Marylanders concen-trated on the careful exploitation of the slaves that they already owned and the skilful utilization of other types of workers, such as servants, hired free labor, and convicts rather than on growing their slave forces through purchase. Christine Daniels shows in a detailed study of the labor practices of John Gresham, a wealthy planter resident in Kent County and the son of an elite member from Annapolis, how native-born planters of sizable estates with inherited slaves found it economically rational to stop buying slaves. Gresham, the master of 34 slaves at his death, owned fewer slaves than he needed but made no effort to increase his slave labor force after 1738. Instead, he supplemented slave labor with bound agricultural debt servants, free laborers, and hired slaves. Planters, even in slave economies, routinely employed large num-bers of wage laborers and tenants.[43] As slaves became ever more expensive, it became risky to purchase new slaves, bearing in mind that new slaves from Africa might not survive the seasoning process and that the demographic chances of survival for native-born slaves were comparatively favorable. Even very wealthy planters, such as the Burwell family of tidewater Virginia, whose slaves Lorena Walsh has studied, stopped buying slaves in the second quarter of the eighteenth century.[44]

Gresham's willingness to supplement slave labor with other forms of bound and hired labor reminds us that slavery and the plantation system in Maryland, if viewed in a broader context over both time and place, was a marginal institution on the mar-gins of the Atlantic system. It was perhaps only in the middle of the eighteenth century and perhaps only among wealthy planters that a full-blown plantation system based on slavery such as dom-inated the economies of plantation societies further south in British North America and the British West Indies ever flourished. Even in this period and among this class, slavery was a comparatively unimpressive institution. In the context of slavery in British North America, slavery in Maryland was peculiar and marginal in several respects. First, the extent of the international slave trade into the colony was very limited. Maryland imported 10,339 slaves direct from Africa in the eighteenth century and 12,210 Africans in the entire colonial period. Undoubtedly, planters received more slaves than enumerated here: Menard estimates that in the two decades around the turn of the eighteenth century alone 4,022 slaves arrived in Maryland. Planters probably acquired slaves from Virginia, and small parcels of slaves probably arrived from the West Indies as part of the cargoes of traders involved in the West Indian trade, as occurred in New York. But even if the slave trade was more considerable than figures show, it paled in comparison to the number of slaves imported into colonies more fully involved in the Atlantic plantation system. Virginia received 84,247 slaves from Africa in the period of the Atlantic slave trade, the Carolinas imported 151,621, Barbados brought in 359,178, and Jamaica landed at least 914,902.[45]

Second, the size of slaveholdings even among the Maryland elite was relatively small. In Maryland, slaveholdings of over 50 were rare, and only wealthy men owned more than 20 slaves. In low-country South Carolina, the average slaveholding in the 1760s neared 20 slaves and the average number of slaves of the wealthiest 10 percent of the population neared 100. Over half of all slaves in the lowcountry by the 1770s lived in plantations comprising 50 or more slaves. In Jamaica, slaveholdings were even larger. In the middle of the eighteenth century, the average slaveholder owned 41 slaves and nearly two-thirds of slaves lived on plantations with 100 or more slaves. The top 10 percent of slaveholders were masters of small armies, with average slaveholdings of 267 slaves each. Peter Beckford, the owner of the biggest slave force in colonial Jamaica, owned 1,669 slaves—nearly as many as every wealthy Marylander in this sample who died before 1726.[46]

Finally, and most tellingly, the structure of both the labor force and the slave population in Maryland showed much greater diversity of forms than in regions more firmly devoted to the production of staple crops. By the mid-eighteenth century, Maryland had not only a diversified agricultural economy but also a diversified labor force. Much more than in other plantation areas, the labor force within Maryland plantation agriculture contained alternative workers to slaves. Planters employed convicts, indentured and debt servants, hired slaves, free wageworkers, and tenants. The labor pattern of colonial and early national Maryland was, to adopt a phrase first coined by Richard Morris, "a shadowland" that was "neither fully slave nor entirely free."[47] Bound labor was never predominant in Maryland, meaning that its eclipse by wage labor in the early national period entailed a gradual rather than an abrupt shift in labor patterns. Most indicative of how slave labor blurred with other forms of labor in the province, even in the colonial period, was the percentage of free blacks in Maryland. In 1755 approximately 4 percent of Maryland's black population was free. In Virginia, South Carolina, and Jamaica, percentages were well under 1 percent. After the Revolution, Maryland diverged further from other plantation societies, especially in the American South, where slavery was increasingly entrenched. The characteristic labor pattern in Maryland was a complex and shifting mix in which the growth of slavery coexisted with circumscribed forms of wage labor, including term slavery.[48]

Even on the margins of the Atlantic plantation system, however, planting offered planters both profit and prestige. From the mid-1740s, planting became more profitable in two ways. First, tobacco and grain prices improved. Second, diversification into other crops besides tobacco gave both additional income and protection from the vagaries of tobacco production. As planting became more appealing, planters became better planters. As Carr and Walsh have demonstrated, the management skills of planters dramatically improved over the course of the eighteenth century. Perhaps this is not surprising, given the increased attention that planters devoted to planting.[49]

What wealthy Marylanders grew changed both over time and place. When we break crops into tobacco, wheat, and corn—the three principal agricultural products found on colonial Maryland plantations—we see considerable diversity by the mid-eighteenth century. In the seventeenth century no such diversity existed. Early colonists were obsessed with the production of tobacco, and the "stinking weede" entered into nearly every aspect of their lives. As an early resident stated in 1699, "tobacco is our meat, drinke, cloathing and monies ... the standard for trade, not only for the merchants, but also amongst ourselves."[50] The production of tobacco, of course, remained important into the eighteenth century. In 1729, Governor Benedict Leonard Calvert could still state: "Tobacco, as our Staple, is our all, and Indeed leaves no room for anything else."[51] Overall, 70 percent of the elite left tobacco in their inventories worth, on average, £88. For those decedents dying before 1708, tobacco was by far the major crop. The average tobacco crop had a mean value of £93 compared to an average corn crop of £17 and a wheat crop of £6. Tobacco lost its overwhelming dominance in the eighteenth century.[52] Wheat crops, in particular, increased in value in elite inventories from an average crop of less than £6 for wealthy Marylanders dying before 1726 to over £40 for wealthy members dying after 1759.

Agricultural diversification led to regional specialization. By the Revolution, wealthy Marylanders in each of the four counties in this study operated substantially different agricultural systems. Planters in Anne Arundel continued to concentrate on tobacco but elsewhere planters moved away from the traditional Chesapeake staple. Baltimore planters began to grow large quantities of wheat. Planters in Somerset turned their attention to corn. In Talbot County, planters spread their attentions evenly among corn, wheat, and tobacco. Wheat and corn did not, however, replace tobacco as a major crop anywhere. Instead, grain growing complemented the production of tobacco. Only 22 of 154 decedents leaving crops in their inventories stopped growing tobacco.

T.H. Breen suggests that the move from tobacco to grain production was a "wrenching cultural process" that created a "crisis of self-perception" for the Chesapeake elite.[53] Breen overstates his case, underestimating the lingering importance of tobacco, even in large grain-producing areas such as the Eastern Shore, and overdramatizing the trauma of the conversion from one agricultural system to another. There is no reason to believe that planters attached any more value to the virtues of tobacco than they did to, say, merchandise, which many of them discarded at about the same time. The very fluidity of New World society made planters in the Chesapeake remarkably adaptable, certainly by European standards, to changes in economic organization. Clemens argues, persuasively, that large planters diversified because of the attractive prospects that grain production offered rather than because of chronically bad tobacco prices or because there was a fundamental crisis in the traditional tobacco economy. Tobacco prices generally kept pace with grain prices until after the Revolution. Planters made a rational choice when deciding to grow grain, taking advantage of the higher profitability and greater security of diversified agriculture rather than reluctantly being pulled away from tobacco. It also allowed planters to cope with declining tobacco output: whereas the average output of tobacco per laborer declined from 1,300 pounds in the first decade of the eighteenth century to about 780 pounds by the American Revolution, Chesapeake grain production benefited from major productivity gains.[54]

Planting also became more attractive as the infrastructures of colonial Maryland developed. Prosperity did not lead to extensive urbanization in the plantation Chesapeake but it did lead to easier conditions for planters. Improvements in transportation, for example, such as public roads, helped the marketing of crops. The expansion and increasing sophistication of both local and British financial arrangements, which made credit more easily available, gave planters the ready capital to improve their plantations and their standards of living, especially as they seldom needed to borrow to acquire labor.[55] Planting, in short, became an easier occupation, especially for men brought up in a planting world and attuned to its rhythms. Planters worked hard as managers and took pride in their skills in planting, but still had time to indulge in other interests, such as gambling and horseracing. Moreover, the growth of settlement reduced the isolation from agreeable company that many earlier planters endured. Planting became increasingly idealized not only as the perfect occupation for a gentleman but as an occupation that promoted virtues desired by colonial Virginians and Marylanders. Native-born elite members thus had many inducements to continue as planters and little to encourage them to pursue other options.[56]

Nevertheless, the professions attracted some interest from wealthy men. Law, in particular, was very lucrative. As Governor Horatio Sharpe explained to the Proprietor in July 1768, law was "the Profession by which a better Income is to be acquired in this part of the World than by any other office in your Lordship's Court." Certainly, talented lawyers such as Thomas Bordley and Daniel Dulany obtained large incomes from the law, probably grossing over £350 per annum by the first third of the eighteenth century. County lawyers grossed between £150 and £200 per annum. Prominent lawyers in Annapolis where the major courts were situated could earn much more. Stephen Bordley, for example, never earned less than £300 per annum between 1742 and 1758. He was probably grossing over £650 per annum by the late 1750s. On average, Bordley took in £493 in fees per annum during these two decades.[57]

For the small number of men who could afford to enter into it, iron manufacturing was also an attractive moneymaking option. But the entry costs were high. Henry Holliday calculated in 1765 that it would cost £7,060 sterling to begin a medium-sized ironworks. He opted not to invest. Not surprisingly, only the very wealthiest men in Maryland had access to such large amounts of capital. The eight men in this sample who were ironmasters owned on average 10,507 acres and had estates worth £5,703, of which £659 was specifically related to iron making. The investment in iron making, once made, however, could be very valuable. It was fundamental in the large fortunes of the Dulanys, Carrolls, Taskers, and Ridgelys. The Baltimore Iron Company was especially profitable. After an investment of £4,480 in the 1730s, Charles Carroll saw his share increase in value to approximately £5,000 with an annual net profit of £400 sterling per annum by the mid-1760s.[58]

Another source of income, almost exclusively confined to the wealthiest men in Maryland, was profit from political office. These offices varied greatly in worth, not only from office to office but within the same office from year to year. Generally, holders of these offices did not have fixed salaries but made money from commissions on provincial and county fees.[59] Proprietary offices were scarce: 21 men obtained posts worth over £100 per annum and 12 earned £300 or more per annum. Patronage was rare in colonial Maryland and was not a significant source of income except for a small number of professional politicians such as Thomas Bordley, Daniel Dulany, and Philip Thomas, all of who probably earned over £500 per annum at the height of their government careers. Not surprisingly, the holders of these posts were far wealthier than the rest of the elite, with average estates of £6,573 (Table 2.7).

Table 2.7 Composition of Maryland Elite Inventories:
Categories of Property as Percentages of TEV[a]

	Pre–1708 (N=36)	1709–25 (N=60)	1726–42 (N=87)	1743–59 (N=102)	1760+ (N=175)	Total (N=460)
Average TEV (£)	1331.19	1829.46	2256.93	1713.49	1935.99	1886.12
Capital (%)	87.7	86.1	87.0	87.8	89.8	88.2
Personal (%)	12.3	13.9	13.0	12.2	10.2	11.8
Livestock (%)	14	12	8	8	8	9
Slaves (%)	19	28	29	33	34	31
Labor (%)	20	29	30	33	34	31
Crops (%)	8	6	7	6	6	6
Merchandise (%)	11	11	9	6	4	7
Debts (%)	29	19	27	28	31	28
Cash (%)	3	4	4	4	5	4
Other (%)	7	8	7	7	7	7

[a]Capital, all goods that are not household or personal goods; labor, slaves and servants; crops, tobacco, wheat, corn, and all other crops. Figures do not add up to 100 percent as some categories overlap.

Source: Inventories and Accounts, Inventories, MHR.

How much, then, did wealthy Marylanders earn? We know, reasonably accurately, the outer limits of colonial wealth. Charles Carroll of Annapolis calculated that he made an annual net profit in 1764 of over £1,800 sterling or £2,700 Maryland currency from an estate worth £88,380.47 sterling. By 1776, he was probably making considerably more than that from interest on loans alone: interest on the £41,000 sterling out on loan was £2,460 sterling at 6 percent interest.[60] Amos Garrett, the richest man in our sample, would have earned as much in the 1720s. Garrett would have made over £1,000 per annum from money lent out on loan, between £500 and £700 per annum from merchandising, and probably around £500 from crops produced by his 41 prime hands and servants.

Few men approached these incomes. Certainly, planting alone was unlikely to produce gross income anywhere near £1,000 per annum. An analysis of 30 planters with inventoried crops worth more than £100 reveals that most planters could not expect to earn more than £200 to £300 gross incomes per annum from planting combined with interest earned from money lent out at 6 percent per annum. The income for an independent merchant or an attorney without other occupations was no higher. Most wealthy Marylanders, especially those devoted to a single occupation, seem to have made between £100 and £500 per annum. They made more only when engaged in several moneymaking activities. Occupational specialization, therefore, merely maintained or reduced elite members' earning potential. Indeed, recent research indicates that the share of wealth held by the richest 10 percent of the population shrank consistently in the first half of the eighteenth century. The top 10 percent of wealth-holders in St. Mary's County owned about the same proportion of wealth between 1745 and 1754 as their predecessors had done between 1658 and 1664. Middling planters—those with assets sufficient to own land and possibly slaves—benefited the most from years of increasing equality and rising prosperity.[61]

Why, then, did elite members not opt to maximize their earning potential? First, native-born Marylanders with handsome but not overwhelmingly large inheritances were unwilling to undertake the considerable risks that accrued to trade when they were able to make a good living at a safer and more genteel pursuit. Second, they needed extra income only when they had additional expenses, such as providing for children and dependants, or when they wanted to acquire consumer goods. Most decedents were able to provide for heirs with little difficulty, at least up until the Revolution. What about the acquisition of consumer goods? As Lois Green Carr and Lorena Walsh have documented, the quest for gentility through the acquisition of genteel consumer goods was constant at all wealth levels of Maryland society throughout the eighteenth century.[62] At a certain level, however, the accoutrements of gentility were obtained. There was no need to go on purchasing consumer items not needed. In addition, there were only so many things that could be bought in a colonial outpost. After an elite member had attained all the consumer goods available on a limited market, he did not need to spend money on consumer goods except to replace broken or old goods. In turn, he did not need to assume large risks in order to expand income. Moreover, with increased population and better markets, consumer goods were both cheaper and more easily attainable by the middle of the eighteenth century.[63]

Despite investing less and less wealth in personal and household goods, the elite lived more luxuriously over the eighteenth century. By the late eighteenth century, many elite members of only middling wealth owned almost all of the domestic goods necessary for gentility: matched china place settings, walnut or mahogany furniture, books, pictures, tea services, clocks, and riding chaises. Thomas Stockett, for example, a planter, died in 1762 worth £1,010 owning a wide assortment of consumer goods, including china and expensive glassware, books, a coat-of-arms, a clock, walnut tables and chairs, and a riding chaise. In sum, Stockett owned all that was necessary to live genteelly on an income of around £150–200 per annum. Because he left debts of just £31 at his death, we can presume that Stockett managed to live within his means. He could, of course, have attempted to increase his income, but for what purpose? He had achieved a genteel life-style, he had managed to provide for his dependents, and he was a respected and prominent member of his community. For Stockett, and for many wealthy planters, the benefits to be obtained from entrepreneurial endeavor were minimal.

An income of £200 per annum placed Stockett comfortably above the mass of men toiling in the Chesapeake. In the late seventeenth century, a landed planter was lucky to gross £20 per annum, and many small planters cleared probably no more than £5 annually.[64] Within their own society, the Maryland elite formed a privileged enclave of wealth, enjoying an income and a life-style commensurate with that income that others could only envy. But within the wider world of Britain and its transatlantic empire, wealthy Marylanders were parvenus. Planters in the South Carolina low country and in the British West Indies were vastly wealthier. In Jamaica, the wealthiest colony in British America, the richest men at the eve of Revolution left estates valued at over £100,000 sterling and the average estate was over £4,000 sterling. The richest planter left land, slaves, debts, and personal property valued at £350,120 sterling, or more than three times as much as Charles Carroll of Annapolis, the richest man in Maryland by some margin, calculated his estate to be worth. British gentry and aristocrats also enjoyed incomes well above those achieved in Maryland. The richest, such as the Duke of Devonshire, jogged along upon around £60,000 per year in the mid-eighteenth century.[65] Some elite members may have fancied themselves as English squires, but more astute observers realized otherwise. Stephen Bordley, from a wealthy family in Maryland, summed up the social status of an elite Marylander accurately when describing the situation of his brother to an English correspondent: "My next bro[ther] is William who lives on his own land which is as good as any in England, and is one whom you would call a gentleman-farmer or in ye old fash'd Stile, a Yeoman."[66]

Bordley's perceptive comment places the Maryland elite in its proper context. Within the transatlantic world of the British Empire, wealthy Marylanders were of middling status. Although they may have been men of substance in colonial Maryland, they counted for very little in the far grander society of metropolitan Britain. Englishmen never accepted them, even grudgingly, as equals, as they were forced to do with West Indian planters and East India Company nabobs. The limited extent of elite wealth in Maryland put considerable constraints on and perhaps determined elite behavior. Not actually gentry, they seldom aspired to live in the grand style of the English gentry, being content with a comfortable sufficiency, a gentleman's "competence." Increasingly it was possible to gain a "competence" from planting alone and eschew the risks of trade. Having obtained most of the consumer goods available on a limited market, wealthy Marylanders for the most part lived moderately by metropolitan and even provincial standards.

A gentleman's "competency" was more than merely being satisfied with a moderate level of wealth. For most wealthy men in mid-eighteenth-century Maryland it also meant being a planter—by implication the most admirable and desirable of all occupations. This belief in what we might call the superiority of the gentleman planter over all other trades and occupations was common among nineteenth-century antebellum planters and indeed is an essential characteristic of the planter culture of the eighteenth century.

From the vantage point of the nineteenth century, the collective choice of most of the elite to concentrate on planting had deleterious effects for both Maryland and for the elite itself. In the nineteenth century, city merchants economically and politically eclipsed planters, especially in Maryland. As Barbara Fields argues, by 1850 there were two Marylands, one founded on free labor and one on slavery. Free labor Maryland, led by the metropolis of Baltimore, was clearly the most dynamic of the two regions. From parity in 1790, northern Maryland, only tangentially linked to slavery and the plantation economy, quickly outstripped the rest of the state in terms of population and economic activity. By 1850, northern Maryland accounted for over 90 percent of the value of Maryland's annual product. The area's per capita output of $85.13 was well above southern Maryland's $16.02 and the Eastern Shore's $10.71. Only through their exploitation of a political system biased in favor of planting interests could planters maintain the power that they had traditionally exercised.[67] Nevertheless, it is only through historians' 20/20 hindsight that those of the Maryland elite who chose to remain planters can be said to have chosen badly. Mid-eighteenth century Marylanders can hardly have been expected to foresee that tobacco would decline quite as precipitously as it did after the Revolution nor to have predicted the rapid rise of Baltimore, a rise that was largely attributable to the special though temporary advantages that war in the federal era provided in the area of foreign trade.[68]

Planters' neglect of trade and business limited their economic horizons and bound them to activities that rendered them unable to strike out into new enterprises when adversity beckoned.[69] But they were not economic innocents. The "market mentality" that was such a feature of the seventeenth-century Chesapeake never abated in the eighteenth century, even if native-born elite members seldom pursued the lure of profit with the same intensity as their acquisitive forebears. Southern planters were eager to take advantage of new market possibilities, as when they introduced grain to complement tobacco in the middle decades of the eighteenth century. Planters were never passive rentiers but were actively involved in all aspects of plantation management, seeking to increase efficiency through the rationalization of plantation activities.

Nevertheless, even if the calculating ethic that Weber considers to be the essential ingredient of the "capitalist spirit" was common among planters, they were ambivalent capitalists. This ambivalence arose in part from the contradictions that slavery engendered, the relationship between master and slave being at bottom a nonmarket and noncapitalist relationship, even if formed within a capitalist world.[70] But planters were also uneasy about the variant of capitalism that developed in the northern United States because they did not share many of the assumptions of emerging capitalists in that area. The myth that planters increasingly created about themselves—a myth of southern honor that emphasized the virtues of hospitality, manly independence, and commitment to a fixed and hierarchical social order—encouraged them to believe that an ability to enjoy life without constant preoccupation with material gain was in itself virtuous and desirable.[71] This myth was increasingly divergent from the values of the northern bourgeois who created their own myths that stressed the dignity of labor, the desirability of constantly striving for material self-improvement, and the availability of middle-class respectability to all those with appropriate talents and character. Planters sought not so much to accumulate profits, as they imagined northern capitalists did, but instead aspired to a comfortable independence or, as they might have put it, to a "gentleman's competency" as planters.[72] In addition, as the next chapter shows, it enabled planters to live within their means and thus attain the independence without indebtedness that colonial Marylanders so cherished.

NOTES

1. For a comparison of standards of living in colonial Maryland, see Lois Green Carr, "Emigration and the Standard of Living: the Seventeenth-century Chesapeake," *JEH*, 52 (1992), 271–91; and idem, "Emigration and the Standard of Living: The Eighteenth-Century Chesapeake," in John J. McCusker and Kenneth Morgan (eds.), *The Early Modern Atlantic Economy* (Cambridge: Cambridge University Press, 2000), 319–43.
2. Charles G. Steffen, *From Gentlemen to Townsmen: The Gentry of Baltimore County Maryland, 1660–1776* (Lexington: University Press of Kentucky, 1993), 77.
3. See Aubrey C. Land, "Economic Base and Social Structure: The Northern Chesapeake in the Eighteenth Century," *JEH*, 25 (1965), 639–54; idem, "Economic Behavior in a Planting Society," *JSH*, 33 (1967), 469–85.
4. Gloria L. Main, "Inequality in Early America: The Evidence from Probate Records of Maryland and Massachusetts," *JIH*, VII (1977), 570; Paul G.E. Clemens, *The Atlantic Economy and Colonial Maryland's Eastern Shore: From Tobacco to Grain* (Ithaca, NY: Cornell University Press, 1980), 135. See also Allan Kulikoff, *Tobacco and Slaves: The Development of Southern Cultures in the Chesapeake, 1680–1800* (Chapel Hill, University of North Carolina Press, 1986), 265; Arthur P. Middleton, *Tobacco Coast: A Maritime History of the Chesapeake Bay in the Colonial Era* (Newport News, VA: Mariners' Museum, 1953), 122; and Ronald Hoffman, " 'Marylando-

Hibernus': Charles Carroll the Settler, 1660–1720," *WMQ*, 3d. Ser., XLV (1988), 219–226.

5. James Oakes, *Slavery and Freedom: An Interpretation of the Old South* (New York: Alfred A. Knopf, 1990), 52; and idem, *The Ruling Race: A History of American Slaveholders* (New York: Alfred A. Knopf, 1982), 153, 190–91.

6. J.A. Schumpeter, *The Theory of Economic Development* (Cambridge, MA: Harvard University Press, 1934), 62–94; Mark Casson, *The Entrepreneur: An Economic Theory* (Oxford: Robertson, 1982), 23; and Peter Kilby (ed.), *Entrepreneurship and Economic Development* (New York: Free Press, 1971), 3. See also C. Lesger and L. Noordegraf (eds.), *Entrepreneurs and Entrepreneurship in Early Modern Times: Merchants and Industrialists within the Orbit of the Dutch Staplemarket* (The Hague, 1995).

7. Oakes, *Slavery and Freedom*, 37; Douglass North, *The Economic Growth of the United States, 1790–1860* (New York: Prentice Hall, 1966), 122–34; Gavin Wright, *The Political Economy of the Cotton South* (New York: W. W. Norton, 1978), 62–74.

8. Inventories and Accounts 27 *MHR* (1707), 246. For elite standards of living in the seventeenth-century, see Lois Green Carr et al., *Robert Cole's World: Agriculture and Society in Early Maryland* (Chapel Hill: University of North Carolina Press, 1991), 97–107.

9. Inventories 1 (1718), 470.

10. Inventories 92 (1766), 251; Wills 33 (1765), 258.

11. Charles Steffen also sees planters as withdrawing rather than being pushed from commercial activities. Steffen, *From Gentlemen to Townsmen*, 94–95.

12. See the articles collected in Jacob M. Price, *Tobacco in Atlantic Trade: the Chesapeake, London and Glasgow 1675–1775* (Brookfield, VT: Variarum, 1995) for changes in the tobacco trade. For the significance of friendship and personal links within the international business community, see David Hancock, *Citizens of the World: London Merchants and the Integration of the British Atlantic Community, 1735–1785* (New York: Cambridge University Press, 1995), 140–41; and Kenneth Morgan, "Business Networks in the British Export Trade to North America, 1750–1800," in McCusker and Morgan (eds.), *The Early Modern Atlantic Economy*, 39–40.

13. Jacob M. Price, *Capital and Credit in British Overseas Trade: The View from the Chesapeake* (Cambridge, MA: Harvard University Press, 1980), 128; Charles Steffen, "The Rise of the Independent Merchant in the Chesapeake: Baltimore County, 1660–1769," *JAH*, 76 (1989), 7–33.

14. Inventories 91 (1767), 149.

15. Charles G. Steffen, "Gentry and Bourgeois: Patterns of Merchant Investment in Baltimore County, Maryland, 1658–1776," *JSH*, XX (1987), 538; idem, "The Rise of the Independent Merchant, 27.

16. Robert J. Brugger, *Maryland: A Middle Temperament, 1634–1980* (Baltimore: Johns Hopkins University Press, 1988), 158–60; Norman K. Risjord, *Chesapeake Politics, 1781–1800* (New York: Columbia University Press, 1978), 8–10; Mary Jane Dowd, "The State of the Maryland Economy, 1776–1807," *MHM*, LVII (1962), 90–132, 229–59; Bayley Ellen Marks, "Economics and Society in a Staple Plantation System, St. Mary's County, Maryland, 1790–1840" (unpublished Ph.D., University of Maryland, 1979); and Steven Sarson, "Landlessness and Tenancy in Early National Prince George's County, Maryland," *WMQ*, 3d Ser., LVII (2000), 569–98.

17. Whitman H. Ridgway, *Community Leadership in Maryland, 1790–1840: A*

Comparative Analysis of Power in Society (Chapel Hill: University of North Carolina Press, 1979), Chapters 1–4.

18. Robert Oliver, an immigrant of the 1760s, is a good example of a man who attained considerable wealth—over $500,000—through trade that he would have been unlikely to achieve as a planter. Robert Gilmor, an immigrant who started out as a factor on the Eastern Shore, later took advantage of the rapidly expanding opportunities in commerce in Baltimore, and ended up with a fortune even larger than Oliver. For Oliver see Stuart W. Bruchey, *Robert Oliver, Merchant of Baltimore, 1783–1819* (Baltimore: Johns Hopkins University Press, 1956). For Gilmor, see Ronald Hoffman, *A Spirit of Dissension: Economics, Politics, and the Revolution in Maryland* (Baltimore: Johns Hopkins University Press, 1973), 79–80. For Charles Carroll of Carrollton, see Ronald Hoffman, *Princes of Ireland, Planters of Maryland: A Carroll Saga, 1500–1782* (Chapel Hill: University of North Carolina Press, 2000), 334–50.

19. Thomas M. Doerflinger, *A Vigorous Enterprise: Merchants and Economic Development in Revolutionary Philadelphia* (Chapel Hill: University of North Carolina Press, 1986), 157.

20. For the profitability of trade see Robert Morris Ledger Book, MHR; Clemens, *Atlantic Economy*, 156; and Edward C. Papenfuse, *In Pursuit of Profit: The Annapolis Merchants in the Era of the American Revolution, 1763–1805* (Baltimore: Johns Hopkins University Press, 1975), 52. Doerflinger, *Vigorous Enterprise*, 127, suggests that 12 percent profit on goods was a realistic expectation.

21. Jean B. Russo, "A 'Model' Planter: Edward Lloyd IV, Talbot County, Maryland, 1770–1796," *WMQ*, XLIX (1992), 62–88.

22. Allan Kulikoff, "The Economic Growth of the Eighteenth Century Chesapeake Colonies," *JEH*, XXXIX (1979), 275–88; idem, *Tobacco and Slaves*, 78–85, 118–22, 132–33; Carville Earle, *Evolution of a Tidewater Settlement: All Hallow's Parish, Maryland, 1650–1783* (Chicago: University of Chicago Press, 1975), 211; John J. McCusker and Russell R. Menard, *The Economy of British America, 1607–1789* (Chapel Hill: University of North Carolina Press, 1985), 121–31; Clemens, *Atlantic Economy*, 231.

23. Lois Green Carr and Russell R. Menard, "Immigration and Opportunity: The Freedman in Early Colonial Maryland," in Thad W. Tate and David L. Ammerman (eds.), *The Chesapeake in the Seventeenth Century* (Chapel Hill: University of North Carolina Press, 1979), 206–42.

24. Carr, "Emigration and the Standard of Living: The Eighteenth-Century Chesapeake," 337–38.

25. Steffen, "Gentry and Bourgeois," 531–48.

26. Hoffman, *Princes of Ireland, Planters of Maryland*, 68.

27. Land varied in quality from area to area and even within individual plantations. Land records seldom make any distinction between improved and unimproved land. In Anne Arundel in 1731, to take one county and one year at random, 3,371 acres changed hands at an average price of 44 pence per acre. The variation in price per acre was immense. One tract of 500 acres sold for just £35 whereas another of 100 acres fetched £173. Data from land records were collated by Historic Annapolis, Inc.

28. A recent article by Lois Green Carr and Russell R. Menard suggests that despite large, generally sequential processes afoot that should have produced rising inequality, equality probably increased between 1710 and 1750 after inequality had risen sharply in the seventeenth century. Nevertheless,

they argue that rising inequality was checked rather than stopped and that evidence of strain mounted as the eighteenth century progressed. By the 1780s no place in the Chesapeake could be described as "good poor man's country." "Wealth and Welfare in Early Maryland: Evidence from St. Mary's County," *WMQ*, 3d Ser., LVI (1999), 106–11. Carr notes in an even more recent article, however, that opportunity at the bottom did not improve over the eighteenth century. "Emigration and the Standard of Living: The Eighteenth-Century Chesapeake," 338. See also Kulikoff, "Economic Growth of the Chesapeake Colonies," 275–88. For landlessness and tenancy, see Sarson, "Landlessness and Tenancy," and Lorena S. Walsh, "Land, Landlord, and Leaseholder: Estate Management and Tenant Fortunes in Southern Maryland, 1642–1820," *Agricultural History* 59 (1985), 373–96.

29. Lois Green Carr, "Inheritance in the Colonial Chesapeake," in Ronald Hoffman and Peter J. Albert (eds.), *Women in the Age of the American Revolution* (Charlottesville: University of Virginia Press, 1989), Table 3, 164–65.

30. Lorena S. Walsh, "Charles County, Maryland, 1658–1705: A Study of Chesapeake Social and Political Structure" (unpublished Ph.D., Michigan State University, 1977), 413. Nevertheless, many small farms remained throughout the colonial period. Lois Green Carr and Russell R. Menard, "Land Labor, and Economies of Scale in Early Maryland: Some Limits to Growth in the Chesapeake System of Husbandry," *JEH*, XLIX (1989), 409.

31. The effects of soil exhaustion required between 20 and 50 acres per worker to maintain productivity. Clemens, *Atlantic Economy*, 155, 195–97; Kulikoff, *Tobacco and Slaves*, 47–48.

32. The post–1760 figures exclude the huge landholdings of Edward Lloyd III, who left approximately 43,000 acres on his death in 1770.

33. This interpretation of Chesapeake slavery follows broadly that outlined in Ira Berlin, *Many Thousands Gone: The First Two Centuries of Slavery in North America* (Cambridge, MA: Harvard University Press, 1998), 109–41; Philip D. Morgan, *Slave Counterpoint: Black Culture in the Eighteenth-Century Chesapeake and Lowcountry* (Chapel Hill: University of North Carolina Press, 1998), 27–101, 261–99; and Lorena S. Walsh, *From Calabar to Carter's Grove: A History of a Virginia Slave Community* (Charlottesville: University of Virginia Press, 1997).

34. Jean Butenhoff Lee, "Land and Labor: Parental Bequest Practices in Charles County, Maryland, 1732–1783," in Lois Green Carr, Philip D. Morgan, and Jean B. Russo (eds.), *Colonial Chesapeake Society* (Chapel Hill: University of North Carolina Press, 1988), 340.

35. Paul G.E. Clemens, "The Operation of an Eighteenth-Century Chesapeake Tobacco Plantation," *Agricultural History*, 49 (1975), 517–31; Christine Daniels, "Gresham's Laws: Labor Management on an Early Eighteenth-Century Chesapeake Plantation," *JSH*, LXII (1996), 213–24, 223, 236.

36. For optimum slave labor force sizes, see Russo, "A 'Model' Planter," 79; Lois Green Carr and Lorena S. Walsh, "Economic Diversification and Labor Organization in the Chesapeake, 1650–1820," in Stephen Innes (ed.), *Work and Labor in Early America* (Chapel Hill: University of North Carolina Press, 1988), 162; and Kulikoff, *Tobacco and Slaves*, 386–87, 396–97.

37. Walsh, *From Calabar to Carter's Grove*, 289.

38. Most of the evidence for the selling of surplus sales comes from after the

Revolution, but a domestic slave trade also flourished in the colonial
period. See Philip D. Morgan, "Slave Life in Piedmont Virginia" in Carr,
Morgan, and Russo (eds.), *Colonial Chesapeake Society*, 433–84; Allan
Kulikoff, "Uprooted Peoples: Black Migrants in the Age of the American
Revolution, 1790–1820," in Ira Berlin and Ronald Hoffman (eds.), *Slavery
and Freedom in the Age of the American Revolution* (Charlottesville: Uni-
versity of Virginia Press, 1983), 147–53, 168–71; Russo, "A 'Model
Planter,'" 79–80; and Michael Tadman, *Speculators and Slaves: Masters,
Traders, Slaves in the Old South* (Madison: University of Wisconsin, 1989).

39. Daniels, "Gresham's Laws"; Lorena S. Walsh, "Plantation Management in
    the Chesapeake, 1620–1820," *JEH* 49 (1989), 393–406.
40. Walsh, *From Calabar to Carter's Grove*, 142–43; Jamaican Inventories,
    1732–86, Inventories, IB/11/3, Jamaica Archives, Spanishtown, Jamaica;
    Morgan, *Slave Counterpoint*, 81.
41. Russo, "A 'Model' Planter," 80n.
42. Ibid, 79.
43. Between 1738 and 1752, Gresham's slave force increased from 17 to 34
    slaves, entirely due to natural increase. Daniels, "Gresham's Laws," 223,
    238. See also idem, " 'Getting his [or her] Livelyhood': Free Workers in
    Slave Anglo-America," *Agricultural History*, 71 (1997), 125–61; Walsh,
    "Land, Landlord, and Leaseholder"; and Hoffman, *Princes of Ireland,
    Planters of Maryland*, 112–19.
44. Walsh, *From Calabar to Carter's Grove*, 140–41.
45. Russell R. Menard, "The Maryland Slave Population, 1658–1730: A
    Demographic Profile of Blacks in Four Counties," *WMQ*, 3d Ser., XXXII
    (1975), 31; Cathy Matson, *Merchants and Empire: Trading in Colonial
    New York* (Baltimore: Johns Hopkins University Press, 1998), 90; and
    David Eltis, David Richardson, Stephen D. Behrendt, and Herbert S. Klein,
    The Trans-Atlantic Slave Trade: A Database on CD-ROM (Cambridge:
    Cambridge University Press, 1999).
46. Russell R. Menard, "Economic and Social Development of the South," in
    Stanley L. Engerman and Robert E. Gallman (eds.), *The Cambridge Eco-
    nomic History of the United States: The Colonial Era* (Cambridge: Cam-
    bridge University Press, 1996), 278.
47. Richard Morris, "The Measure of Bondage in the Slave States," *Mississippi
    Valley Historical Review*, 41 (1954), 220.
48. For the varieties of forms of labor in colonial Maryland, see Christine
    Daniels, "Alternative Workers in a Slave Economy, Kent County, Mary-
    land, 1675–1810," (unpublished Ph.D., Johns Hopkins University, 1990).
    For transformations in slavery in Maryland, see T. Stephen Whitman, *The
    Price of Freedom: Slavery and Manumission in Baltimore and Early
    National Maryland* (Lexington: University Press of Kentucky, 1997). For
    the number of free blacks, see "Maryland Census, 1755," *Gentlemen's
    Magazine*, 1766, 261; Robert Olwell, "Becoming Free: Manumission and
    the Genesis of a Free Black Community in South Carolina, 1740–1790,"
    Slavery and Abolition, 17 (1996), 1–19; and Gad Heuman, *Between Black
    and White: Race, Politics, and the Free Coloreds in Jamaica, 1792–1865*
    (Westport, CT: Greenwood Press, 1981), 7.
49. Allan Kulikoff, "The Economic Growth of the Eighteenth-Century Chesa-
    peake Colonies," *JEH*, XXXIX (1979), 282–88; David C. Klingaman,
    "The Significance of Grain in the Development of the Tobacco Colonies,"
    JEH, XXIX (1969), 268–78; Carr and Walsh, "Economic Diversification

and Labor Organization in the Chesapeake," 144–88; Carr, "Diversification in the Colonial Chesapeake: Somerset County, Maryland in Comparative Perspective," in Carr, Morgan, and Russo, *Colonial Chesapeake
Society*, 342–82.

50. Edmund S. Morgan, *American Slavery–American Freedom: The Ordeal of
Colonial Virginia* (New York: W. W. Norton, 1995); Gloria L. Main
Tobacco Colony: Life in Early Maryland, 1650–1720 (Princeton, NJ:
Princeton University Press, 1982); and Michael Kammen (ed.), "Maryland
in 1699: A Letter from the Reverend Hugh Jones," *JSH*, 29 (1963), 369–70
(quote). Jones overstated his case, as Lorena Walsh points out. Tobacco
may have been the chief source of market income and the primary export
crop but export earnings accounted for just over one-third of total revenues
in the late seventeenth century. Moreover, farm building was the greatest
source of increased wealth for most farmers. Lorena S. Walsh, "Summing
the Parts: Implications for Estimating Chesapeake Output and Income Subregionally," *WMQ*, 3d Ser., LVI (1999), 56–57.

51. *AM*, 25, 602.

52. Clemens, *Atlantic Economy*, 168–205.

53. T.H. Breen, "Back to Sweat and Toil: Suggestions for the Study of Agricultural Work in Early America," *Pennsylvania History*, 49 (1982), 253; and
idem, *Tobacco Culture: The Mentality of the Great Tidewater Planters on
the Eve of Revolution* (Princeton, NJ: Princeton University Press, 1985),
30–31, 82.

54. Clemens, *Atlantic Economy*, 169–205; Walsh, "Plantation Management,"
395.

55. Kulikoff, *Tobacco and Slaves*, 122–27, 209–14.

56. Breen, *Tobacco Culture*, 251–61; and Rhys Isaac, *The Transformation of
Virginia, 1740–1790* (Chapel Hill: University of North Carolina Press,
1982), 34–42, 74–79, 58–138.

57. *AM*, XIV, 522–23; Figures extrapolated from Alan F. Day, "A Social Study
of Lawyers in Maryland, 1660–1775" (unpublished Ph.D., Johns Hopkins,
1976), 244–253.

58. Hollyday Papers, Note, 1765, Mss. 1317, MHS; Hoffman, *Princes of Ireland, Planters of Maryland*, 109–10, 229–34.

59. Donnell M. Owings, *His Lordship's Patronage: Offices of Profit in Colonial Maryland* (Baltimore: Johns Hopkins University Press, 1953), 12.

60. Hoffman, *Princes of Ireland, Planters of Maryland*, 122, 263.

61. Carr and Menard, "Wealth and Welfare," 110.

62. Lois Green Carr and Lorena S. Walsh, "Changing Life Styles and Consumer Behavior in the Colonial Chesapeake," in Cary Carson, Ronald
Hoffman, and Peter J. Albert (eds.), *Of Consuming Interests: The Style of
Life in the Eighteenth Century* (Charlottesville: University of Virginia Press,
1994), 59–166.

63. T.H. Breen, " 'Baubles of Britain': The American and Consumer Revolutions of the Eighteenth Century," *Past and Present* 119 (1988), 73–104.

64. Clemens, *Atlantic Economy*, 161; Gregory A. Stiverson, *Poverty in a Land
of Plenty: Tenancy in Eighteenth Century Maryland* (Baltimore: Johns
Hopkins University Press, 1977), 45–48.

65. For wealth in lowcountry South Carolina, see Philip D. Morgan (ed.), "A
Profile of a Mid-Eighteenth Century South Carolina Parish: The Tax
Return of Saint James', Goose Creek," *South Carolina Historical
Magazine*, LXXXI (1980), 51–65. For the wealth of Jamaica, see Trevor

Burnard, "'Prodigious Riches': The Wealth of Jamaica in 1774 Once Again," *EHR*, LIV (2001), 505–23. For the wealth of the Duke of Devonshire, see Amanda Foreman, *Georgiania Duchess of Devonshire* (London: HarperCollins, 1998), 17. Philip Jenkins estimates that £1,000 per annum was the lower level of gentry incomes in mid-eighteenth-century Glamorgan, in the British periphery, where incomes were much lower than in England. Philip Jenkins, *The Making of a Ruling Class: The Glamorgan Gentry, 1640–1790* (Cambridge: Cambridge University Press, 1983), 49–50.

66. Bordley to an unknown correspondent, 20 November, 1750, Stephen Bordley Letterbook, Mss. 81, MHS.

67. Barbara Jeanne Fields, *Slavery and Freedom on the Middle Ground: Maryland during the Nineteenth Century* (New Haven: Yale University Press,1985), 1–22.

68. Ibid, 7.

69. Doerflinger, *Vigorous Spirit of Enterprise*, 344–64.

70. Morgan, *Slave Counterpoint*, 273–84.

71. For a thought-provoking analysis of the values that animated southern planters, see Bertram Wyatt-Brown, *Southern Honor: Ethics and Behavior in the Old South* (New York: Oxford University Press, 1982).

72. The ideal of competency was widespread at all levels of society. But competency was tied not to a logic of endless accumulation but to individual and family decisions about the maintenance of a desired level of independence and well-being. The material needs of wealthy planters were greater than those of small planters but their interpretation of competency—an interpretation that gave much greater priority to propertied independence than to profit maximization—was the same. A shared vision of competency, of course, did not preclude competition and disagreement about how individual, family, and class aspirations for competency were to be achieved. Daniel Vickers, "Competency and Competition: Economic Culture in Early America," *WMQ*, 3d. Ser., XLVII (1990), 7, 12, 28.

CHAPTER 3

"A Species of Capital Attached to Certain Mercantile Houses"

Elite Debts and the Significance of Credit

To be wealthy meant more than just having money. It meant being independent from the demands of others and being free from excessive indebtedness. But if substantial indebtedness was inimical to independence, some indebtedness was crucial to gain independence. Credit was extremely important in the growth and development of early America and in fostering the rise of southern planter elites. All enterprise in the early modern era was founded upon a bedrock of credit.[1] The British-American colonies were land rich but poor in capital and labor. Labor was mainly achieved through the importation of, first, servants and, second, slaves. Capital was gained through borrowing and through reinvestment of plantation profits. Without capital acquired through borrowing, American colonists, especially in plantation colonies, would have been unable to develop their land, to obtain labor to cultivate their crops and build industries, or to market their produce and gain a satisfactory standard of living.[2]

The language that southerners invoked to discuss credit and debt ignored the positive benefits that credit allowed and focused almost obsessively on the destructive moral impact of debt. But despite their rhetoric, few wealthy Marylanders were overly indebted. Even fewer had sacrificed their independence to British creditors. On the contrary, wealthy Marylanders actively if cautiously employed credit as a tool for achieving concrete and attainable goals that supported rather than threatened their independence and integrity.[3] This finding is at odds with a longstanding historiography that insists that Chesapeake planters were heavily in debt to British merchants and that relies on the groans of Chesapeake planters during and after the Revolutionary conflict to bolster that claim. This chapter analyzes the real amount of debt that wealthy Marylanders owned and attempts to reinterpret their hostility toward indebtedness, especially to British merchants, in light of the actual debt that they owed.

Jefferson's comments on debt are the most famous planter groans. Writing to a French correspondent in 1786, he claimed that before the Revolution Chesapeake planters "were a species of capital annexed to certain mercantile houses in London," with hereditary debts passing "from father to son for many generations."[4] Jefferson's comments have often been linked with statements made in 1766 by his father-in-law, John Wayles, a merchant-planter who associated debt with "luxury and extravagance."[5] Together, they have been taken as evidence of the increasing indebtedness of planters in the Chesapeake as a consequence of both the manipulations of British merchants and the enticements of high living. Such comments did, of course, have some foundation in fact. Chesapeake debts to Britain were growing in the last quarter century before the Revolution and were large in comparison to debts owed to Britain by other mainland colonies.[6] Some planters, most notably William Byrd III, owed huge sums to British merchants, although these planters were few in number with large amounts of assets to cover their debts. Moreover, they usually got into difficulty only through a combination of extravagance, incompetence, and overoptimistic business decisions.[7]

Even if we dismiss Jefferson's views as paranoiac Whig propaganda and as founded mostly out of the particular family circumstances that he found himself in after his marriage and assumption of his father-in-law's debts,[8] the existence of such views needs to be explained. As T.H. Breen has pointed out, if we approach debt from the standpoint of the anthropologist rather than the accountant and accept that what a man owed was less important than what he thought about debt and how "he defined relations with people to whom he happened to owe money," then Jefferson's and Wayles' fulminations can be seen as ideological statements, verbalizations of deep-seated planter fears. Many Chesapeake planters were obsessed by fears of excessive indebtedness, believing that debt would compromise their personal autonomy, integrity, and virtue.[9] Credit involves human exchanges not just of pounds and pence but of values as well and was discussed in such terms in the Chesapeake. Nevertheless, debt was also a concrete reality— money lent that had to be repaid. It is a mistake to assume that planters did not realize this or that ideological preoccupations with the meaning of debt dominated their thinking. As rational economic actors, wealthy men in the Chesapeake realized that credit and debt were necessary. Credit in the Chesapeake should be viewed not only as a series of moral relationships between guileless planters and avaricious British merchants but also as a "highly rational, mutually advantageous relationship for both clear-sighted lenders and intelligent borrowers."[10]

In a developing economy, credit is necessary for economic growth, and the questions of how, to whom, in what amounts, and for what purpose credit was granted are highly significant. Capital was necessary to acquire land and slaves, to improve plantations, to buy trading vessels, to begin a mercantile operation, to build houses, and to improve standards of living. Even when wealthy men had sufficient cash reserves to make these purchases without borrowing, they often found it quite advantageous to continue to borrow. Land, for example, was comparatively cheap and plentiful in Maryland, especially given the scarcity of labor and capital, but was continually increasing in value, and it was a sensible business decision to buy land on loan, improve it, and wait for higher land prices to occur before repaying the loan. Usually, the long-range annual increment in land was more than the 5 percent maximum interest rate for loans, especially if the land was improved (which took relatively small expenditures of labor to accomplish). Borrowing also allowed the diversion of income for other purposes, such as the acquisition of more labor and more consumer goods.[11]

In addition, credit allowed planters and merchants to engage in money lending. The greatest fortune made in colonial Maryland, that of Charles Carroll of Annapolis, was largely derived from lending out money at interest. In 1764, Carroll had £24,000 sterling out at interest. By 1776, that sum had increased to £41,000 sterling, of which six loans over £1,000 sterling took up nearly half of the total.[12] Lending money also created a network of people in some way obligated to the creditor, with important social and political ramifications. Finally, the multiplier effect of credit benefited the local economy and stimulated further development. Surplus capital could be invested in local goods and services. It could be used both to aid settlement on the frontier and also to attract productive artisans. These developments helped to centralize and increase trade, to found and expand towns, and, in turn, to attract further capital into the region.[13]

We need, therefore, to look at credit as a desirable but occasionally dangerous resource and determine what access to capital various segments of the population had and what use they made of that credit. As Andrew Beveridge has stated, "the allocation of credit is directly tied to social structure and to the dynamics of change in a capitalist society."[14] Fortunately, a source exists— administration accounts: the accounts by executors of estates of debts owed by decedents and costs incurred in the administration of estates—that enables an examination of the debt networks of wealthy Marylanders. From these accounts we can assess the real incidence of indebtedness among wealthy men in the northern Chesapeake.

Both the procedures used in utilizing these remarkably informative documents and some of their limitations as sources need to be outlined. Over 70 percent of the Maryland elite left administration accounts. Their accounts detailed the size of the estate and the costs of estate settlement, and listed the debts owed by the estate to creditors. A careful analysis of each account has been made, distinguishing between debts incurred in the administration of the estate as a result of the decedent's death, legacies and bequests made by the deceased, and debts owed to creditors. Because many of the elite owed money or tobacco to a large number of people or institutions, a distinction has been made between small and large debts owed. Large debts are defined as over £8 for any decedent who died before 1737 and over £10 for any decedent dying after 1736—the increase being designed to take into account inflation in the second half of the eighteenth century. The name and status of each large creditor were noted, along with the amount of money or tobacco owed. The numbers and amount of small debts were also tabulated. I have been careful to ensure that each account contained a complete listing of all debts by comparing the total value of the estate listed in the account to the value of an accurate inventory and by excluding accounts that did not delineate each individual debt to the estate. Very few accounts made an accurate separation between types of debts such as bonds, mortgages, and unsecured loans, but each account had to distinguish between debts owed to creditors and debts that were bequests or legacies in order to be used. Bequests and legacies cannot be considered as liabilities on the estate but were assets to be disposed as the decedent dictated. Fortunately, executors were invariably scrupulous in their enumeration of debts and in their distinctions between debts and bequests.

Were administration accounts representative? It is likely that they were. Wealthy people had much more at stake in the proper settlement of their estates than poor testators and therefore more often tended to put their estates through probate. A glance at any administration account book shows that the majority of testators who put their estate through probate were wealthier than the average decedent. The costs of settling an estate could be considerable and only those testators with either substantial property or significant indebtedness would want, or be required, to go through probate. In addition, the central government, the Commissary General, and local sheriffs, who collected sizable fees for each estate that went through probate based on the size of the estate, had more interest in ensuring that large estates went through probate than they did with less lucrative estates. Creditors were also anxious that their debtors go through the prescribed legal processes so that their money could be secured. Thus wealthy testators, who had larger aggregate debts than the general populace, went through probate more frequently than less wealthy people. Nevertheless, there is some unrepresentativeness in the sample, as a number of the very richest merchants and planters in eighteenth-century Maryland did not have their estates probated. Even when the very rich did leave inventories of their estates, they often left no accounts.[15] Why some of the very rich did not leave administration accounts is unclear, but may be related to their good fortune in having enough cash reserves to be able to avoid borrowing from others. Dr. Charles Carroll, Charles Carroll, the Settler, and Charles Carroll, Barrister, for instance, all stated in their wills that their debts were few and requested that no inventory of their estate be taken and no accounts be made.[16] The effects of the underrepresentation of the very rich in administration accounts are hard to measure. The inclusion of the missing very wealthy decedents would probably lower indebtedness because it does not appear that any of the absent very wealthy were seriously in debt. One suspects that they were similar to the richest man in this sample, Amos Garrett of Annapolis, who left an estate in 1729 of £24,450 and disbursements of only £1,777, amounting to 7.3 percent of his total estate.

Differences in the likelihood of leaving an administrative account do exist over time: 55 percent of the decedents who died before 1726 left accounts, compared to 77 percent of the decedents dying after 1725. Members of the earlier group had disbursements and desperate debts that amounted to 27 percent of average total estate value (TEV). Members of the latter group had debts that took up 37 percent of the average estate. Thus, variances in reporting rates probably led to a slight overestimation of elite indebtedness. Wealthy men who did not leave accounts probably had fewer debts compared to assets than those that did leave accounts, but court records show that at least some wealthy men not in this sample did leave considerable debts at death. The roguish Thomas Macnemara, for example, died in 1720 deeply in debt, causing his widow great trouble in settling his estate. In Baltimore County, the executors of John Stokes, who died in 1732, had to sell most of his land to pay a large debt of £1,300 sterling (undeflated) to Philip Smith, a London merchant. Without more evidence, however, it seems reasonable to assume that wealthy men who left accounts were representative of the whole, especially because most wealthy men did leave accounts.

One problem with using administration accounts is that the fact of dying in and of itself caused considerable expense. The Commissary General, the Deputy Commissary in each county, and local sheriffs were all entitled to fees at the death of the decedent. Moreover, the executor of the estate was allowed a percentage of the estate as well as reimbursements for legitimate expenses in settling the estate. Such expenses could include paying for the funeral of the deceased, the costs of maintaining and educating the deceased's children, or the expenses of managing the deceased's plantation. These miscellaneous charges on the estate were often substantial: £95 on average. Just less than one-third of total disbursements were on average miscellaneous charges. A large proportion of these charges consisted of the share of the estate allowed to be taken by the executors. A desire to keep that share within the family may be one reason why the majority of the elite appointed either a wife or an of-age son as an executor. The costs of settling an estate were charges on the estate and were important obligations to the extent that they reduced heirs' inheritances. Yet their inclusion as debts increases the amounts of elite indebtedness artificially and makes it appear that elite members at death were more indebted than they were when they were alive. Thus, they have been excluded from this analysis of elite debts.

Accounts provide a fascinating picture of wealthy Marylanders' debt, overturning many preconceptions about indebtedness based on planter complaints. Using accounts we can test whether wealthy Marylanders were so overwhelmed by debt that they could not pay or service their debts without either selling large amounts of property or passing on burdensome debts to a future generation. In addition we can examine whether wealthy Marylanders were able to borrow sufficient capital to carry on their business operations or whether they were hindered by a chronic lack of working capital. Three measures have been used to judge the extent of a wealthy Marylander's indebtedness: net worth after disbursements and desperate debts (debts owed to the estate that were unlikely to be collected) have been subtracted, net worth as a percentage of TEV, and disbursements as a percentage of TEV. The first measure shows how many of the elite slipped into another wealth category after debts were paid; the latter two measures indicate the importance of debt to any individual estate.

As Tables 3.1 and 3.2 show, most wealthy Marylanders were not excessively indebted. Although nearly 36 percent of elite members had net worth less than £650 after disbursements and desperate debts were subtracted from TEV, only 13 percent had net worth under £100 and 7 percent had debts totaling more than their assets. These figures overestimate elite downward mobility. Of 74 decedents with net worths between £225 and £650, two-thirds had TEVs less than £1,000 and 42 percent had TEVs less than £750. These men were not particularly wealthy to begin with.

Table 3.1 Measures of Indebtedness

	Anne Arundel	Baltimore	Somerset	Talbot	Total
Net worth[a] by amount					
Under £0 (%)	5	10	2	14	7
£0–225 (%)	7	3	2	7	5
£225–650 (%)	21	28	22	21	23
£650+ (%)	67	60	73	58	65
Disbursements[b] as a percentage of TEV					
Under 5 (%)	27	10	42	21	24
5–20 (%)	31	32	36	33	32
20–50 (%)	23	35	13	17	23
50+ (%)	20	23	9	29	21
Net worth as percentage of TEV					
Over 75 (%)	56	33	78	56	54
50–75 (%)	20	30	11	14	20
25–50 (%)	9	16	7	5	9
Under 25 (%)	16	20	4	25	17

[a]Net worth is defined as TEV minus disbursements.

[b]Disbursements are all debts not concerned with the settlement of the estate and the burial of the deceased.

Source: Inventories and Accounts, Accounts, *MHR.*

Table 3.2 Changes in Various Categories of Indebtedness over Time

	Net worth[a]	Disbursements[a]	Desperate debts and disbursements[a]
Pre-1726	73	25	29
1726–1742	63	34	37
1743–1759	65	28	35
1760+	63	30	38
1691–1777	65	30	35

[a]As a percentage of TEV.

Source: Inventories and Accounts, Accounts, *MHR.*

Their indebtedness was unlikely to alter their status greatly. If debts were taken from assets, they would still remain landowners and slave owners but on a smaller scale. Of course, if we add landed wealth to personal wealth, then the percentage of men seriously indebted falls even further. It was a rare member of the elite who carried so many debts that at his death his heirs would have been seriously inconvenienced or would have had to dispose of substantial portions of property.

Nevertheless, the amount of debt a man carried might have been less important than how debt affected his assets. It might explain why planters in particular were prone to lament their sorry state as compromised debtors. We can measure these effects by looking at the percentage of TEV taken up by disbursements. Here again, the majority of the elite were left with most of their estate intact when debts were subtracted from TEV. Over 40 percent of decedents owed less than 10 percent of TEV to creditors, and 72 percent owed less than 40 percent. When we take into account all charges on the estate—disbursements and desperate debts—excessive elite indebtedness increases only marginally: 17 percent of men had fewer than 25 percent of TEV remaining after liabilities to the estate were subtracted. If we take a net worth of under £225, disbursements greater than 50 percent of TEV, or net worth less than 25 percent of TEV as qualifications for substantial indebtedness, just over one in five wealthy Marylanders had debt problems that may have caused them to sell land or slaves.[17] To keep these data in perspective, the numbers of the heavily indebted should be compared to the number of wealthy men who avoided what Virginia planter Richard Corbin in 1761 called the "Evil of being in Debt."[18] If we take the very low figure of disbursements under 5 percent of TEV as the qualification for complete independence from debt, then 24 percent of the Maryland elite heeded Corbin's warning. To put it another way, for every member of the elite who was substantially indebted, there was another who was nearly completely debt free and who could achieve the financial independence that William Byrd II celebrated in 1726 as crucial to the social goals of a slave-owning patriarch.[19]

Table 3.3 outlines the characteristics of the substantially indebted and those with very little debt. The typical substantially indebted wealthy man was significantly different from his

Table 3.3 Comparisons of Elite Members Who Are Seriously Indebted
and Those with Little Debt

	Seriously indebted (N = 64)	Little debt (N = 78)
Occupation (%)		
Principally planter	34	55
Merchant-planter	26	40
Principally merchant	35	3
Professional	5	3
Age (%)		
Under 30	8	0
31–40	15	5
41–50	38	27
51–60	29	15
61+	10	53
Percentage of TEV in form of debts (%)		
None	10	23
Under 20%	30	49
21–60%	35	26
61%+	26	3

Source: Inventories and Accounts, Inventories, *MHR.*

counterpart who had little debt in age, occupation, and in the extent of his involvement in money lending. He was likely to be a merchant or merchant-planter, under 45, with debts due to him comprising over 40 percent of his personal estate. An elite member with little debt, on the other hand, was much more likely to be a planter, over 60 years in age, with very little of his estate (under 20 percent) lent out to others. Levels of indebtedness, therefore, were very much a reflection of an individual's age and involvement in the commercial world.

Differences in age are especially revealing. Young men embarking on their careers, especially those involved in trade, needed capital with which to finance their businesses and consequently tried to borrow as much as they possibly could. They assumed that they would be able to repay these loans when they were properly established. If they died at a young age, the repayment of debts was disrupted. A number of the most seriously indebted elite members died young. Consequently, they were much more indebted than they might have been had they lived to old age. Their indebtedness does not demonstrate so much extravagance or living beyond their means as it does their access to ample amounts of credit (which, with luck and skill, could be used to turn a comfortable inheritance into a considerable fortune) and their misfortune in dying young.

William Nicholson II, for example, died with very large debts of £4,060 on assets of £2,016. He was the only wealthy man who at first glance seems to fit within Jefferson's picture of planters owned completely by avaricious British merchants: 89 percent of his debt was owed to the London merchant, William Hunt. The fact that his only son, Beale, died at age 33 with a meager personal estate of £24 suggests that Nicholson had seriously overextended himself. Yet his indebtedness was the result of his dying at age 27 when he was still establishing himself as a merchant in Annapolis. What is most revealing about his indebtedness is that he was able to borrow such a large sum from an English merchant at such a young age. Nicholson had certain advantages as a credit risk. He was the son of a prominent merchant-planter and was married to the heiress of John Beale, a second-generation legislator and officeholder. London merchants knew him to be a good risk because of his kin links to other good credit risks.[20] Much of his borrowed money was put out on loan, was employed to finance his mercantile operations, and was used to purchase over 6,000 acres in Anne Arundel and Baltimore Counties. Very little of it was used on personal expenditure: personal goods comprised only 5 percent of his TEV. Nicholson used other people's money to increase his wealth and to carve out a position for himself as a dominant merchant on the Western Shore. Quite possibly, he would have achieved his goal if he had not died so young. Land prices rose considerably over the course of the eighteenth century, and Nicholson obviously had bought land on the assumption that the increase in the value of his land would be more than the cost of servicing his debts. His indebtedness, therefore, was a calculated risk—the major risk being that he would live to take advantage of an improving Chesapeake economy.

James Heath is another example of someone with a sizable fortune, important connections, a secure place within Maryland society, and considerable debts resulting from death at a young age. The son of a large planter from Cecil County and the son-in-law of Attorney General Daniel Dulany, Sr., he was a legislator in his twenties and had acquired extensive real estate (over 5000 acres). He left a TEV of £3,454 when he died in his 29th year, 56 percent of which was in the form of debts due to him. He also owed large sums and left a negative net worth of −£615 when his estate was settled. Again, the point to make about his indebtedness is that he had such easy access to credit while a young man. He was sufficiently credit-worthy to be able to borrow heavily from some of the richest men in the province, including Edward Lloyd III, Daniel Dulany, Sr., Charles Carroll, Sr., Bennet Chew, and John Beale Bordley. Little of this borrowed money was diverted to conspicuous consumption—he had personal goods worth less than 4 percent of his TEV—being instead used to finance his business dealings. Presumably, if he had not died before he was 30 years old, his connections and large inheritances would have made him, like his brother-in-law Daniel Dulany, Jr., a major political and economic player. Then, he would have been easily able to repay his creditors and become a large creditor himself.

Both Heath and Nicholson, therefore, hoped to enlarge their fortunes by taking advantage of their ability to attract capital. Credit, if employed creatively, could augment their fortunes and social standing. Levin Gale, from Somerset County, is another man who used credit in this manner. He died at age 40, a powerful figure not just in Somerset but also in the province as a whole. Gale left the largest estate in colonial Somerset—£9,651—and had by far the largest amount of debts of any Somerset resident—£12,057. He had overextended himself, clearly, and may have been more of a warning than an example to other gentlemen. Yet his career was one of the most successful in colonial Somerset. A prominent attorney and the chief merchant on the lower Eastern Shore by the late 1730s, he forged extensive links with prosperous Western Shore and British merchants. He married the daughter of a very prominent member of the elite of Accomack County, Virginia, and became one of only three men from Somerset to become a member of the Upper House. In addition, he obtained many choice political offices both in Somerset and in Annapolis. His indebtedness did not hinder his rise to provincial prominence. He needed to borrow extensively for his merchant operations, but these operations seem to have fostered his rise into provincial leadership. For Gale, borrowing money on a large scale expanded his business and allowed him entry in the higher reaches of provincial politics. None of his brothers was as economically and politically conspicuous, suggesting a correlation between his use of credit and his political success.

Indebtedness at death was therefore largely determined by time of death within the life cycle. An ambitious young man, especially if he was involved in trade, often borrowed heavily in the early stages of his career, calculating that by the time he was withdrawing from an active life, he would be in a position to repay the debts that had financed a successful increase in his wealth. A number of wealthy Marylanders achieved what Nicholson, Heath, and Gale sought to do before early death interrupted their plans. John, Thomas, and William Worthington, for example, died at advanced ages with few debts, having considerably enhanced their wealth from what they had inherited. They were the sons of John Worthington I, who left an estate of £691. After careers as merchant-planters in Anne Arundel County, they died worth £2,458, £2,142, and £2,385 respectively. They all left minimal debts but had sizable percentages of their estates tied up in desperate debts and debts receivable. Presumably, by a combination of business acumen, careful deployment of capital resources, and surviving past 60, they had obviated the need to borrow and had become large-scale creditors rather than debtors. The varying degrees of indebtedness between the Worthingtons, on the one hand, and William Nicholson, James Heath, and Levin Gale, on the other, do not seem to be a result of different business policies, attitudes to credit, or as Jefferson or Wayles believed, alternative levels of indulgence. Rather, they were a function primarily of age.[21]

Occupation was also important. Merchants needed (or were able to acquire) more credit than planters. Over a third of the substantially indebted were merchants. Planters did not borrow so heavily, especially if they inherited land and slaves. Entering into trade, on the other hand, required not only a large initial investment but also constant applications of capital in order to make purchases both in Maryland and in Britain. Few men in colonial

Maryland could finance mercantile operations entirely out of their own pockets. Consequently, most merchants needed to borrow to remain in business. Wealthy native-born Maryland planters hesitated before involving themselves fully in the confusing and increasingly complex swirl of commerce. The movement of the elite away from direct involvement in commerce only heightened their ambivalence about what seemed to them to be the vagaries of a rapidly changing Atlantic credit system, a system, moreover, that bypassed the majority of planters who did not have close links to British merchants.[22]

Another contrast between the substantially indebted and those with little debt is that the substantially indebted were heavily involved in the local money market as both borrowers and lenders. Nearly half of substantially indebted men had over 40 percent of their TEV tied up in the form of desperate debts or debts receivable compared to 14 percent of those with little debt. Because "not one person in a hundred pays ready money for the things he buys in a store," merchants were forced to extend generous credit terms to their customers.[23] Sometimes this practice led to financial problems. John Inch, for example, a silversmith in Annapolis, left a negative net worth of –£83, most of which was the result of the nearly two-thirds of his estate that had to be written off as desperate debts.[24]

It is a mistake to take notice only of the rhetoric of a few late eighteenth-century planters who feared that debt would lessen personal autonomy without noting that wealthy men in the Chesapeake were active players in creating the extensive credit networks that were a vital part of the functioning of the international Atlantic economy.[25] Indeed, it was not only necessary but also desirable to lend money in order to make surplus capital work and to borrow to maintain the liquidity of assets. It is hardly coincidental that Somerset County was both the least prosperous of the four counties in this study and had the highest proportion of wealthy men with few debts. Disbursements there took up on average 15 percent of the average TEV, half of the average for wealthy Marylanders as a whole. Only four wealthy men from Somerset, including Levin Gale, were seriously indebted. The marginality of Somerset's economy allowed little opportunity for aspiring entrepreneurs to borrow the money needed to raise their fortune and social standing. In a spiraling effect, the lack of credit within the Somerset economy compounded the poverty of the county.

Much of the rhetoric about debt in the Chesapeake has concentrated on the professed desire of gentlemen to be free from financial dependence on others and so reach a state in which they had "no Bills to pay" and where "half-a-Crown would rest undisturbed in my Pocket for many Moons together."[26] Yet if a gentleman believed that it was best if he had no bills to pay, he seldom practiced what he preached. Most of the elite, while having more than enough assets to cover their debts, owed money to a large number of people. Moreover, those with greater wealth than usual (TEVs between £5,000 and £10,000: the very richest Marylanders, those with TEVs greater than £10,000, tended to have little debt but extended credit on a large scale) not only were creditors with extensive networks of debtors but also had more than average indebtedness. Their debts, on average, amounted to 47 percent of their TEV.

Even more so than the population as a whole, wealthy Marylanders grew more affluent over the course of the eighteenth century, especially after 1750. Wealthy Marylanders were dominant actors in the economic expansion of the period. Credit borrowed by rich men led to increased economic development, as planters improved their plantations, further settled the frontier, and helped make the society of the Chesapeake both more complex and more British than in the seventeenth century.[27] The growth of debt among the wealthy after mid-century, nevertheless, should not be exaggerated. Comparatively few rich men seriously overextended themselves and average net worth did not decrease greatly over time: three-quarters of men dying after 1759 were not substantially indebted. Most great planters, merchants, and professionals were able to increase the amount of debt they held without greatly compromising their independence.[28]

Given the dramatic expansion in credit available between 1750 and 1776 in the Chesapeake as British firms competed for advantage in the lucrative tobacco trade, it is on the surface surprising that wealthy Marylanders took little advantage of these favorable borrowing opportunities.[29] British credit was distributed liberally throughout the region. According to Kulikoff, merchants and gentlemen— the men most likely to be involved in transatlantic trade—owed just 47 percent of Virginia's British debt even though they accounted for well over half of the total wealth in the colony. A majority of British credit was lent to poorer planters, especially to planters on the frontier. Scottish factors were particularly prominent lenders, willing to take far greater risks than local merchants and planters were seemingly willing to do.[30]

The result was rising debt levels among middling to poor planters. Glaswegian traders recognized the risks they were taking in extending credit by deducting from their annual accounts 20 percent on all balances even after desperate and doubtful debts had been deducted.[31] Defaults on loans became much more common from the mid-eighteenth century. Before 1726, desperate debts accounted for 3 percent of the average wealthy Marylander's estate. That percentage nearly quadrupled for decedents dying after 1743. Indeed, the dramatic increase in desperate debts— invariably owed by poor Marylanders—accounts for virtually all of the increase in wealthy Marylanders' indebtedness after mid-century. Experience with increasing numbers of bad debts would have encouraged wealthy Marylanders' growing aversion to trade, would have lessened whatever limited enthusiasm they had for becoming involved themselves in the burgeoning market for credit, and would have heightened their predilection for lending money only to people like themselves on whom they could rely to pay their debts. Instead of taking advantage of new credit opportunities that could enable them to indulge in speculation and in the pursuit of luxury, as critics claimed, third- or fourth-generation Maryland planters were careful to use credit cautiously in order to moderately improve their properties. If anything, planters were more wary than their seventeenth-century ancestors were about the complex commercial changes that were occurring in the Chesapeake, principally because they had purposely removed themselves from a commercial world increasingly distasteful to them and had been supplanted by indigenous merchants and British factors in the lucrative but risky business of extending credit to planters on the developing frontier.

In addition, the equation that John Wayles made between elite indebtedness and conspicuous consumption seems totally unfounded in Maryland.[32] Lois Green Carr and Lorena S. Walsh have shown that although consumption of luxury goods by the wealthy increased as the eighteenth century progressed, both the total amount invested in consumer goods and the percentage of consumer goods in TEV decreased over time. This study confirms those findings. Wealthy Marylanders who died after 1759 had decreased the proportion of their estate that was composed of consumer goods to two-thirds of what men dying before 1726 owned. Anne Arundel elite members dying after 1759—men living closest to the urban delights and shops of Annapolis—had only 9 percent of their wealth tied up in consumer goods. Moreover, overlarge investment in luxury goods was not significant even for those who were substantially indebted. Wealthy Marylanders were able to immerse themselves in the consumer revolution of the eighteenth century without getting into debt. In Maryland, at least, the cries of commentators concerned that personal indulgence was leading to financial ruin were misplaced.[33]

What types of debt networks did wealthy Maryland men create? Most—97 percent—were debtors. Two-thirds owed money to more than 10 creditors and over one-third died indebted to more than 20 creditors. A small number of men owed money to lots of people: 19 decedents had over 50 creditors each at death. The average wealthy Marylander had 14 small creditors and 5 large creditors (large creditors being people owed more than £8 or £10, depending on the time period). Differences over time and by county were minimal, except that decedents with very large estates, worth over £5,000, had a greater number of large creditors. The very rich had on average 14 large and 18 small creditors.

Small creditors were not very important in the overall makeup of elite debt. Elite men owed small creditors on average 6 percent of their debts, amounting to 1.4 percent of TEV. Small creditors could be paid off without substantially diminishing assets. Large creditors were not so easily accommodated. The average decedent owed 22 percent of his personal estate to large creditors. His relationships with these large creditors were thus important and helped to define his attitudes to indebtedness. We need, therefore, to know whom these large creditors were and how they interacted with their debtors. To approach this question systematically, I have made a careful analysis of each large creditor of the elite and have assigned each, if he or she could be identified, to specific categories defined by status and area of residence. Tables 3.4 and 3.5 tabulate my results.[34]

Table 3.4 Principal Creditors of Elite Members
with Disbursements over £100: Large Debts Only

Debts	Pre-1726	1726–42	1743–59	1760+	Total
Widely dispersed	22	28	50	22	27
Over 50% debt to specific categories of creditors (%)					
Elite own county	33	25	17	22	27
Maryland elite	51	54	46	62	53
British merchants	27	18	4	16	20
Maryland state	5	0	0	4	3

Source: Inventories and Accounts, Accounts, *MHR.*

Table 3.5 Principal Creditors of Elite Members
with Disbursements over £100: Total Debt

Debts	Pre-1726	1726–42	1743–59	1760+	Total
Widely dispersed	53	46	75	53	53
Over 50% debt to specific categories of creditors					
Elite own county	15	16	4	13	14
Maryland elite	31	41	21	38	34
British merchants	17	13	4	9	13

Source: Inventories and Accounts, Accounts, *MHR.*

Historians have assumed that the principal creditors of wealthy men in the Chesapeake were British merchants.[35] British merchants were an important but by no means dominant group of elite creditors. There were 238 wealthy men who left debts of more than £100. Of these, one in five owed over half of all large debts to British merchants. Slightly more men with significant indebtedness spread their principal debts widely and mostly within local networks. Another one in five elite members did not owe over half of their large debts to any one of the following: fellow wealthy Marylanders, British merchants, a provincial agency, or a representative of the Maryland government. Thus, claims that Maryland planters were over their heads in hock to British merchants do not hold up.

If there was to be anyone to whom a wealthy man would feel

dependent because of debt obligations, it was likely to be another Chesapeake gentleman. Over half of those with over £100 in disbursements owed over half of their large debts to other wealthy Marylanders. Moreover, 27 percent owed over half of their large debts to wealthy men from their own county. Of large debts the share that debt to British merchants took up was significant but not substantial: 13 percent of those with disbursements over £100 owed half of their large debts to British merchants. Put another way, 9 percent owed more than a quarter of their personal estate to British merchants. If real estate is added into the equation, then British merchants had a claim to very little of the average wealthy Marylanders' estate. Instead, wealthy Marylanders were remarkably creative in the patterns of indebtedness they developed. We can isolate seven different types of debt patterns among wealthy men, ranging from the debt patterns of those without debt to the debt patterns of those who were seriously indebted to one creditor.

Just over one in six men had minimal debts and no large creditors. In general, these men were poorer, more likely to be planters, and especially likely to be older than average. George Irving, a planter who died at age 65 with a TEV of £919, was typical. Irving owed £6.91 to nine small creditors. His lack of indebtedness could signify two somewhat opposed conditions. On the one hand, he had lived long enough to pay off any large debts he may have contracted and to achieve a satisfactory income. Alternatively, he may have been hampered by an inability to obtain credit and thus expand his estate to obtain more than moderate wealth. Being a moderately well-off planter with no other sources of income living in the backwaters of rural Somerset on the Eastern Shore may have made credit difficult to come by—lenders were hardly likely to maximize their returns by investing in such a person in such a place.

Over a quarter of elite members had small debts (less than £100) with no more than one or two large creditors. It is difficult to discern any particular differentiating characteristics about this group except that they tended to have to a lesser degree some of the features of those members with very little debt. Consequently, they were slightly poorer, slightly more likely to be native born, slightly more likely to be planters, and slightly older than the elite as a whole. Yet none of these features was pronounced. This category included men such as the planter John Worthington I, who left a TEV of £691 with one large creditor and total debts of £52, and the doctor and merchant Dr. George Buchanan, an immigrant with an estate of £2,545, debts of £62, and two large creditors. These men were far more likely to borrow from other wealthy men than from English merchants: 29 percent owed large debts to English merchants compared to 71 percent who had other wealthy Marylanders as creditors. Some combined debts to English merchants with debts to wealthy Marylanders. But a more frequent strategy was to borrow only from fellow wealthy men, as did Thomas Jobson. Jobson owed debts of £204 at his death, of which £158.50 was owed to Benjamin Allen and Vachel Denton, fellow elite members from Anne Arundel.[36]

A third strategy, favored by one in ten men and most common before the mid-eighteenth century, was to borrow money from between five and seven large creditors, as well as from a large number of small creditors. Reflecting the fact that men in the earlier cohorts were most likely to fall into this category, a high number of immigrants and merchant-planters followed this pattern. Wealth and age were not significant variables here. Once again, men owing money to English creditors—36 percent—were heavily outnumbered by the 97 percent who had rich Marylanders as creditors. Richard Jones can be taken as typical. A native-born merchant-planter, Jones left a TEV of £1,222 and debts of £177. He owed three wealthy Anne Arundel men, Samuel Peele, Charles Carroll the Settler, and William Bladen, £150, with the largest creditor, Peele, owed £57.[37] Although they owed money to a number of people, these men did not owe large sums to one or two people and seldom owed much to British merchants. They used credit advantageously, choosing between varieties of potential creditors. They did not become so indebted to any one man that they lost their financial independence.

A substantial minority of men, although not indebted to any great degree, had one or two principal creditors among five to eight large creditors. This strategy was common in mid-age and while attempting to consolidate an already established estate. In general, men who followed this debt pattern tended to be younger than average and tended to have mid-range estates, with a TEV between £1,501 and £5,000. In a number of cases the principal creditor was a British merchant. Darby Lux, for example, with a TEV of £2,492, owed £1,027 out of a total indebtedness of £1,171 to the English firm of Sydenham and Hodgson. Basil Dorsey, who had debts of £328 on an estate of £3,671, owed £261.68 to John Stuart & Campbell. Yet overall only one-third of men in this category had British merchants as their chief creditors. Just over one-half owed anything at all to British merchants. More commonly, the chief creditor was a fellow wealthy Marylander. James Lloyd I, for instance, owed £153 to the wealthy Eastern Shore merchant-planter Richard Bennett out of total debts of £354. Lloyd was in good company. Bennett was the chief creditor of six other wealthy men.[38] Even though this group depended on good relations with one or two creditors, this pattern of indebtedness was a rational approach to keep debt networks manageable and avoid overdependence. No man in this category had debts large enough to weaken assets seriously.[39] Indebtedness was more of a problem for the 15 percent of men who borrowed from a large number of creditors. John Beale, for example, the father-in-law of the heavily indebted William Nicholson, owed £1,397 on an estate of £1,301 to 30 creditors, of whom 19 were large creditors. Richard Bennett and Daniel Dulany headed the list of creditors, and no large creditor was an English merchant. Nevertheless, not all men in this category were like Beale. Some, such as Thomas Bordley, Samuel Peele, and Edward Dorsey, were very wealthy men whose extensive business interests would have necessitated dealing with a large number of creditors but who would have had sufficient wealth to avoid becoming financially compromised. Dorsey, for example, owed £404 to 41 creditors, including 15 large creditors. It barely made a dent in his estate of £12,231.[40]

One in twelve or thirteen wealthy Marylanders borrowed from a large numbers of creditors with one or two predominating. Men falling into this category tended to be richer than average, were often immigrants, and were often merchants or merchant-planters. Over 45 percent left estates worth over £2,500 and over two-thirds were merchants or merchant-planters. Immigrants outnumbered the native born. Men who needed or who could gain access to greater credit than average favored this strategy. Merchants needed more credit to undertake the risks of trade than did planters, while immigrants, needing to establish an estate from scratch, would also require more credit than the native born. Yet although they may have relied on one principal creditor for the bulk of their debt, they also borrowed from a number of other creditors, leading to a diversified debt structure. Thus, whereas William Peele, an immigrant merchant, owed £255 to Samuel Galloway, a fellow merchant from Anne Arundel, he also owed £195 to another three creditors, including eight large creditors. The chief creditor was more often British than in other types of debt structure, but the 42 percent who had a British merchant as their chief creditor were still outnumbered by the 47 percent who had as chief creditor a fellow wealthy Marylander. Often the sums owed to the principal creditor were quite large, with six men owing over £1,000 to their chief creditor. The very wealthy merchants Kensey Johns and John Morton Jordan both owed over £2,500 each to an English merchant and to Lord Baltimore, respectively.[41]

Finally, there were a small number of men—14 in total—who resembled the heavily indebted planters of historiographical legend, being dependent on one creditor. They tended to be poorer than average, with three-quarters having TEVs less than £1,500, were unlikely to be immigrants, but were often merchants or merchant-planters. They were also less likely to die in middle age, with higher than average percentages dying under 36 and also over 65. In many respects, they form a counterpoint to those men with no debt. Mordecai Hammond, a planter from the powerful Hammond family, should have been able to achieve a comfortable sufficiency without being burdened by debts. Yet he proved to be a wastrel (or unlucky), with debts amounting to £956, including one to Lord Baltimore of £536, out of an estate worth £1,390. Similarly, Moses Hill, the son of an elite member and a planter, died owing the Baltimore merchant Richard Moale £689. He died with total debts of £905 on an estate worth £870. More often than not, these men, heavily indebted to one man, had wealthy Marylanders as their principal creditors. Only four men—William Nicholson II, George Stokes, Patrick Creagh, and Henry Dorsey I—were principally indebted to British merchants, with William Nicholson II the only wealthy man over his head in debt to a single English merchant. The other ten elite members in this category all had major creditors from within Maryland.[42]

British merchants, therefore, played a relatively small role as suppliers of credit to the Maryland elite. Yet there might be some basis for Chesapeake fears about the dominance British merchants supposedly exercised over them if British merchants tended to be the foremost creditors of wealthy men. The largest creditor had by law first priority when debts were paid off and if, as was often the case, the largest debt was sizable, then the type of relationship the debtor had with that creditor would be crucially important. If the creditor was a far-distant merchant with few personal dealings with the debtor, he had small incentive to treat the debtor favorably because of personal, neighborhood, and family connections. In such situations, a planter could feel oppressed and dependent on the whims of a stranger.

If we look just at the major creditors of wealthy men, the importance of British merchants as creditors does increase. An examination of the 282 decedents who had at least one large creditor shows that over one in five had a British merchant as the largest debtor. British merchants were more important when we look at men who owed major creditors a considerable portion of their estates. One-third of wealthy Marylanders who owed a single creditor more than 10 percent of their TEV owed that money to an English or Scottish merchant. Nevertheless, the most likely type of person to be the major creditor of a wealthy Marylander was another wealthy Marylander. Over half of wealthy Marylanders, especially those dying in the second and third quarters of the eighteenth century, owed their single largest debt to a person much like themselves.

In light of evidence drawn from administration accounts, the importance of British merchants in wealthy Marylanders' debt networks needs to be reevaluated. Indeed, their importance as creditors seems unremarkable. Investigation instead should focus on two related issues. First, why did planters have such deep-seated fears about rich cosmopolitans when they were not heavily indebted to them? Second, what significance was attached to debts to local creditors? What can wealthy Marylanders' debt patterns tell us about Maryland social structure and about commercial relationships in a small, provincial community?

To answer the first question, we need to look less at the amount and structure of debt to Britain and concern ourselves more with planter ideology and what meanings people attached to debts. Business transactions in the eighteenth century were conducted in informal, highly personal ways. The "meaning" of a specific debt was fashioned through a combination of the size of the debt and the nature of the relationship between the creditor and the debtor. More often than not, the person to whom wealthy men owed most was a fellow wealthy Marylander. The great planter or merchant in the Chesapeake, however, was less concerned about that type of debt than he was about a debt to a British merchant, because his relationship with a British merchant was often (to him at least) unclear. When a debtor owed money to another wealthy man, the relationship was between equals, two men who operated within a common culture with shared moral and social imperatives. A gentleman may conceivably have lost some of his independence in going into debt to another gentleman (although it seems unlikely that many conceptualized debt in this fashion) but the resulting relationship was one of mutual dependence rather than, as with a debt to a British merchant, reduction to a "state of Vassalage and Dependence."[43]

Great planter reliance on British merchants, however, was a curious sort of "Vassalage and Dependence." They were notoriously touchy and ungrateful dependents, as eager to drive a hard bargain with merchants when trade was in their favor as quick to take offense when the shoe was on the other foot. Charles Carroll of Annapolis and his son—possessors of the first fortune in Maryland, with real and personal assets probably over £100,000 by the Revolution—relentlessly pushed for the most lucrative arrangements with London mercantile houses, dealing with seven firms in the 1760s and 1770s. They had no hesitation in changing suppliers and in using their wealth to leverage highly advantageous deals for themselves. As the Carrolls knew, the size of their crop made merchants fall over themselves to try and obtain it. The Carrolls did not need to go to them; they always applied to the Carrolls.[44] George Washington's prerevolutionary dealings in the British tobacco trade also shows the hardheaded approach that Chesapeake planters adopted in their dealings with British merchants. Breen has shown how compassionate and financially generous Washington could be to fellow Virginians down on their luck, even when that misfortune was entirely deserved. He was much more demanding of his British correspondents. Whereas Washington and other planters discussed commercial relationships through the metaphor of "commercial friendship," British merchants could not be unaware that that friendship was very one-sided: merchants were expected to remain loyal to planters in times of adversity but planters could demand the highest standard of service from their agents and terminate accounts with these merchants at their pleasure. Despite the many and vitally important services that Washington's principal agent, Robert Cary & Co., provided for him—a wide variety of imported goods, extensions of credit to enable Washington to expand his landholdings, remarkably efficient and accurate fulfillment of complicated instructions—Washington's letters to the firm are full of complaints about damaged goods, poor prices for tobacco, and lectures on what he considered to be proper commercial practice.[45]

It may have given Cary & Co. perverse satisfaction when Washington temporarily found himself distressed in the early 1760s and was forced to rely on the good graces of a firm he had so recently maligned. Washington's gratitude to British merchants, however, was limited and short-lived. At the same time as Cary & Co. were allowing Washington latitude in the payment of a sizable debt, Washington was prepared to cease doing business with another firm over an error that he refused to let that firm explain or apologize for. When Washington's fortunes revived in the mid-1760s, not only did Washington resume his complaints about the service he was receiving in the consignment trade but also he began to seek alternatives to Cary & Co. When Washington terminated his account with Cary & Co. in 1773, the British merchants may have had cause to bemoan the nature of the friendship that they had with a man destined to severely disrupt their business.[46]

How do we explain planter antagonism to British merchants? Part of the reason for resentment toward people who provided colonial gentlemen with valuable goods and who did important services for them was political. Many gentlemen were convinced that British merchants had persuaded Parliament to adopt commercial, monetary, and immigration policies that favored their mercantile interests over colonial interests. Resentment against British mercantilism and the burden of the Navigation Acts reached its height in the last decade before the American Revolution—the decade in which complaints by Virginians against British merchants and Scottish factors were at their peak.[47] Another cause of resentment was the success enjoyed by English and especially Scottish storekeepers in the Chesapeake piedmont. Wealthy men found themselves displaced as middlemen by specialist merchants either born in America or sent over as factors from Britain.

More important than either of these two reasons for resentment were long-term structural changes in the Chesapeake economy. Wealthy Chesapeake planters could afford to treat British merchants in the cavalier fashion exemplified by Washington because they were increasingly marginal players within the rapidly expanding and extremely dynamic Atlantic economy of mid-eighteenth-century imperial Britain. Despite the Chesapeake's recovery from recession after 1755 and despite booming prices for tobacco in the mid-1760s and early 1770s that fed expanded settlement and a remarkable increase in the purchase of goods of conspicuous consumption, British merchants, especially the biggest and most dynamic merchants in the largest commercial centers, turned away from investment in the Chesapeake. Planter fulminations against the devilish practices of British merchants should not hide the fact that after mid-century Chesapeake planters were not especially important to British merchants and British merchants did not intrude very much into the business affairs of Chesapeake planters.

From the British point of view, the northern colonies and the Chesapeake were not where the action was in the Atlantic economy in the decades immediately preceding the Revolution. David Hancock has made a study of a group of leading London merchants heavily involved in the British Atlantic economy in the second and third quarters of the eighteenth century, a group that was both typical of large-scale merchants operating in the period and a group that was especially thrusting and entrepreneurial in its pursuits of the best opportunities for investment in the empire. Significantly, this group of dynamic merchants showed little interest in investing in the Chesapeake after the mid-1750s. Before the outbreak of war in 1755, Hancock's associates had traded primarily with the Chesapeake. Within nine years, however, they had turned their backs on the tobacco colonies and had decided to focus on the rice and sugar economies of the Lower South and the Caribbean. The Ceded Islands gained after the Peace of Paris, especially Grenada, were particularly appealing places for business, as were the suddenly available markets under the ambit of the East India Company. The Associates were not alone, as "many similarly situated merchants moved out of the northern and Chesapeake colonies at the same time."[48]

From the perspective of British merchants, sugar was a more appealing trade than tobacco. Both staple industries boomed in the mid-1760s, but sugar was easily the most sizable and valuable import. Moreover, participation in the sugar trade offered two substantial benefits that were unobtainable in the tobacco industry: fresh lands and profits from the slave trade. The conclusion of the Seven Years' War had opened up new land ideally suited to the cultivation of sugar along the eastern edge of the Caribbean. British investors rushed eagerly to fill the vacuum. By 1772, the most productive island, Grenada, contained 334 plantations with 26,211 slaves. Most of these plantations had been established in the previous decade. The debts new Grenadian planters owed to British creditors indicated the eagerness with which British merchants sought out opportunities in this small island. In 1772, Grenadians owed more than £2,000,000 to British creditors—a sum approximately equal to the entire British debt of the Chesapeake, a region with nearly 400,000 whites to Grenada's 1,600 and a region, moreover, that had been involved in the Atlantic economy for over 150 years. Put another way, each white resident of Grenada was, within one decade, able to attract nearly £1,300 sterling and each white resident of the Chesapeake attracted just £5.[49]

The British West Indies was an attractive area for British investment not only because of the profits that could be made from sugar. It had a signal advantage over the Chesapeake for British merchants in that it was a region that avariciously consumed slaves. In the last decade before the Revolution, British merchants shipped 279,100 Africans to British America. Of these, 87 percent went to sugar-producing colonies, 11 percent went to the rice-producing economies of the Lower South, and 1.8 percent went to the Chesapeake. Moreover, only a very small fraction of the slaves that went to the Chesapeake was sold to tidewater planters. Planters in the piedmont seeking to establish properties bought most Africans. The Chesapeake in general and wealthy tidewater planters in particular had abandoned the Atlantic slave trade. The result is that wealthy Marylanders were virtually removed from the major area of commerce that British traders had with British America. They were able to afford to buy increased amounts of consumer goods from British merchants without needing to borrow money, as their ancestors had done and as their compatriots in other plantation colonies were still doing, for the far more expensive and much more necessary purchases of the slaves they needed to run their estates. Another consequence of the virtual ending of the slave trade in the tidewater Chesapeake was that British merchants were less and less likely to have personal dealings with Chesapeake planters, would be less likely to have reason to extend credit to them, and would have considerably less knowledge of their credit-worthiness and credit standing. The British Atlantic economy in the second half of the eighteenth century was characterized by a startling sophistication in financing commerce, a closer intertwining of business networks, and a greater emphasis on establishing reliable knowledge on the credit-worthiness of individuals and firms. In conditions of high risk, merchants put a premium upon a matrix of personal trust and obligation and increasingly restricted their dealings only to people whom they knew well. By the middle of the eighteenth century, few Chesapeake planters fitted the bill.[50]

Borrowing to purchase luxury goods may have created ideological problems for men devoted to republican ideas of austere frugality, but it allowed planters a degree of latitude to their British creditors that would have been impossible earlier in the century and impossible also in those parts of the British empire in which British credit was still essential to obtain slaves. Luxury goods were desirable but not necessary. When times became hard, as they did in the early 1770s when a combination of a major credit crisis in Britain in 1772 and a fall of tobacco prices due to a glut in the market heralded a drop in tobacco prices, Chesapeake planters were easily able to cut back on items of consumption that they did not really need. In 1773, residents of the Chesapeake cut back British imports by 47 percent, primarily as a result of a contraction in the tobacco trade in the previous two years. The Chesapeake's response to the Coercive Acts a year later—a boycott on importing British manufactures and a boycott on exporting tobacco—lowered imports to just £2,000 sterling and lowered tobacco exports to virtually nothing. The result was a dramatic rise in the price of tobacco (jumping 67 percent between April 1774 and April 1775) and a bumper tobacco crop that included unsold tobacco grown in 1773 and 1774. The result was the largest trade surplus in Chesapeake history, a surplus that allowed Chesapeake planters to substantially reduce their obligations to British merchants. Chesapeake planters were able to embark upon such a strategy—one that combined the appearance of economic sacrifice while solving an immediate problem of economic recession—only because they were not dependent on British merchants for the purchase of necessities and because they produced a crop that was not produced by foreign suppliers and that had the advantage of not being perishable. Neither option was available to colonials who were truly dependent on British finance. South Carolinians refused to allow a ban on the export of rice to Britain, knowing that this was their only market and that they needed money from rice to buy slaves. West Indian planters, dependent on protective tariffs for their monopoly of the British sugar market and much more closely tied to British merchants than was the case in British North America, could not afford to even contemplate such an assertion of economic pique against Britain. Not surprisingly, their outrage against the Coercive Acts was very muted.[51]

Thomas Jefferson memorably called himself the slave of British merchants, declaring that inherited debts to British merchants made white Virginians like himself "species of property annexed to certain mercantile houses in London." As was so often the case, Jefferson extended a proposition that was true in his own case to the population at large, where the proposition fails. Jefferson was one of the rare Chesapeake planters who were seriously indebted to British planters. By the late 1780s, he faced the prospect of ruin. His situation was in large part due to his own foolishness as well as to unforeseen bad luck. He agreed to take over the large debts that his father-in-law owed to British merchants (much of which arose from a disastrous incursion into slave trading in 1772) in return for control over a large estate. Unwilling to sell land or slaves and gambling that future profits from a large, if encumbered, estate would allow repayment of debts, Jefferson ran into severe financial trouble during the Revolution when uncontrollable inflation made his plans turn to dust. Jefferson added to his woes through extraordinary extravagance.[52]

Jefferson was unusual in his indebtedness to British merchants.

He was not unusual, however, in expressing his anger toward British merchants and their supposed misdeeds and was not unusual in behaving toward them in a way that was anything but servile. The Chesapeake elite did not act toward British merchants as if they were slaves. Indeed, their actions toward British merchants were less those of slaves than of cantankerous opponents, unfamiliar with commercial ways and determined to stake out their commercial independence. They continually went out of their way to aggravate London merchants, especially as the Revolutionary conflict neared.[53]

Business relationships with fellow gentlemen were conducted in ways that were more akin to friendship. This is not to say that debts contracted between colonial gentlemen could not provoke resentment or that large-scale Maryland creditors were not sometimes disliked. The behavior of Charles Carroll of Annapolis, the most significant money lender in Maryland, won him few friends among his peers. They especially resented his insistence that unpaid interest had to be added to the principal of the loan and feared his feisty willingness to foreclose or sue in court without hesitation. Yet none of his many critics challenged his right to charge compound interest or to pursue delinquent debtors. They did not do so because they had a personal involvement with Carroll. James Dilling, for example, was prepared to accept a renegotiation of a loan on harsher terms mostly, it seems, because he could deal directly with his creditor. Even when conflict arose, both sides could be certain that they were members of a shared culture and that each could exert some influence over the other's behavior. In this culture, sometimes creditors had the advantage and sometimes debtors. Carroll found out how debtors could have an advantage over him in 1777 when the Revolutionary legislature passed a legal tender bill that within a year cost Carroll nearly £4,000 sterling.[54]

The importance of these mutually dependent relationships can be seen in an examination of wealthy Marylanders as creditors. As the only group in colonial Maryland with substantial liquid assets, wealthy Marylanders regularly put this capital to work for them by lending it out at interest. Fewer than 10 percent of wealthy Marylanders were not owed money: 61 percent had debts receivable of over £100, 27 percent died with debtors owing them over £500, and 14 had debts receivable worth more than £1,000. The average decedent had 29 percent of his TEV and 32 percent of his capital goods in debts receivable. When desperate debts are added to these figures, the totals rise to 37 percent and 41 percent, respectively. Assets and liabilities balanced each other almost exactly: liabilities took up on average 35 percent of TEV.

Merchants were the most heavily involved in money lending. So too were the very rich. The wealthiest men in this sample (those with TEVs over £5,000) invested 47 percent of their nonlanded wealth in recoverable loans. Decedents with TEVs under £1,000, on the other hand, lent out on average 13 percent of their non-landed wealth in debts receivable. One reason for the disparity is that increased wealth led to more disposable income. Nevertheless, wealthy investors had a number of other options open to them. The fact that the most common choice for men with disposable wealth was to become a large-scale money lender suggests that money lending was more profitable and more likely to be the basis for a large fortune than other activities. Maryland law set interest rates at 6 percent. As long as courts were willing to uphold credit arrangements, money lending was a relatively risk-free way of ensuring a decent income—providing, of course, that creditors could gain a true appreciation of the financial circumstances and personal probity of borrowers.

What type of people borrowed money from wealthy planters and merchants? It is more difficult to make a systematic analysis of the distribution of debtors to the elite than it is with their creditors. Some inventories do not itemize each debtor but merely list the sum of all debts. Nevertheless, enough decedents did leave itemized lists of debtors to make an analysis possible. I have selected a sample of 48 men who left debts receivable at death and have made a breakdown of their creditors into various wealth categories. The sample is by no means representative, being confined to the Western Shore, principally to Baltimore County, and is biased in favor of larger creditors, who were more likely to have their debtors enumerated, than to small creditors. Yet it does offer evidence on who borrowed money from wealthy men, how much they borrowed, and the role that wealthy Marylanders played as providers of credit. The mean debt receivable—£1,148—is considerably higher than the average in the total sample—£557—but much of this disparity is due to the inclusion of Amos Garrett and

William Hall in the sample. Both of them lent money on a grand scale and have been included in the sample in order to examine the credit networks of substantial money lenders. Excluding these two brings average debts receivable to £638.

Most men were owed money by a large number of debtors: over half had networks of fifty debtors or more. The average amount of debts receivable was also considerable, with 44 percent having debts receivable of over £500. Over 80 percent of debtors in the average estate borrowed only small sums.[55] Small debtors were not generally very important. The only two creditors to have substantial debts lent out to mainly small debtors were Nicholas Rogers, who had debts receivable of £3,728, of which £1,498 was lent to 437 small debtors, and Thomas Talbott, who had debts receivable of £952, of which £514 was owed by 294 small debtors. Moreover, the importance of small debtors lessened over time, perhaps due to the increasing presence of Scottish traders vying for poor planters' attentions. Large debts predominated. Over 70 percent of this small sample had more than 50 percent of their debts receivable lent out to debtors who owed them more than £20, while 37 percent lent over 50 percent of their debts receivable to debtors who owed them over £100.

An examination of the debts owed to John Hall and Dr. Josias Middlemore illustrates the importance of large debtors in elite credit networks. John Hall lent £703 to 27 debtors. The majority of that sum was tied up in two debts: one of £431 to Francis Holland, a merchant and legislator from Harford County, and one of £158 to Corbin Lee, a Baltimore ironmaster and legislator. Dr. Josias Middlemore was one of the largest money lenders in Baltimore County, with debts receivable of £2,930, lent out to 127 debtors. Of these, 73 debtors owed him less than £10, accounting for less than 5 percent of total debts receivable. The largest debtor, Col. John Hall, was a prominent planter and legislator. Hall owed Middlemore £617, which was 21 percent of Middlemore's total debts receivable.[56] Each of the above large debtors was a member of Baltimore County's political elite. Who did and did not obtain credit was a measure of social standing, and the fact that wealthy Marylanders chose to give most of their credit to other wealthy men while allotting comparatively little to small debtors suggests that financial interactions in the Chesapeake functioned in much the same way as other types of interactions between different social and economic groupings. Although colonial Marylanders shared certain important commonalities of experience, much of their existence was spent in separate spheres: slaves within a slave community, tenants among tenants, yeomen with other yeomen, and gentlemen in the company of other gentlemen. These spheres overlapped and intersected at numerous points and shared many similarities but did not function under identical amalgams of operating principles and values. At the highest level, small debtors may have been actively discouraged. Charles Carroll of Annapolis lent virtually nothing to small debtors. Of the over £40,000 sterling he had out on loan in 1776, less than a quarter of the loans, amounting to under 3 percent of the total money loaned, was borrowed by people who owed him less than £100. The bulk of his money out on loan was in the form of mortgages of more than £500.[57]

The exclusiveness of wealthy Marylanders' debt networks can be seen when we look at the significance of credit relationships both within groups and between different ranks in society. Allan Kulikoff describes the relationship with regard to credit between yeomen and gentlemen as reciprocal in nature, but it was a very limited sort of reciprocity.[58] Small planters may have relied on the generosity of wealthy men for necessary credit, but wealthy men were not similarly reliant on loans to small planters. For wealthy planters and merchants, such transactions were not very important as parts of their business operations, but were a personal favor, a kind of patronage great planters were expected to provide to their less wealthy neighbors.[59] Even if a debt to a small planter was large in relation to the small planter's total wealth, it would not be more than a small fraction of a wealthy man's wealth. Moreover, it is yet to be proved that small planters obtained much of their credit from large planters and local merchants instead of Scottish factors. Probably, also, they were unable to acquire the credit they needed to improve their estates because they lacked the resources that wealthier Marylanders possessed. Even if they did borrow from wealthy men, it is not certain that they thought of their indebtedness as requiring them to be deferential to their supposed betters. It is likely that they borrowed in much the same rational manner as their wealthier contemporaries. The attitudes that such debts engendered should not be presupposed without systematic analysis of the structure of small planters' debts.

An initial examination of debt at lower wealth levels in 1750, just before the influx of Scottish merchants into the Chesapeake, is suggestive about the nature of nonelite Marylanders' debt networks. The 47 men who left accounts in that year in the four counties under study fall into two distinct categories, based on wealth. The first group, 20 men leaving estates between £70 and £650, were remarkably free from debt, a fact that might indicate sturdy independence but is more likely to signify lack of access to credit. Just two men had debts amounting to more than 40 percent of TEV, whereas 17 had minimal debts of less than 15 percent of TEV. Significantly, only Richard Ruff, with a high TEV of £402 (thus, a man in the wealth category immediately below the elite and functionally different from poorer elite members), owed anything at all to British merchants. His debts amounted to 7.5 percent of his TEV. Not only are British merchants conspicuously absent, but also few middling Marylanders listed major money lenders such as Charles Carroll, Daniel Dulany, or Josias Middlemore as creditors. Even fewer seem to have been substantially indebted to wealthy Marylanders—only five men, all of whom had comparatively large estates over £225, borrowed more than £10 from any wealthy man. It is possible that middling Marylanders chose not to deal with large planters and merchants out of an ideological or social commitment to men of their own kind, but it is more likely that their choice was made for them. Yeomen were good credit risks, but wealthy Marylanders did not lend to them. They confined most of their money lending to other wealthy men. Deprived of credit but solvent and with appreciating assets, middling planters and artisans were ideal clients for the Scottish factors and indigenous merchants who filled the vacuum that wealthy Marylanders voluntarily vacated after 1750.

Poor Marylanders—27 men with estates of less than £70—were more likely than middling yeomen to be heavily indebted, often with wealthy men as their creditors: 10 men had debts amounting to over 40 percent of TEV. Their precarious financial position made it necessary to borrow from many people and they established more elaborate debt networks than those immediately above them socially—poor men had, on average, 5.4 creditors compared to middling men's 4.3 creditors. For these men, credit functioned in the ways that Kulikoff and Breen posit, with wealthy men extending credit as a kind of personal favor or patronage toward the less fortunate. Usually, poor men borrowed small sums from many men, as did Vincent Stewart, who owed small sums of no more than one or two pounds to twelve men. Occasionally, however, the majority of credit was obtained from a single creditor. Moses Ringrose, for example, died with a debt of £20 to elite member William Govane, a debt that amounted to over two-thirds of his TEV.

Such extensions of credit to poor men may have helped to cement deferential ties between the wealthy and poor and even facilitate a spirit of friendship, albeit between unequal parties. But the likelihood that the debt would not be repaid surely dampened good feelings between client and patron. Francis Street, for example, died with an estate of £38 and owed Baltimore merchant Richard Gist the enormous sum of £83. Liquidating the estate would not satisfy the debt. For Gist, friendship or patronage toward Street entailed the loss of a sizable amount of money. Therefore, one needs to be wary of imagining debt merely as a means of structuring social relationships and creating a web of interdependent relationships from which wealthy men could profit. Such benefits would have been lost on Richard Gist, who died with Street's debt unpaid and with desperate debts of £158 reducing the value of his estate. At Gist's death the greater majority, in value, of both the debts he owed and the debts owed to him were with fellow wealthy Marylanders who were undoubtedly better credit risks than the unfortunate Francis Street.[60]

In short, the important credit relationships for the wealthy Marylanders were with large debtors from status and background similar to themselves. It was nearly as important for Dr. Josias Middlemore that Hall repay him as it was important for Hall that Middlemore continue to loan him large sums and not insist on the immediate repayment of the debt. Consequently, it was in these circumstances that intangibles such as a man's reputation for integrity and honesty were important. Debt for the elite did involve human exchanges and was looked at in "highly moral terms," but it was not an abstraction, divorced from the everyday conduct of business.[61] Attitudes related directly to the size of an individual debt and to the importance such debt had to both the debtor and the creditor. Mercantile dealings in the eighteenth century consisted of a great number of transactions that were carried on with regard to one's estimation of another's capabilities and moral character. When it involved the loan of a significant portion of one's estate in a business atmosphere in which the acceptance of a high degree of risk was the norm, the nature of one person's relationship to another became vital. One can assume that Middlemore placed a good deal of trust in Hall's ability to repay his loan and that he trusted Hall—a fellow gentleman—more than he did other people to whom he lent less money. If Hall defaulted, Middlemore's estate would be severely encumbered. Therefore, Middlemore needed to be certain that Hall's credit was good if he did not want to court financial embarrassment.

Credit in Maryland should be seen as a scarce resource, the allocation of which was the result of careful choices made by creditors regarding the safety and profitability of their investments. Whoever controlled the distribution of capital and the beneficiaries of their largesse were able to play important roles in the social and economic development of the region. To a large degree, wealthy Marylanders played the part of both distributors and beneficiaries in the disposal of credit in eighteenth-century Maryland. When they needed credit they largely obtained it from within their own ranks. This chapter has focused on the questions of their involvement in credit networks and what the membership of these networks was. But many important questions remain. Were wealthy men able to acquire sufficient capital resources for their purposes? For what purposes did they want credit? What meanings were attached to debt and did they vary according to the size of the loan and from whom it was borrowed? Most importantly, what does the structure of debt in the Chesapeake tell us about social organization and interactions among social groups over time? These questions can be answered only by merging the perspectives of accountant, anthropologist, and historian and by looking not only at the rhetoric planters used when talking about debt but also at the reality of the uses debt played in a developing society and the meanings colonists attached to it. A first step toward a more informed understanding of the purposes and meanings of debt in the Chesapeake is more systematic investigation, as has been attempted above, into the actual amounts and functioning of debt between individuals, especially within the vitally important local commercial world.

NOTES

1. For credit in the seventeenth-century Atlantic economy, see Nuala Zahedieh, "Credit, Risk and Reputation in Late Seventeenth-Century Colonial Trade," in Olaf Janzen (ed.), *Merchant Organisation and Maritime Trade in the North Atlantic, 1660–1815* (St. John's, Newfoundland: International Maritime Economic History Association, 1998), 53–74.
2. See especially Jacob Price, *Capital and Credit in British Overseas Trade: The View from the Chesapeake, 1700–1776* (Cambridge, MA: Harvard University Press, 1980).
3. Much of the debate has focused on debt as part of general republican discourse. Historians interested in the discourse of debt have found much evidence of planter discontent with indebtedness in the writings of prominent Virginians such as Landon Carter, George Washington, and especially Thomas Jefferson. See T.H. Breen, *Tobacco Culture: The Mentality of the Great Tidewater Planters on the Eve of Revolution* (Princeton, NJ: Princeton University Press, 1985); Bruce A. Ragsdale, *A Planters' Republic: The Search for Economic Independence in Revolutionary Virginia* (Madison: University of Wisconsin Press, 1996), 23–29; Woody Holton, *Forced Founders: Indians, Debtors, Slaves, and the Making of the American Revolution in Virginia* (Chapel Hill: University of North Carolina Press, 1999), 41–44, 50–51, 66–67, 79–88; Emory G. Evans, "Planter Indebtedness and the Coming of the Revolution in Virginia," *WMQ*, 3d. ser., XIX (1962), 511–33; and Herbert Sloan, *Principle and Interest: Thomas Jefferson and the Problem of Debt* (New York: Oxford University Press, 1995). All take at face value Virginia planter laments about the scale of their indebtedness to British merchants. The wealth of qualitative evidence about planter attitudes about debt and credit available for Virginia is scarce for Maryland. Quantitative data about levels of debt, however, are abundant in Maryland and almost totally absent in Virginia. The relative lack of comment in Maryland about the evils of indebtedness may reflect different realities in the two colonies. Nevertheless, I believe that Marylanders and Virginians shared the same republican beliefs about debt. The few comments that do survive concerning debt and credit from the Maryland elite suggest that Marylanders were just as resentful of Scottish and English merchants as were Virginians and that personal characteristics of honesty and integrity rather than ability to pay on time were just as essential in business. See, for example, Stephen Bordley Letterbook, Mss. 81, MHS, 1/11/1741; 7/26/1744; 1/31/1750; 10/31/1750; 7/28/1756.
4. Paul L. Ford (ed), *The Works of Thomas Jefferson* (New York, 1904–05), V, 28.
5. John M. Hemphill II (ed.), "John Wayles Rates His Neighbors," *VMHB*, 66 (1958), 302–306.
6. Price, *Capital and Credit*, 7–16; Richard B. Sheridan, "The British Credit Crisis of 1772 and the American Colonies," *JEH*, XX (1960), 163.
7. James H. Soltow, *The Economic Role of Williamsburg* (Williamsburg, VA: University Press of Virginia, 1965), 148. It is possible that wealthy Virginians were more indebted than rich Marylanders in the last decade before the Revolution, although without firm quantitative evidence it is difficult to test such suppositions. Virginia, however, can be distinguished from Maryland in this period in two respects. First, Virginian gentlemen were heavily involved in westward speculation. Maryland gentlemen were not. For all those who made a fortune in the Shenandoah Valley and the Upper Ohio Valley, others,

especially after the Proclamation of 1763 that prohibited land grants being issued at a line west of the Appalachian Mountains, lost enormous sums. Losing investors included William Byrd III, Thomas Jefferson, George Washington, Richard Henry Lee, George Mason, and Patrick Henry. Second, in 1766 Virginia faced the greatest scandal in its history when it was revealed that the Speaker of the House of Burgesses, John Robinson, had stolen more than £100,000 from public funds, most of which was lent to wealthy Virginians. The effect was a local credit crisis among the Virginia gentry, as the House of Burgesses demanded that Robinson's administrators chase up debts and immediately repay the Virginia Treasury. For western land speculation, see J. Russell Snapp, *John Stuart and the Struggle for Empire on the Southern Frontier* (Baton Rouge, 1996); Eric Hinderaker, *Elusive Empires: Constructing Colonialism in the Ohio Valley 1673–1800* (Cambridge: Cambridge University Press, 1997); and Holton, *Forced Founders*, 3–38. For the Robinson scandal, see David J. Mays, *Edmund Pendleton, 1721–1803: A Biography*, 2 vols. (Cambridge, MA: Harvard University Press, 1952), I: 174–208; and Joseph Albert Ernst, *Money and Politics in America, 1755–1775: A Study in the Currency Act of 1764 and the Political Economy of Revolution* (Chapel Hill: University of North Carolina Press, 1973), 174, 177–78.

8. For a full discussion of Jefferson and debt that tends to equate Jefferson's plight with Virginia gentlemen generally, see Sloan, *Principle and Interest*.

9. Breen, *Tobacco Culture*, 29, 91.

10. Price, *Capital and Credit*, 16.

11. See Lorena S. Walsh, "Land, Landlord, and Leaseholder: Estate Management and Tenant Fortunes in Southern Maryland, 1642–1820," *Agricultural History*, LIX (1985), 373–96.

12. Aubrey C. Land, "Economic Base and Social Structure: The Northern Chesapeake in the Eighteenth Century," *JEH*, XXV (1965), 469–85; Ronald Hoffman, *Princes of Ireland, Planters of Maryland: A Carroll Saga, 1500–1782* (Chapel Hill: University of North Carolina Press, 2000), 122–23, 262–64.

13. Allan Kulikoff, *Tobacco and Slaves: The Development of Southern Cultures in the Chesapeake, 1680–1800* (Chapel Hill: University of North Carolina Press, 1986), 125, 127.

14. Andrew A. Beveridge, "The Social Effects of Credit: Cheshire County, New Hampshire, 1825–1860," *Working Paper from the Regional Economic History Research Center*, 1, 1 (1977), 1.

15. For examples of the former: Richard Bennett, Dr. Charles Carroll, Charles Carroll, Sr., Benjamin Tasker, Philip Hammond, Edmund Jennings, Stephen Bordley, and Robert Goldsborough, Sr. Falling into the latter: Daniel Dulany, Sr., Edward Lloyd II, and Edward Lloyd III.

16. Wills 16 (1721)/176; Edward Papenfuse et al. (eds.), *A Biographical Dictionary of the Maryland Legislature, 1635–1789* (Baltimore: Johns Hopkins University Press, 1979–1985), I: 194–95, 197.

17. These measures for substantial indebtedness probably overestimate elite indebtedness compared to other elites. Wealthy landowners, merchants, and businessmen were much more indebted. It was not unusual for an aristocrat or landed gentleman to borrow very large sums—several tens of thousands of pounds for the largest landowners—on the security of their estates. See J.V. Beckett, "English Landownership in the Later Seventeenth and Eighteenth Centuries: The Debate and the Problems," *EHR*, 2d. ser., XXX

(1977), 567–81; idem, *Coal and Tobacco: The Lowthers and the Economic Development of West Cumberland* (Cambridge: Cambridge University Press, 1981); Christopher Clay, "Marriage, Inheritance and the Rise of Large Estates in England, 1660–1810," *Economic History Review*, 2d. ser., XXI (1968), 503–18; idem, "The Price of Freehold Land in the Later Seventeenth and Eighteenth Centuries," *EHR*, XXVII (1974), 173–89; H.J. Habbakuk, "English Landownership, 1680–1740," *EHR*, X (1939–40), 2–17; L. Holderness, "Credit in a Rural Community, 1600–1800: Some Neglected Aspects of Probate Inventories," *Midland History*, 3 (1975), 94–115; G.E. Mingay, *The Gentry: The Rise and Fall of a Ruling Class* (Oxford: Oxford University Press, 1978); and Peter Roebuck, *Yorkshire Baronets 1640–1800: Families, Estates and Fortunes* (Oxford: Oxford University Press, 1980).

18. Richard Corbin to Robert Dinwiddie, 10 July 1761, Richard Corbin Letterbook, 1758–1768, Colonial Williamsburg, Inc., cited by Breen, *Tobacco Culture*, 91.

19. William Byrd to Charles, Earl of Orrery, 5 July 1726, in "Virginia Council Journals," *VMHB*, XXXII (1924), 27.

20. For a penetrating evaluation of how merchants in the early modern world assessed risk and credit-worthiness, see Peter Mathias, "Risk, Credit and Kinship in Early Modern Enterprise," in John J. McCusker and Kenneth Morgan (eds.), *The Early Modern Atlantic Economy* (Cambridge: Cambridge University Press, 1900), 15–35. See also Trevor Burnard and Kenneth Morgan, "The Dynamics of the Slave Market and Slave Purchasing Patterns in Early Jamaica," *WMQ*, 3d Ser., LVIII (2001), 205–28.

21. For the importance of age on investment and borrowing patterns in Britain, see Peter Earle, "Age and Accumulation in the London Business Community," in Neil McKendrick and R.B. Outhwaite (eds.), *Business Life and Public Policy: Essays in Honour of D.C. Coleman* (Cambridge: Cambridge University Press, 1986), 62–63; and ibid, *The Making of the English Middle Class: Business, Society, and Family Life in London, 1660–1730* (London: Methuen, 1989), 144.

22. Breen, *Tobacco Culture*, 73 n. 74, 84–123; Kenneth Morgan, "Business Networks in the British Export Trade to North America, 1750–1800," in McCusker and Morgan (eds.), *Early Modern Atlantic Economy*, 52–56. For the importance of gaining privileged access to the insider's world of international trade—a world that was shaped by personal contacts, confidential kinship relations, personal trust, and status in the trade, all gained only through long involvement in business—see Mathias, "Risk, Credit and Kinship," in McCusker and Morgan (eds.), *Early Modern Atlantic Economy*, 15–35.

23. Richard B. Sheridan, "The British Credit Crisis of 1772," 163.

24. Inventories (1764) 84/298; Accounts (1764) 51/189, (1764) 52/80, (1765) 54/296, (1775) 73/55.

25. Jacob M. Price, "What Did Merchants Do? Reflections on British Overseas Trade, 1660–1790," *JEH*, XLIX (1989), 273–74, 278–282.

26. Byrd to Orrery, 5 July 1726, in "Virginia Council Journals," 27.

27. Kulikoff, *Tobacco and Slaves*, 118–29.

28. Nevertheless, debt was a financial drain on the resources of some of the elite. The usual rate of interest for money on loan was 6 percent. A debt of £1,000, therefore, cost the borrower £60 per annum to service. The average amount of debt for an elite member was £450, costing £27 per annum to service. Some of the substantially indebted would have been forced to divert

large amounts of their income to service their debts. William Nicholson, for example, would have had to allocate £219 per annum to service his debts. Levin Gale would have spent £354 to service his debts.

29. Price, *Capital and Credit*, Chapter 1; and Allan Kulikoff, "The Economic Growth of the Eighteenth Century Chesapeake Colonies," *JEH*, XXXIX (1979), 286–88.

30. Kulikoff, *Tobacco and Slaves*, 128; Allan Karras, *Sojourners in the Sun: Scottish Migrants in Jamaica and the Chesapeake* (Ithaca, NY: Cornell University Press, 1992); Jacob M. Price, *Perry of London: A Family and a Firm on the Seaborne Frontier, 1615–1763* (Cambridge, MA: Harvard University Press, 1992). For a study of the retail trade in the colonial southern backcountry that emphasizes the independent role of frontier merchants, see Daniel B. Thorp, "Doing Business in the Backcountry: Retail Trade in Colonial Rowan County, North Carolina," *WMQ*, 3d Ser., XLVIII (1991), 387–408.

31. Price, "The Last Phase of the Virginia-London Consignment Trade," 94.

32. Evans, "Planter Indebtedness and the Coming of the Revolution in Virginia"; idem, "Private Indebtedness and the Revolution in Virginia, 1776 to 1796," *WMQ*, 3d. ser., XXVIII (1971), 349–74; Rhys Isaac, *The Transformation of Virginia, 1740–1790* (Chapel Hill: University of North Carolina Press, 1982), 247; Breen, *Tobacco Culture*, 105–106, 129–132; Kulikoff, *Tobacco and Slaves*, 118; and Holton, *Forced Founders*, 70–90.

33. See Lois Green Carr and Lorena S. Walsh, "Changing Life Styles and Consumer Behavior in the Colonial Chesapeake," in Cary Carson et al. (eds.), *Of Consuming Interests: The Style of Life in the Eighteenth Century* (Charlottesville: University of Virginia Press, 1994), 69–104; Lorena S. Walsh, "Urban Amenities and Rural Sufficiency: Living Standards and Consumer Behavior in the Colonial Chesapeake, 1643–1777," *JEH*, 43 (1983), 109–117; and Lois Green Carr, "Emigration and the Standard of Living: The Eighteenth Century Chesapeake," in McCusker and Morgan (eds.), *The Early Modern Atlantic Economy*, 326–33. For an important article that assumes that increased consumption led to increased indebtedness with wide political implications, see T.H. Breen, "'Baubles of Britain': The American and Consumer Revolutions of the Eighteenth Century," *Past and Present*, 119 (1988), 87–91.

34. Status was determined first by wealth indicated in probate records. A creditor was considered to be an elite member if he or she left over £650 in inventoried wealth or was a legislator, prominent merchant, or professional.

35. Aubrey Land is a notable exception. See "Economic Behavior in a Planting Society," 479.

36. Accounts (1750) 28/10, *MHR*.

37. Inventories and Accounts (1714) 36a/150.

38. Beatrix Betancourt Hardy, "A Papist in a Protestant Age: The Case of Richard Bennett, 1667–1749," *JSH* LX (1994), 209–10, 222–23.

39. Accounts (1726) 7/268, (1753) 33/419, (1767) 57/149, (1768) 60/207.

40. Accounts (1735) 14/69, (1740) 17/494, (1764) 51/90.

41. Accounts (1755) 37/143, (1765) 53/318, (1765) 54/29, (1767) 55/29, (1767) 57/372, (1773) 68/276, (1774) 71/219.

42. Accounts (1755) 37/132, (1767) 59/47, (1769) 61/281.

43. Robert Beverley to John Bland, Beverley Letter Book, cited in Breen, *Tobacco Culture*, 134. For the importance of face-to-face contacts in deter-

mining credit-worthiness in the British transatlantic trade, see Mathias, "Risk, Credit and Kinship," 16, 25, 28–35.

44. Hoffman, *Princes of Ireland, Planters of Maryland*, 260–61.
45. Breen, *Tobacco Culture*, 97–101; Bruce A. Ragsdale, "George Washington, the British Tobacco Trade, and Economic Opportunity in Prerevolutionary Virginia," *VMHB*, 97 (1989), 133–62.
46. Ibid.
47. Holton, *Forced Founders*, 54–55.
48. David Hancock, *Citizens of the World: London Merchants and the Integration of the British Atlantic Community, 1735–1785* (Cambridge: Cambridge University Press, 1995), 121, 144.
49. Richard B. Sheridan, *Sugar and Slavery: An Economic History of the British West Indies, 1623–1775* (Bridgetown, Barbados: Caribbean Universities Press, 1974) 458, 464.
50. Mathias, "Risk, Credit and Kinship."
51. For the decline of the Atlantic slave trade in the Chesapeake in the eighteenth century, see David Richardson, "The British Empire and the Atlantic Slave Trade, 1660–1807," in P.J. Marshall (ed.), *The Oxford History of the British Empire: the Eighteenth Century* (Oxford: Oxford University Press, 1998), 456–57; Philip D. Morgan, *Slave Counterpoint: Black Culture in the Eighteenth-Century Chesapeake & Lowcountry* (Chapel Hill: University of North Carolina Press, 1998), 59–62; and Herbert S. Klein, "Slaves and Shipping in Eighteenth-Century Virginia," *JIH*, 3 (1975), 383–412. For a first-rate study of the transition of slavery in the Chesapeake to one dominated by native-born slaves, see Lorena S. Walsh, *From Calabar to Carter's Grove: The History of a Virginia Slave Community* (Charlottesville: University of Virginia Press, 1997). Holton points out that Jefferson and other Virginia gentlemen embarked upon a five-year legislative effort to curb the slave trade to Virginia by raising the import duty. Such actions were not calculated to endear wealthy Virginian planters to merchants involved in Atlantic commerce; Holton, *Forced Founders*, 66–73. For West Indian quietude prior to the Revolution, see Andrew O'Shaugnessy, *An Empire Divided: The American Revolution and the British Caribbean* (Philadelphia: University of Pennsylvania Press, 2000), 72–77, 126–30.
52. Sloan, *Principle and Interest*.
53. Holton, *Forced Founders*, 77–128; Ronald Hoffman, *A Spirit of Dissension: Economics, Politics, and the Revolution in Maryland* (Baltimore: Johns Hopkins University Press, 1973).
54. Hoffman, *Princes of Ireland, Planters of Maryland*, 122–23, 262–64, 318–30.
55. Excluding Amos Garrett and William Hall, who had 902 and 442 creditors, respectively, these figures are 61 and 52.
56. Inventories (1760) 70/336, (1769) 101/280, (1771) 106/180.
57. Hoffman, *Princes of Ireland, Planters of Maryland*, 263.
58. Kulikoff, *Tobacco and Slaves*, 288–89.
59. Breen, *Tobacco Culture*, 95.
60. Inventories (1741) 26/413, (1743) 28/54, (1744) 29/20, Accounts (1744) 20/455.
61. Breen, *Tobacco Culture*, 94–95.

CHAPTER 4

Patriarchy and Affection

The Demography and Character of Elite Families

In a preindustrial society, wealth was acquired by individuals and transferred over time through families. The characteristics of individual families largely determined how fortunes were accumulated and whether they were preserved. Large families or a paucity of heirs could diminish or extinguish estates, and the time of death of the head of the family could have significant effects on the transmission of property to future generations. The type of marriages made within families could also alter wealth patterns and change power relations within a community. In looking at whether the Maryland elite preserved their wealth and power over time, therefore, we need to examine family patterns and inheritance practices. In seeking to understand how they comprehended themselves and what their relations were like with others, we also need to appreciate the forms of elite family life and the meanings that wealthy men attached to such family life—families being, after all, not only the primary economic unit within society but also the principal arena in which individuals learned social rules and gained affection and love.

The character of the elite family was determined by its demography and by prevailing familial ideology. My understanding of both the demography of elite families and the ideologies that undergirded such families can be quickly summarized. The demography of the elite family demonstrated both change and continuity from the seventeenth century. Continuities were more important. The most fundamental continuity was continuing high mortality. Life expectancies for wealthy Marylanders and their children remained low, with over half of the elite dying before reaching old age or before their children had grown to maturity. The results for family structure, as will be explored below, were ambiguous. On the one hand, continuing high mortality did not necessarily lead to instability within the family; in most cases it actually contributed to family stability and allowed the smooth transfer of assets and affections over the generations. On the other hand, remarriage was frequent and complex families, made up of stepparents and stepchildren, were common. The comparatively early death of fathers meant that children gained independence early and accentuated strong ideological trends toward independence as a primary value. Patriarchal authority was thus both reinforced and undermined by continuing high mortality.

Frequent remarriage was another continuity between the seventeenth and eighteenth centuries. Wealthy Maryland men were invariably married gentlemen and tended to marry again once widowed. Whom they married did not change appreciably over time, either. They tended to marry people from their own social level. Nevertheless, elite families were not exclusive clans unwilling to allow entry to outsiders. Intermarriage was not customarily between people already related to each other but was between unrelated people from similar social backgrounds. Increases in wealth and an expansion in the number of people who could be considered respectable in Maryland led to an expansion of the pool of potential marriage partners but the character of that pool remained the same over time. Sociability was more important than family economic and political strategies in determining marriage practices. Indeed, wealthy Marylanders had a limited understanding of what constituted kinship. Devoted to immediate family members, they had more distant relations with more distant kin. Households tended to be open and associations with nonkin (associations usually predicated on shared modes of behavior) were both extensive and intimate.

The other important continuity shaping the elite family was the ideological strength of patriarchy as a fundamental value.[1] Patriarchy was the dominant social ethos and cultural metaphor of sev-

enteenth- and eighteenth-century Anglo-America and was an ethos
actively subscribed to by wealthy men. In its domestic form, it may
be defined as the historically specific authority of the father over
his household, including the right to punish family members and
enforce their obedience to his dictates.[2] Although the powers of the
father were close to absolute within the household, at least theoretically, the doctrine also involved protection, guardianship, reciprocal obligations, and love between family members. Even if the
power of Anglo-American heads of household was weak compared to those of ancient Mesopotamia or Rome, it was still formidable, akin in the domestic realm to the power of authority
figures in the political realm. By the beginning of English settlement in the colonies, the power of the household head was extraordinarily strong, with few countervailing obstructions from
church or state likely to lessen its sway. In the seventeenth century,
demographic and social difficulties in the settlement of the Chesapeake may have lessened the ability of fathers, husbands, and masters to enforce their authority, although recent scholarship has cast
doubt on whether the diminution of patriarchal authority was as
severe as once thought even in this period.[3] Whether patriarchal
forms of government were hindered or not, belief in it as an ideal
practice of household governance remained strong and men
implanted patriarchal ideals and practices into society as soon as
they could and reinforced the powers of the household head as
strongly and as often as they were able. By the end of the seventeenth century and throughout the eighteenth century, patriarchy
was a dominant form of household and political governance.
Indeed, social and demographic changes in the eighteenth century,
especially the growth of slavery and increases in the proportion of
children in the population, meant that the American colonies had a
far greater percentage of dependents in their populations than was
the case in England.[4] Nevertheless, the harshness that often characterized patriarchal social relationships remained tempered by the
limitations placed on patriarchal government early in the settlement process and, more importantly, by the eagerness of wealthy
men to adopt symbols and modes of behavior that denoted genteel
or respectable status. The ideology of patriarchal governance
required unthinking subordination to a patriarch's will. The reality
of elite Maryland family life presupposed that family relationships

would be governed by affection, mutual respect, and love. Only in this way could wealthy Marylanders achieve the "domestic tranquility" that they yearned for in their familial relationships.[5]

If the elite family remained stable over the latter colonial period, it did not remain static. Changes in elite demography accompanied continuities in structure and ideology. The most notable changes concerned women rather than men. In the late seventeenth and early eighteenth centuries the rise of a native-born elite was accompanied by a lowering of the age of female first marriage. The consequence was longer marriages and more children. Family size increased appreciably over time, Nevertheless, by the end of our period, Maryland men and women were beginning to realter their marrying and childbearing patterns so as to reduce the size of elite families—a trend that coincided with the beginnings of a slight Malthusian pressure on land to devise to children, especially sons. Thus, even change was neither remarkable nor long lasting.

Perhaps the most surprising feature about the elite family in the late seventeenth and eighteenth centuries is that it continued to be shaped by high mortality rates. These were not as calamitous as those of the first years of settlement of the Chesapeake, but early death remained a constant fact throughout the eighteenth century.[6] The majority of elite members, at all time periods, died before their society would have considered them elderly, even though there was an improvement in life expectancy over time with male life expectancy increasing from 50 to 53.[7] A year of birth and an approximate age at death for 268 wealthy Marylanders can be determined.[8] Over 50 percent of wealthy Marylanders died between ages 36 and 55, years of early middle age when a man was likely to have at least some children who were not yet adults. Another one in ten men died before they had reached the age of 36, when any of their children would still be young. Less than two in ten men died over 65 years of age, when it could be expected that their children would be adults (Tables 4.1 and 4.2).[9]

To avoid biases inherent in the sampling procedure,[10] I have also analyzed the life expectancies of those sons of the elite for whom accurate birth and death dates can be determined and who survived to adulthood. Bearing in mind that this sample is biased toward the prominent, the survivors, the stay at homes, and the longer lived, the creation of a life table for the sons of the elite

Table 4.1 Age at Death for Elite Members over Time

	Pre-1726	1726–42	1743–59	1760+	Total
Known (number)	56	46	57	107	268
Known (%)	58	53	56	62	58
Average age at death	50	52	52	53	52
Under 36 (%)	4	15	7	15	11
36–45 (%)	34	22	22	18	23
46–55 (%)	36	22	42	27	31
56–65 (%)	16	24	12	19	18
66+ (%)	11	17	18	21	18
36–55 (%)	70	44	63	45	54
46–65 (%)	52	46	54	46	49

*Categories based on year of decedent's death.
Source: Probate Records, *MHR*; Genealogical Records.

Table 4.2 Age at Death for Sons of Maryland Elite over Time[a]

	Pre-1691	1691–1708	1709–25	1726–42	1743+	Total
Known (number)	32	59	72	109	72	341
Average age at death	52	50	54	49	50	51
Under 36 (%)	22	17	14	19	19	18
36–45 (%)	9	17	19	18	19	18
46–55 (%)	28	27	19	18	19	22
56–65 (%)	16	22	19	23	14	19
66+ (%)	25	17	28	20	29	24
36–55 (%)	38	44	39	39	39	40
46–65 (%)	44	39	47	43	43	41

[a]Categories based on year of son's birth and includes only those sons who survived past 20 years.
Source: Probate Records, *MHR*; Genealogical Records.

shows that their average age at death was essentially the same as for the elite sample. The average age at death for the 341 sons whose birth and death dates are known was 51, with no increase in age at death over time. In fact, the average age at death for sons of the elite who were born after 1725 was 1 to 5 years *lower* than for those sons born before 1726. A higher proportion of the sons of the elite reached old age than in the elite sample, but the numbers were not very large and did not show any discernible increase over time. Less than one-quarter of the sons of the elite reached the age of 65. Just over one-third died between ages 20 and 45, with the percentage reaching age 45 declining over time. Most sons died at roughly the same age as their fathers, with most dying between ages 36 and 65. Not only was it likely that a man would die in his early fifties, but his son could not expect to live to a more advanced age.

The elite's continuing low life chances show, first, that life was precarious in the Chesapeake throughout the *whole* of the colonial period. Elite Marylanders continued to have considerably shorter life spans than their contemporaries, certainly in New England and also in England, although they far outdistanced their fellow planters living in Jamaica. The differences between life expectancy for males in New England and in Maryland were striking. The son of an elite member in Maryland could expect to live 20 years less than the average male in New England.[11] Less work has been done on the population process in the Middle Colonies, but male life expectancy appears higher in Pennsylvania, New Jersey, and New York than in Maryland.[12] The opposite is truc for Jamaica, where mortality persisted at epidemic proportions throughout the colonial period (Tables 4.3 and 4.4).[13]

The Maryland elite also fares badly compared to the English

Table 4.3 Life Expectancy from Age 20 of Elite Sons[a]

Age	Pre-1691 (N=32)	1691–1708 (N=59)	1708–25 (N=72)	1726–42 (N=106)	1743+ (N=72)	Total (N=341)
20	32	31	34	29	31	31
30	24	24	26	24	27	22
40	17	18	21	19	20	19
50	14	13	15	13	17	15
60	13	11	12	11	12	11
70	5	8	8	9	8	8

[a]Includes only those sons known to have reached age 20 and for whom both a year of birth and a year of death are known. Categories determined by date of birth of son.

Source: Probate Records, *MHR*; Genealogical Records.

Table 4.4 Comparative Life Expectancies

Age	(1)	(2)	(3)	(4)	(5)	(6)
20	26	29	21	44	45	18
30	20	19	16	41	39	15
40	16	13	12	33	31	13
50	12	8	10	24	24	10
60	9	6	7	16	15	8
70	7	4	4	10	10	6

(1) Males born Charles County, MD, 1652–99, preferred estimates, Menard and Walsh, "Death in the Chesapeake, 213; (2) Males born Middlesex Co., VA, 1650–1710, Rutmans, "'Now-Wives and Sons-in-Law'," 178; (3) Males born Charles Parish, VA, 1665–99, Smith, "Chesapeake Mortality," 415; (4) Males born Andover, MA, 1640–69, Greven, *Four Generations*, 27; (5) Males born Andover, MA, 1670–99, ibid, 110; (6) Children born St. Andrew Parish, 1666–1750, Burnard, "'The Countrie Continues Sicklie,'" 60.

elite, although there were some short-term similarities, especially during the demographic crisis for the English aristocracy and gentry in the late seventeenth century. Life expectancy at 20 for male members of the British aristocracy born between 1650 and 1674 was 29 years, which was lower than for any birth cohort of the Maryland elite. Nevertheless, life expectancy both before the late seventeenth century and certainly after 1700 was considerably higher for the British aristocracy than for the Maryland elite. A son of a Maryland elite member born after 1743 could expect to live to 51 if he survived to age 20. His contemporary in England who survived past 20, however, could expect to reach 59. Moreover, the Maryland elite—the most privileged group in their society—could expect to die 6 to 8 years before not just elite Englishmen but also Englishmen taken as a whole.[14]

If mortality for the Maryland elite remained high throughout the eighteenth century, we need to revise the common assumption that mortality improved greatly in the eighteenth century from the disastrous rates that prevailed in the seventeenth century. As Anita Rutman points out, the carefully tested and validated works that established the presence of a severe demographic crisis in the seventeenth-century have not been accompanied by similarly precise analyses of eighteenth-century rates.[15] Without such detailed studies, the connections between increasing life expectancy and transformations in the Chesapeake are necessarily tentative.

A closer examination of the work that does pertain to eighteenth-century mortality rates combined with the evidence on elite life expectancy presented above suggests that the differences in mortality between the seventeenth and eighteenth centuries were not great. Life tables constructed for other populations in the Chesapeake confirm that life expectancy remained low throughout the eighteenth century. The Rutmans' study of Middlesex, Virginia, puts life expectancy for males at 20 who were born between 1650 and 1710 (many of whom would have died in the eighteenth century) at 29 years. Menard and Walsh's life table for males born in Charles County, Maryland, between 1652 and 1699 estimates a life expectancy for males at 20 of 26 years, while Daniel Blake Smith has found that males born in York County, Virginia, between 1665 and 1699 could expect to live only another 21 years after they reached the age of 20.[16] A problem with all of these life tables is that they cover large time spans. As a consequence, they have been principally used to explain low life expectancy in the seventeenth century. Yet the majority of cases in all of the above life tables, as only the Rutmans emphasize, deal with men born at the end of the seventeenth century and who died in the second and third quarters of the eighteenth century, supposedly at the height of gentry domination of the Chesapeake. Few studies of life expectancy for native-born Marylanders born after 1710 exist, and those that do are unsatisfactory in several respects.[17] The life table for elite sons presented here indicates that improvements in mortality in the eighteenth century have been seriously overemphasized.

The standard argument, derived in the main from David Jordan's seminal article on the emergence of a native-born elite in Maryland, is that Maryland politics were initially dominated by relatively young immigrants who failed to leave adult sons who could capitalize on their fathers' brief successes, but by the early eighteenth century political control was being taken over by a Creole elite. Improving elite life expectancy underlays Creole political dominance but is asserted rather than proven.[18] Moreover, Jordan uses a very narrow definition of a successful transfer of status from generation to generation: the holding of provincial political office by both father and son. By adopting a broader definition of intergenerational status and asking whether descendants of early legislators obtained appointments as justices of the peace (J.P.s) and vestrymen and obtained wealth sufficient for elite status, we can see that early legislators were not so much isolated individuals who enjoyed transitory success than founders of powerful Maryland families.

An examination of the careers of the legislators in office between 1676 and 1682 (the period of Bacon's Rebellion in Virginia) illustrates this point. Over one-third of legislators whose birth and death are known reached the age of 60, with a slightly greater percentage leaving at least one full-grown adult son. Of these, nearly half left sons or grandsons who were prominent in colonial Maryland society and government. These included the establishment figure Philemon Lloyd, who had numerous legislators among his descendants, and Quakers like Samuel Chew, William Richardson, and John Edmundson, all of whom established important merchant-planter families but whose sons were denied political office because of their religious beliefs. It also includes legislators such as William Burgess, who left a son who did not become a legislator but who attained the rank of J.P. Jordan rightly emphasizes the significance of the changes in political behavior that resulted when native-born politicians replaced immigrants in the legislature but he underestimates the achievements of those immigrant politicians in establishing themselves and their descendants in Maryland society. If seventeenth-century Maryland legislators failed to pass their political power on to their children it was due less to underlying demographic conditions than to changes in political organization that excluded Catholics and Quakers from political power. Moreover, if we accept that low life expectancy significantly influenced the development of political institutions and the evolution of political stability in the colony, it is difficult to explain the rise of the most prominent political family in colonial Maryland—the Lloyds.[19] Not until the fourth generation of Lloyds did a father live long enough to see his son come of age. Both Philemon and Edward Lloyd II died when their eldest sons were well under age and Edward Lloyd I, though living to 76, left the province permanently before his son had attained political office.

Low life expectancy and high mortality had important repercussions for marriage and the procreation of children. It ensured
that a continuing high proportion of marriages ended abruptly or
before all children were adults. The majority of the Maryland
elite—92 percent—married. As colonial commentators such as
Benjamin Franklin pointed out, marriages in the colonies were
"more general . . . than in Europe."[20] Certainly the proportion of
wealthy Marylanders who married was considerably higher than
in the general population in England and in the British aristocracy,
where the proportion of males never marrying by the age of 40 was
seldom lower than 15 percent and often as high as 25 percent.[21]

Unmarried elite members tended to be younger than the total
sample. Nearly half of immigrants, moreover, remained unmarried. Nearly three-quarters were merchants or professionals. Why
merchants and nonplanters were so much more likely to remain
unmarried than planters is unclear. Faced with the considerable
demands of running a plantation, planters possibly needed a wife
more than merchants did. In addition, merchants, some of whom
were factors for British merchants, possibly did not feel they had
the same stake in society as planters and may have had less contact
with the networks of friends and kin within which most planters
chose their partners.

Many elite members married more than once, although the
incompleteness of marriage records makes it difficult to determine
precisely how frequent second or third marriages were. Nevertheless, we can establish that nearly 18 percent of married men remarried, with 2 percent remarrying more than once. The percentage
remarrying gradually declined over time from one in five wealthy
Marylanders remarrying to one in ten for those dying after 1760.
Because there was no instance of divorce among the elite, this
decline probably reflects an improvement in the longevity of their
marriage partners (a consequence of lower ages of first female
marriage around the turn of the eighteenth century) and a reduction in the number of women who died in childbirth.[22] Over half
of those who did remarry married a second wife before they were
36. In exactly half the cases, a wealthy widower remarried a
widow. Marrying a widow often entailed taking responsibility for
her children by a previous marriage and resulted in households
with complicated ties of blood and affection between parents and

children, with stepparents and stepsiblings common.[23] The drop in remarriages that occurred for elite members dying after 1760 reduced the likelihood of such mixed and complex households.

More crucial than the incidence of marriage was the age at which men and women married. Demographers have found that the age at first marriage is the most crucial determinant of fertility and population growth.[24] They have established that the European pattern was, by modern standards, one of relatively late marriage; the mean age at first marriage in England in the seventeenth and eighteenth centuries was around 28 for men, declining slightly over time, while the average age for women at first marriage was around 26.[25] Aristocrats married even later.[26] Contemporary commentators asserted and later historians have shown that age at first marriage was lower in the New World than in England, although considerable variations existed between regions, especially in the age of first marriage for women. Whereas female teenage marriage was rare in New England, teenage brides were frequent in the Chesapeake, especially in the late seventeenth and early eighteenth centuries (Table 4.5).[27]

Although the ages at first marriage of only a small proportion of the wives of the elite can be determined, we have reasonably full information concerning the age at first marriage of a large number of elite members' daughters. The average age at first marriage for native-born elite women in Maryland was several years younger than for women in both England and New England. The daughters of the Maryland elite married at an average age of 20 years and 6 months compared to 26 years for women in England

Table 4.5 Age Distribution at First Marriage of Elite Children

Sons (N = 54)		Daughters (N = 95)	
Age	%	Age	%
Under 21	9	Under 18	22
21–25	49	18–20	39
26–30	26	21–24	21
31–35	11	25–30	13
36+	5	31+	5

Source: Probate Records, *MHR*; Genealogical Records.

and 22 years in New England.[28] Age at first marriage changed considerably over time. Elite teenage brides were common in the seventeenth century but less so in the eighteenth century. The average age at first marriage for daughters of the elite cohort that died before 1726 was 18 years. Several daughters married as young as 14, 15, or 16 in the seventeenth century. The two daughters of Henry Darnall, for example, married when they were respectively 15 and 16 years old. By the mid-eighteenth century, daughters of the elite were more likely to marry in their twenties. Less than one-third of the daughters of wealthy Marylanders who died after 1760 married in their teens.

The average age of first marriage for men did not change so dramatically and was more similar to European and New England patterns. The mean age at marriage was 26, with no discernible variation over time. This age was 5 or 6 years younger than the average age of first marriage for the British aristocracy but only 1 to 2 years earlier than for British men as a whole.[29] Few men married before they were of age, with nearly half marrying between the ages of 21 and 25 and a quarter marrying between 26 and 30.

The gap in age between husband and wife was thus around 5 to 7 years. Where we have complete information regarding the age at first marriage for both partners in an elite marriage, the average age of the husband was 27 years and the average age of the wife was 20 years. The gap was higher for elite marriages in the late seventeenth and early eighteenth centuries, when there were more teenage brides. The marriage of Joseph, the son of William Richardson I, to Sarah Thomas in 1695 was typical. The groom was 27 and the bride was 16—a gap of 11 years. By mid-century, the two participants were likely to be closer in age, as in the marriage in 1774 of Nicholas, the son of Henry Dorsey I, to Lucy, the daughter of Colonel Edward Sprigg of Prince George's County. He was 24 and his bride 22.

Marriage was the principal means whereby different kin groups could become associated, and the growth of close-knit kinship networks linking wealthy families to other genteel families in the area was essential for elite class formation. Moreover, marriage in a premodern society was, along with inheritance, almost the only way to increase individual wealth quickly. One traditional way to acquire instant wealth through marriage was to marry a widow.

As historians of the early Chesapeake have pointed out, marrying a widow allowed many otherwise impecunious men to leapfrog into landed and wealthy status. This was especially true in the seventeenth century, so much so that Edmund Morgan and Daniel Blake Smith have characterized Chesapeake social structure as a form of "widowarchy."[30] Women tended to outlive men, at least according to data taken from Charles County, Maryland, between 1658 and 1705, which meant that there was always a sizable number of widows on the marriage market. More importantly, the overwhelming majority of immigrants into Maryland in the seventeenth century were men. Inheritance practices in the seventeenth century also encouraged men to marry a widow, because widows were often provided for handsomely in their husbands' wills.[31]

A significant proportion of the elite married widows: 13 percent of all first marriages were to widows, with the percentage nearing 30 percent for elite members who died before 1708. Widows tended to be of high status, with 45 percent being the widows of legislators or other elite Marylanders. A number of elite members who died before 1726 attained sizable benefits from marrying a widow, especially the Reverend John Henry, who married the very wealthy widow of Colonel Francis Jenkins. Almost all of those who gained wealth and status from marrying a widow were immigrants, and all, except Daniel Dulany, Sr., who died in 1753 after a very prominent career, died before the first third of the eighteenth century. Widows became less attractive marriage partners in the eighteenth century, mainly because they were less likely than their predecessors to inherit property outright.

Unsurprisingly, even if they did not marry widows, many elite members married well. Nearly 40 percent married daughters of other elite members with 6 percent marrying daughters of legislators. This estimate is clearly low because there were surely elite wives whose fathers' name and position are unknown who were of elite status. Certainly few wealthy men married women from much inferior social backgrounds, with only one in ten wedding a woman whose father is known to have left a total estate value (TEV) of less than £400. Marrying above oneself was more common. John Welsh, for instance, the son of a medium-sized landowner who left a TEV of £358, married first the daughter of Gerrard Hopkins, who left an estate of £2,035, and then the daughter of John Hammond II, a provincial legislator. As a son of a poor but well-connected planter, Aquilla Paca I also married well, marrying the daughter of James Phillips, who left an estate of £1,387. The Pacas became a prominent family in Baltimore County. Despite the ability of some immigrants and native-born men of low status and, presumably, considerable potential, to marry daughters or widows of prominent Marylanders, native-born men of high status enjoyed a distinct advantage in the marriage market, with nearly twice as many proportionately marrying within the Maryland elite than migrants and elite members not from elite backgrounds.[32]

Many elite families established kinship networks through marriage with other families of similar status in the local area. The extent to which the Maryland elite married among themselves is most usefully examined through an analysis of the marriages of elite children. Here we can see to what degree the Maryland elite were able to create a hereditary ruling class of wealthy gentlemen, separating themselves from the mass of Chesapeake society through shared kinship ties. Once again, we are hindered by the incompleteness of our sources. We are thus more likely to know the identities of prominent brides and grooms than those of humbler origin. Nevertheless, the children of the elite intermarried frequently, with at least 284 marriages between children of elite members or legislators. In sum, 197 elite members—53 percent of those with surviving children—had at least one child marrying a child from another wealthy or politically prominent family.

Elite intermarriage was more common on the Western Shore than on the Eastern Shore, with Anne Arundel having the highest and Talbot the lowest percentage of elite children marrying other elite children. One reason for this is purely statistical: a larger proportion of the population in Anne Arundel qualified for elite status in the terms set by this study than was the case in either Talbot or Somerset. The second reason is somewhat paradoxical. Although a number of men reached elite status in Talbot, entry into the highest level of society seems to have been more difficult than elsewhere in the province. As Paul Clemens has shown, a few very powerful merchant-planter families dominated Talbot society, economy, and politics. These families—the Lloyds, Hollydays, Tilghmans, Chamberlaines, Goldsboroughs, Robinses, and

Nichollses—were linked by numerous kinship ties and formed an exclusive, interlocking enclave that other wealthy men in the county found difficult to penetrate. Within this narrow group of families, intermarriage was extremely high and the linkages stronger than for elites in other counties.[33]

Elite intermarriage declined over time, with elite members dying after 1760 much less likely than earlier cohorts to have children intermarrying with other wealthy Maryland families. This decline in elite intermarriage is somewhat at odds with the accepted view of the Chesapeake elite as becoming more entrenched over time. The growth of population and the increase in wealth in the region over the course of the eighteenth century combined to allow a larger pool of potential spouses for elite children by mid-century than was possible in the poor and sparsely populated Chesapeake of the late seventeenth century. Elite children who did not marry other elite children did not marry beneath themselves. Generally, they married children of well-established native families who were not of elite status but who were both landowners and slave owners and who left TEVs over £225. In the early Chesapeake, the number of families in middling to rich wealth categories was very small.[34] Marylanders of elite status who wished to marry people from respectable backgrounds had only a limited pool of prospects from which to choose. Not surprisingly, they usually chose their spouse from one of the few wealthy merchant-planter families in the region. Later, that pool of potential partners was enlarged, principally as a result of the growing wealth of a larger percentage of the community and by the inclusion of the children of middling slave-owning planters and professionals into the marriage market. Indeed, the Maryland elite was remarkably *inclusive*, welcoming new additions so long as they satisfied basic criteria of wealth and status.[35]

A number of fathers had more than one child marrying into another elite family, headed by Caleb Dorsey I, who had 10 children intermarrying with other elite children. Overall, one-fifth of elite members with children had at least two children marrying other elite children. Elite intermarriages served two purposes in terms of cementing elite bonds. Extensive intermarriage connected a family with a number of other prominent families. The marriages of Caleb Dorsey's children, for example, linked the Dorseys with the Worthington, Hill, Nicholson, Beale, Chew, Woodward,

Todd, and Ridgley families, as well as with other branches of the Dorsey family. In Talbot County, the daughters of the wealthy merchant-planter George Robins married into the Hollyday, Hayward, Chamberlaine, and Nichols families. Elite intermarriage not only broadened the networks connecting wealthy Marylanders with other members of their own class but also helped to cement ties with what amounted to a merger of the property and power of two important families in a single marriage. Thus, the two most powerful provincial politicians in mid-eighteenth century Maryland, Daniel Dulany, Sr., and Benjamin Tasker, Sr., allied themselves together in a very fundamental sense when Dulany's eldest son Daniel married the daughter of Tasker. Not surprisingly, Daniel Dulany, Jr., quickly entered politics himself, obtained a number of lucrative posts, and, after the death of his father-in-law, emulated the example of his father in becoming the dominant politician in the province.

Nevertheless, wealthy Marylanders' unwillingness to confine themselves to a narrow group of increasingly interrelated families when choosing marital partners indicates that sociability was more important than family economic and political strategies in making marriages. The importance of sociability can be ascertained by measuring the extent of cousin marriage with the elite. Allan Kulikoff asserts that the desire to keep family property within the kinship group encouraged cousins to marry each other. He finds a remarkable level of cousin marriage in Prince George's County, despite it being denounced by some observers. The Anglican divine, Peter Fontaine, for example, declared that such marriages were "not only of pernicious consequence to the government, but contrary to the true spirit of Christianity." In Prince George's County marriages between blood relations gradually increased during the eighteenth century until 28 percent of all marriages between 1760 and 1790 were between already related people.[36]

Wealthy men and their children elsewhere in Maryland did not replicate Prince George's high rate of cousin marriage. In sum, from 403 marriages made by children of the elite, 14 percent were between blood relations.[37] Moreover, there is no evidence that cousin marriages were arranged so as to consolidate or retain property within the family, as might be expected in a highly patriarchal and kin-focused society. The type of cousin marriage that most effectively retained property within the kin group was parallel-cousin marriage (marriages by sons to daughters of mother's sisters or father's brothers). Parallel-cousin marriages were the most common form of cousin marriage within the English peerage. Such marriages preserved patrilineal wealth by preventing female property from leaving the kinship group. Cross-cousin marriages (marriages by sons to daughters of mother's brothers or father's sisters), however, tend to dilute wealth by preventing the infusion of other families' property, in the form of dowries, into the kinship group. The children of wealthy Marylanders were just as likely to make cross-cousin marriages as they were to make parallel-cousin marriages. Of 55 cousin marriages, 27 were parallel-cousin marriages and 28 were cross-cousin marriages.

Thus, although the rate of cousin marriage was high by European standards and high even by the standards of isolate populations, this merely reflected social structures prevailing in rural communities.[38] Parents divided their land among their sons, who would then set up new plantations on this land, which was often near the property of relatives. The people with whom the newly established sons would come into contact and form emotional attachments would be nearby relatives. But, given a choice, children of the elite did not necessarily prefer to marry relatives rather than neighbors. Significantly, sibling exchange (where two siblings from one family marry two siblings from another) was as prevalent as cousin marriage, with 58 separate examples, amounting to 14 percent of all marriages made by elite children. Sometimes two families seem to have virtually merged, as when three children of William Hammond married three children of Reverend John Lillingston and three daughters of John Ensor married sons of Nicholas Merryman. Occasionally, there were multiple sibling exchanges within one family, such as when two children of Nathan Hammond married children of Mathew Hawkins, two children married children of John Raitt, and a further child married John Raitt's widow. Sibling exchange resulted from great friendliness and sociability between two families rather than a design to merge two families. Little or no gain in overall family wealth was gained through sibling exchange.

The economic and social benefits that could be attained by an alliance to a wealthy family through the marriage of a child were substantial, and many parents were anxious that their children marry someone whose position and estate they could approve. The issue of the extent of control exercised by parents over who their children married has been much debated because it is an historical litmus test for determining the nature of the elite southern family. Those who argue that great planters in the Chesapeake moved from a family life "characterized by a strong sense of order, authority and self restraint" to one in which there was "a strikingly affectionate family environment" see a shift by the mid-eighteenth century from families presided over by unchallenged patriarchs, determining marital and career decisions according to "paternal preference, economic class and social status, rather than companionship or romantic love," to families in which parents had "a growing belief in the autonomy of sons and daughters, especially regarding the selection of marriage partners."[39] On the other hand, those who hold that southern planter families became increasingly patriarchal over the eighteenth century argue that parental control over the marriage choices of their children increased as parents lived longer, sex ratios became more normal, and slavery became firmly established as the principal labor system in the region.[40] The extent of control that elite members were able to maintain over their children, especially when and whom they were to marry, is crucial to understanding the nature of colonial family life in the Chesapeake.

One way to analyze this issue is to see how many sons delayed marrying until after their fathers died. Many fathers died at a comparatively young age, so it is difficult to determine whether sons who married in their mid- to late twenties waited until their father died before marrying or whether they would have married at that time with or without their father being alive. Only three sons, however, married when they were over 30 years of age and within 2 years of their fathers' death, suggesting that there was in general little delay of marriage because of either parental disapproval or a lack of financial independence. Indeed, a considerable number of sons married while their fathers were still alive. Of those sons whose age at marriage is known, one-third married before their father was dead, at an average age of 24 years. This is slightly younger than the overall average age at first marriage but can be explained by the nature of the sample. Sons were less likely to have their fathers alive at the time of their marriage if they married after their mid-twenties. More significantly, marriage while fathers were still alive did not necessarily mean that such sons were able to marry because they received their inheritance at that date rather than at the time of their father's death. On the contrary, 58 percent of sons who married while their fathers were still alive and whose fathers later made a will received substantial amounts of property at their fathers' death. Some elite sons, of course, such as Samuel Chew II, Edward Lloyd IV, James Lloyd Chamberlaine, and Samuel Chamberlaine II, were sons of extremely wealthy men who could afford both to devise property to a son at the date of marriage and also leave substantial assets to that son at their death. Nevertheless, quite a number of elite members made a conscious choice not to devise property at the time of their sons' marriages but at the date of their own death. John Hammond II, for example, left an estate of £978.75, but did not devise sizable amounts of property to his married son, Thomas John, before his death, despite living for 22 years after the date of his son's marriage.

It was unusual for a father to survive for so long after his son's marriage. Less than half of the elite with married sons lived more than 10 years and just two-thirds survived more than 5 years after their sons' marriages. In all likelihood, the gap between date of marriage and a son's inheritance was short and seldom a serious source of friction between fathers and sons, as seems to have occurred in some New England families from the late seventeenth to the mid-eighteenth centuries.[41] Continued early death in the Chesapeake meant that parental control over children's behavior, even when consciously exercised by would-be patriarchs, was in practice severely limited, with sons usually entering their inheritance within, if not before, a few years of marriage. However much men might have wished to behave in the manner of patriarchs, their ability to do so depended in large measure upon circumstances largely beyond their control. For eighteenth-century elite Marylanders, demographic fortuities curtailed their ability to prolong paternal authority to the extent that New England farmers were able to achieve.

The end result of marriage and one of the principal reasons for entering that state was the procreation of children. Four out of five men who married also left children. Childlessness was higher than in New England but considerably below that within the British elite, whose rate of childless marriages reached epidemic proportions in the early eighteenth century.[42] Average family size for elite families gradually increased during the colonial period. Less than one-third of those who died before 1726 left more than four surviving children, with just five wealthy Marylanders dying before 1726 leaving families of seven or more children. As the century progressed, large families became less unusual: 47 percent of elite members dying between 1743 and 1759 and 50 percent of those dying after 1760 left families with more than four surviving children. By the mid-eighteenth century two-thirds of wealthy Maryland men managed to successfully replace their family and add to a gradual population increase by leaving three or more surviving children (Tables 4.6 and 4.7).[43]

Increasing family size among the Maryland elite presents somewhat of a conundrum in light of other vital demographic facts, notably life expectancy, which did not change appreciably over time. To some degree, the paradox of increasing family size results from the different samples used to explore death, marriage, and family size among the elite. I have been able to use data both from elite members and from their children for deaths and marriages, whereas I have treated family size only for elite members and not for their children. Elite members included immigrants who tended to marry later and die sooner than native-born Marylanders, thus

Table 4.6 Family Size of Elite: Number of Surviving Children

	Pre-1726	1726–42	1743–59	1760+	Total
Number married	90	77	99	159	425
Surviving children					
None (%)	16	8	12	13	13
1–2 (%)	28	37	25	18	25
3–4 (%)	23	17	19	18	19
5–7 (%)	26	29	22	32	29
8+ (%)	6	10	25	18	15
3+ (%)	54	56	67	69	63
5+ (%)	31	35	48	50	44

Source: Probate Records, MHR; Genealogical Records.

Table 4.7 Family Size of Elite: Number of Surviving Sons

	Pre-1726	1726–42	1743–59	1760+	Total
Number married	90	77	99	159	425
Sons					
None (%)	24	22	22	21	22
1–2 (%)	47	46	41	32	40
<3 (%)	71	68	64	54	62
3+ (%)	29	33	36	47	38
4+ (%)	17	22	22	25	22
Total number of sons	30	31	25	29	28

Source: Probate Records, *MHR*; Genealogical Records.

reducing the possible years they could father children.[44] Also, within the elite members' sample, the numbers of wealthy Marylanders dying before they reached the age of 45 decreased over time, although, overall, average age at death did not change. As a consequence of these two factors, the duration of elite members' marriages increased over time, from 22 years for those dying before 1726 to 28 years for wealthy Marylanders dying after 1760. The average length of marriage for elite children, however, did not increase over time, with the cohort born before 1708 having the longest average duration of marriage—32 years—of all four cohorts of elite children, suggesting that increasing family size might be to some extent a statistical illusion. Increases in family size were probably the result of a combination of short-term factors rather than a reflection of a long-term trend.

Nevertheless, family size probably did increase. Although it is difficult to document, infant mortality surely decreased over the course of the eighteenth century. The only studies made of infant mortality suggest that there was some decrease in total mortality for children and youths by the turn of the eighteenth century.[45] An increase in the number of nearby kin, neighbors, midwives, and doctors who could help in the childbirth process also may have helped reduce the incidence of death in childbirth, although, even for elite women, the medical and physical help received was, even by the close of the colonial period, still quite primitive in nature.[46] If the proportion of elite men remarrying can be used as a crude measure, the numbers of women dying in childbirth seem to have declined. The percentage of men remarrying (usually by 36) dropped after the first quarter of the eighteenth century from a quarter to a tenth, indicating a greater survival rate for women before menopause. The replacement of the immigrant population of the seventeenth century with the native-born population of the eighteenth century also aided females through the rigors of childbirth. Of the 57 daughters of the elite whose date of marriage and age at death are known, 28 percent died within 20 years of marriage and 10 percent died before they had been married 10 years. If these rough figures accurately estimate female survival rates, then by the eighteenth century most native-born women were likely to live until their childbearing years were almost over.

Female age at marriage was the most important determinant of fertility and family size. Elite members dying in the mid-eighteenth century were the beneficiaries of an increase in fertility as a result of the comparative plenitude of teenage brides in the late seventeenth and early eighteenth centuries. There is little information about elite wives, but we can surmise from other evidence that immigrants, who constituted a larger part of the early Maryland elite than they did later on, tended to marry immigrant women who were in their early twenties.[47] Those wealthy Marylanders dying after 1726 were more likely to have married a native-born bride who was a teen when she married and who would be likely to have a lengthy childbearing period. Moreover, elite members dying after 1726 were more likely to marry before the age of 26 than were members of the earliest cohort. This change increased the possibilities that both parents would be alive and married during a woman's peak childbearing years.

The increase in the average age of marriage for women after the mid-eighteenth century probably led to a decrease in family size for the generation of elite Marylanders dying after 1776. Evidence collected by Allan Kulikoff supports this assertion. He sees a decline of 25 percent in family size from 7.4 children for native-born women marrying between 1700 and 1750 to 5.5 children for native-born women marrying in the latter half of the century.[48] Attitudinal changes toward fecundity accompanied changes in the length of the marital childbearing period. After 1760, crude birth rates in the thirteen colonies rapidly declined, a decline that Susan Klepp convincingly attributes to female agency whereby pregnancy came to be seen by women as less a natural than an alien experi-

ence. Women deliberately began to limit fertility in the revolutionary period. In the North, women began to view high fertility as
linked with brutishness and lack of self-control. In the South,
women began to limit their families out of a fear of death in childbirth and were less successful in family limitation than their northern sisters, using breastfeeding as a way of increasing the space
between children.[49] Another reason why women (and men) may
have consciously or subconsciously wanted to limit family sizes by
the Revolution was to avert a possible Malthusian crisis of too
little land for too many sons. No such Malthusian crisis existed
before the war: wealthy Marylanders had usually more than sufficient land to disperse to all their sons. Nevertheless, a gradual
increase in the age of female first marriage, decreasing fertility, and
increased family limitation illustrate that wealthy Maryland
women did assert some agency in altering elite demography in
order to fit changed circumstances.

This survey of the demography of elite families in the eighteenth century suggests that continuity coincided with moderate,
gradual, and occasionally reversable changes. Elite men and
especially elite women were able to alter their demographic
behavior in some areas, notably as regards age of marriage and
fertility, but continued to be handicapped by relatively high mortality and by a perpetuation of fragile and complex family structures. Even if demographic change had been substantial, however,
we should be wary of drawing large-scale conclusions about the
character of the elite family purely from demographic evidence,
as many students of the colonial southern family have been wont
to do. For example, historians have been anxious to make the
supposed achievement of more normal demographic conditions
by the early eighteenth century a necessary precondition for a
wide array of social, political, and economic changes, transforming the inherently unstable world depicted in Edmund
Morgan's *American Slavery, American Freedom,* where social
conflict raged between repressive adventurers on the make and
their sullen and rebellious white servants, to the established, traditional, and hierarchical world of Rhys Isaac's *Transformation
of Virginia,* where the authority of "proud men on horseback"
and the values they espoused were widely accepted as the basis
for considerable social order.

Leaving aside the question of whether "normal" demographic

conditions were ever established in the Chesapeake or whether Morgan's and Isaacs's depictions of the Chesapeake are accurate, demographic "crisis" conditions are not necessarily indicative of instability. On the contrary, studies of British politics and elite social structure show that growth in political stability and a demographic crisis for the landed elite went hand in hand in the early eighteenth century. The inability of the British gentry and aristocracy to reproduce themselves did not lead to a diminution of their power but rather increased the wealth of those members who managed to survive. Heiresses were common and tended to marry eldest sons. The result was the amalgamation of large estates within a small circle of very wealthy aristocrats who dominated British society and politics to an extent unparalleled either before or after in British history.[50]

Even early parental death was not as socially disastrous for the British elite as it has been argued to be in Chesapeake society.[51] At times, the early death of the head of the family could be advantageous, allowing an estate time to recuperate from the heavy expenditures of extravagant landed gentlemen: maintaining a minor as the family head was comparatively inexpensive.[52] Thus we should be careful in making bold claims about changes in social structure from apparent demographic shifts. Relationships between the two are complex and more resistant to sudden changes in direction than historians have imagined. Moreover, similar demographic conditions often effected quite different changes.

What an analysis of the structure of elite families does tell us is that Maryland elite members were able to form extensive family ties among themselves, creating a close-knit group linked in numerous ways. Many of the elite were linked directly either intergenerationally as father and son or intragenerationally as brothers. There were 178 elite members who were either fathers or sons of other elite members, with another 20 being brothers of wealthy Marylanders. Overall, 43 percent of the elite had a direct blood link with another elite member, with 5 percent having both their father and their paternal grandfather as elite members. Other wealthy Marylanders, although not directly related by blood to other wealthy Marylanders, were indirectly or affinally related to other cohort members, either marrying the daughter of an elite member or having a child marrying either an elite member or the child of one. Only one-quarter of the sample does not seem to have kinship ties to other elite members, and a few of this number were connected to elite members in other counties. Edmund Key, for example, does not seem to have any blood or affinal relations within the elite sample, but his membership in a very prominent family in St. Mary's County makes it difficult to see him as unconnected. In total, one in five wealthy Marylanders of the elite did not have kinship ties to other elite members.

A further breakdown of unconnected wealthy Marylanders emphasizes how close-knit a group the Maryland elite really was. Only 15 percent of native-born elite Marylanders failed to establish familial links with other elite families. These men tended to be among the poorer elite members with estates worth less than £1,500. Moreover, they seldom attained either local or provincial office. Robert Smith, who died in 1707 when Maryland was essentially a frontier society and who left only a daughter to survive him, was the only unconnected wealthy Marylander in this sample to attain membership in the Maryland legislature.

But if the elite were closely connected, they did not retreat into exclusive clans. Immediate family members and kin relations were important, but they were important only in certain situations connected with family affairs. Outside of immediate family matters, wealthy men sought out people with whom they may not have shared a common genealogy but with whom they shared common values, notably an aspiration toward gentility and respectability. If a person had the requisite attributes of gentility and could demonstrate gentility through wealth, status, and behavior, then that person—even an outsider or newcomer—could easily be incorporated into elite society. That culture was based less on family than on an explicitly male political culture, focused around taverns, hospitality, rough sports, and, by mid-century, genteel gathering places. Genteel newcomers, like the Scottish immigrant, physician, and accomplished Enlightenment gentleman Alexander Hamilton—the eminence grise of Annapolis's Tuesday Club—found it easy to enter into elite circles, circles characterized by inclusivity rather than exclusivity.[53]

Understanding the demography of wealthy Marylanders' families is important, but we also need to try to understand what values Marylanders attached to families and family life. Unfortunately, qualitative evidence on the nature of familial relationships for wealthy Marylanders is very limited, and it is difficult to state with any certainty how Marylanders thought of other family members and what they expected the family to represent. Moreover, what they did write down has not often been preserved. The abundance of public papers for colonial Maryland is matched by the paucity of private papers for even the most prominent colonial Marylanders.

What emerges from the limited records of family life is that family life remained essentially the same throughout the colonial period. I am unconvinced by claims that the elite family changed remarkably over time—the customary analysis being that patriarchy was under great attack in the seventeenth century, was rehabilitated around the late seventeenth century, and crumbled again in the onslaught of Revolutionary change around mid-century. In my opinion, relationships between women and men and parents and children did not vary radically over this period. The major change in family relationships came from the shift from the Old World to the New and the development of much looser family relationships. Kin networks were small or nonexistent, and the scarcity of women led to a lessening of sexual role differentiation, while the likelihood of early death as well as the increased geographical and social mobility of a frontier society were much greater than in Europe. The result, as historians of the seventeenth-century Chesapeake have documented, was some diminution in paternal authority in fact (although not in theory, where patriarchy as an ideal form of governance remained a constant to strive for) and a concomitant increase in the freedom of wives and especially children within the family. Children, in particular, had an increased ability to enter into new familial arrangements without the consent of their fathers.[54] These patterns, early established, remained true throughout the colonial period. But that did not mean that the fundamental values that undergirded family governance in England were overturned in the new colonies of the Chesapeake. I agree with James Horn that "the move to America did not undermine patriarchalism, the theoretical basis of male dominance, or alter in practice the somewhat more ambiguous social relations between men and women."[55] As kin networks expanded as a function of time, the importance of emotion as the cement keeping families together increased, although it appears to have been a fundamental characteristic of Chesapeake families from the seventeenth century onward. Smith and Lewis contrast the strongly affectionate and companionate family life of the late eighteenth century with the Chesapeake family of the early eighteenth century in which they believe "emotional attachments between family members were muted" because of "an overriding concern for order and for clear lines of authority."[56] Yet what limited evidence exists concerning the family life of the Maryland elite suggests that wealthy Marylanders at all times placed great if not paramount importance upon love and affection in family relationships. Letters preserved in the Hollyday Papers dating from as early as 1697, when Andrew Tilghman wrote in some detail to his kinsman Richard Tilghman about his fond feelings for his wife and children, throughout the 1730s until the 1790s and involving various Hollydays, Tilghmans, and Lloyds, are full of references to family members that indicate that affection was extremely important.[57]

The most notable collection of family correspondence of wealthy Marylanders points to the significance of affection as a fundamental value undergirding the patriarchal Maryland family. Charles Carroll of Annapolis conducted an intense epistolary correspondence with his son, Charles Carroll of Carrollton, from the late 1740s until the early 1780s, much of which has been preserved. Letters were the Carrolls' lifelines, the tangible manifestations of the ties that bound them. For each man, the other was the emotional center of his life. The younger Carroll's relationship with his wife and family were noticeably less effusive and less important than his connection to his irascible but loving father. His father was a tough taskmaster, tirelessly dictating his expectations about his son's education, conduct, and future prospects, concerning himself endlessly with his son's mental, moral, and social development. Yet his letters do not so much portray a stern patriarch as a tenderhearted father, wishing to cajole and implore rather than command. The elder Carroll could be both irascible and imperious—he was insistent for a long time that his son would complete studies in law. But he was inclined to treat his son as an equal more than a dependent and the correspondence between the two was marked less by commands and instruction than by a shared intimacy and a delight in each other's thoughts.[58]

Other collections of family papers also show how sentimental early elite families were. A letter written by Richard Grafton, a wealthy landowner, to his daughter, Mary, later the wife of Walter Dulany of Annapolis, a letter designed to be read after his death, is an excellent example of such sentiment. Written with a great deal of pathos, Grafton bemoaned that he will "no more . . . delight himself in your dear company" nor "behold your sweet disposition and temper of mind." He then proceeded to give his daughter advice on her future conduct but, importantly, couched this advice not as instructions that a stern patriarch has a right to expect will be obeyed but as maxims of conduct learned "from my own experience" and offered to a daughter free to make up her own mind concerning her conduct. Indeed, the only command Grafton gave to Mary was to treat her mother with "respect and duty." Even then, the command was hardly binding because he "lay[ed] no injunction on you not foreseeing what may happen." This letter was written in 1737 by a man brought up in the late seventeenth century and indicates that even before the mid-eighteenth century love, mutual respect, and intense affection, rather than subordination to patriarchal authority, bound families together.[59]

Strong statements of emotional love continued throughout the period.[60] In 1757, for example, Thomas Robins, studying in Edinburgh, fairly gushed in a letter to James Hollyday II about how much "joy" he received from letters from America and declared that he could "see the Mother, the Father, the Sister in their several letters" and admitted "how happy am I in having them still living."[61] When the circle was broken by death, the grief was real and deeply felt. The fragility of life in the early Chesapeake did not make loss any easier to accept. Dr. Charles Carroll, for instance, was distraught when his 18-year-old son, John Henry, died in 1754 and, when writing to his sole surviving son, Charles, who was studying law in London, expatiated at length about the death "in my arms" of a son about whom he had "never heard or Saw the least offensive word or Behavior." Carroll "was resigned to the will of God" in the matter, but it had affected him deeply, making him aware of his own mortality and the importance of his family to him. He implored his remaining son to return as soon as possible "least my eyes should close before I see you they begin to be dim long since but this last stroke has added Dimness to my Sight and Senses." Yet even here parental authority was muted. Carroll did not command his son to return but left this decision to his son "as your own Judgmt will best suggest to you what is proper to be done."[62]

Chesapeake gentlemen liked to think of themselves as all-powerful patriarchs. The extent of their authority was immense in relationship to their slaves, as challenges to master authority were determinedly resisted in slave societies. Their authority was less certain within the immediate family, as Katherine Brown has detailed for Virginia. In part, gentlemen focused so intently on achieving domestic harmony and mutual affection with their wives and children because their powers to compel immediate family members to do their will were always circumscribed by the circumstances of family life. In particular, fathers often found it difficult to assert their authority over their children, especially their sons, primarily because they insisted that their commands be obeyed freely from affection, duty, and loyalty. Sons did not always return that affection and when they did not, fathers were left with little recourse besides the grave threat of disinheritance to compel obedience. The Virginia planter Landon Carter's tribulations with his children are especially well known. Carter could never reconcile his desire for control over his children with his insistence on intensely affectionate relations with his adult children. Chesapeake gentlemen were anxious patriarchs because their theoretical powers were never matched by practical abilities. Children, especially sons, were quite as willing as their fathers to insist on independence and resist the authority of others.[63]

One indication of children's independence came when making marriages. In practice children married when they wanted to rather than at the behest of their parents, even if they tended to marry people of whom fathers would approve. The vagaries of demography necessitated such freedom of choice for children, but parental decisions to give children wide latitude in the choice of a spouse also contributed. The ability of young Maryland elite members to choose spouses freely can be seen in the very few examples of courting and marriage selection described in private papers. Charles Carroll of Annapolis, for example, gave his son Charles

Carroll of Carrollton much freedom in his eventually unsuccessful pursuit of a West Indian heiress. The elder Carroll left all negotiations to his son, offering merely advice about what a man should look for in a wife. This advice points to a companionate view of marriage. More important than her pedigree and her fortune was her character, which should be "sensible [and] sweet tempered," for without these characteristics "Domestick Peace and Content [,] Matrimony must prove a Curse instead of a Blessing." A decent marriage settlement was essential but, even for the avaricious Carrolls, money was not the crucial ingredient in a happy marriage: "As to her Fortune whatever it may be you know it does not with me enter into any sort of Comparison with virtue good nature and Good Sense."[64] A wife was a companion, a partner (if a subordinate one and one who accepted the essential tenets of patriarchal authority), and a marriage was designed to promote "Domestick Peace and Content Matrimony." Other writers echoed Carroll's view that a wife first and foremost needed to be emotionally compatible with her husband. Stephen Bordley advised his brother John in 1745, on hearing of his forthcoming marriage, that he should "regard well the Character first, and then the temper of the Girl; as to fortune, if there were any, it serves to be considered but in the third place."[65]

The tone of Bordley's letter clearly indicates that the final decision for marriage rested in his brother's hand, not in the nominal head of the family. Insistent on their own independence, elite Marylanders recognized and were willing to extend to family members a good deal of freedom in choosing mates and indeed in almost every sphere relating to personal and family concerns. Although within families clear lines of authority existed (husbands were superior to wives, children were subordinate to parents), the family was not just an economic unit but was the primary social institution in the region, providing much of the meaning to wealthy Marylanders' existence. This was perhaps more true of the southern colonies than elsewhere in mainland America because competing institutions such as churches, the state, schools, and other networks of community interaction were relatively weak.[66] The family was ideally a firm emotional support, and what evidence exists of attitudes to the family by colonial Marylanders suggests that family relationships played a vital role in their emotional life. The principal value of such relationships was to promote domestic happiness. The affectionate character of the elite family is evident in inheritance provisions, the most concrete indication of the importance of family and family members that has been left by wealthy Marylanders.

NOTES

1. My understanding of the workings of patriarchal social relations in the Chesapeake has been influenced by Kathleen Brown, *Good Wives, Nasty Wenches, and Anxious Patriarchs* (Chapel Hill: University of North Carolina Press, 1996); Mary Beth Norton, *Founding Mothers and Fathers: Gendered Power and the Formation of American Society* (New York: Alfred A. Knopf, 1996); Kenneth Lockridge, *On the Sources of Patriarchal Rage: The Commonplace Books of William Byrd and Thomas Jefferson and the Gendering of Power in the Eighteenth Century* (New York: New York University Press, 1992); and Carole Shammas, "Anglo-American Household Government in Comparative Perspective," *WMQ*, 3d. Ser. (1995), 104–44.

2. The family and the household were defined both narrowly and broadly in the plantation societies of Anglo-America in the seventeenth and eighteenth centuries. The broad definition included all people subjected to the same household head. It included not only wives and children but also servants, tenants, and, depending on context, poorer men, especially those employed by or indebted to wealthier men. It also included slaves. The narrow definition of family, and the one used here, is the more familiar one (to us at least) of the nuclear family of husband and wife, parents and children. The narrower definition, however, was always encaptured within the broader one.

3. See Norton, *Founding Mothers and Fathers*. Her account of gendered power shows seventeenth-century Maryland males determined to assert their power. I am not sure, however, that the actual workings of the seventeenth-century Maryland family were as proto-Lockean as she suggests. Even if families were too truncated and peculiar to allow in practice the family to serve as a model for the state, there is little evidence that Maryland leaders were willing to give up the ideal that the two were equated and even less evidence that they saw family and public life as being conceptually distinct.

4. Shammas, "Anglo-American Household Government," 122–23. If Shammas had included the British West Indies in her analysis, then the percentages of both the total population and the adult population who were dependents increase even further, from 80.4 percent to 83.8 percent for the former, and from 54.4 percent to 64.5 percent for the latter.

5. For the importance of domestic tranquillity, see Brown, *Good Wives, Nasty Wenches, and Anxious Patriarchs*, 324–28.

6. For the seventeenth century, see Terry Lee Anderson and Robert Paul Thomas, "The Growth of Population and the Labor Force in the Seventeenth Century Chesapeake," *Explorations in Economic History*, XV (1978), 290–312; Lorena S. Walsh and Russell R. Menard, "Death in the Early Chesapeake: Two Life Tables for Men in Early Colonial Maryland, *MdHM*, LXIX (1974), 211–27; idem, "The Demography of Somerset County, Maryland: A Progress Report," *Newberry Papers in Family and Community History*, 81–82 (1981); Darrett B. Rutman and Anita H. Rutman, "Of Agues and Fevers: Malaria in the Early Chesapeake," *WMQ*,

3d. Ser., XXXIII (1976), 31–60; idem, " 'Now-Wives and Sons-in-Law': Parental Death in a Seventeenth-Century Virginia County," in Thad W. Tate and David L. Ammerman (eds.), *The Chesapeake in the Seventeenth Century* (Chapel Hill: University of North Carolina Press, 1979), 153–82; and Daniel Blake Smith, "Mortality and Family in the Colonial Chesapeake," *JIH*, VIII (1978), 403–27. For the eighteenth century see Allan Kulikoff, *Tobacco and Slaves: The Development of Southern Cultures in the Chesapeake, 1680–1800* (Chapel Hill: University of North Carolina Press, 1986), 49–63, 167–74.

7. Colonial Americans defined "old age" in chronological terms that were similar to contemporary ideas about old age. For New Englanders, "old age" started at 60. Southerners saw less people reach old age than in New England (although the percentage of the population aged 60 and over in Maryland in 1776 was slightly higher than the percentage of old people in the United States as late as 1840) but still thought of old age as beginning at 60. David Hackett Fischer, *Growing Old in America* (New York: Oxford University Press, 1977), 27, 222. One Carolinian commented that "there are few old men or women to be found in the province . . . we cannot say that there are many in the country who arrive at their sixtieth year." Alexander Hewatt, *An Historical Account of the Rise and Progress of the Colonies of South Carolina and Georgia*, 2 vols. (London, 1779), II, 294. The age of 65 has been used here as the date of old age principally to ensure that men in this category would be very likely to have no nonadult children at the time of death.

8. Dates at death are usually taken from date of probate and thus overestimate the life span of the deceased. Yet the lag between actual death and probate was generally short and the error seems tolerable, perhaps reducing life expectancy by between one-eighth and one-quarter of a year. Walsh and Menard, "Death in the Chesapeake," 212. Also, since only the years of birth and death are known, not the exact dates, the actual length of an elite member's life could vary by as much as 2 years. Daniel S. Levy, "The Life Expectancies of Colonial Maryland Legislators," *Historical Methods*, 20 (1987), 26, n.6.

9. Jane Turner Censer, *North Carolina Planters and Their Children, 1800–1860* (Baton Rouge: Louisiana State University Press, 1984), 20, suggests that early death was still significant in southern families in the mid-nineteenth century.

10. The sample excludes some older men who had retired from business at the time of their death and who may have diverted considerable portions of their wealth to adult sons and it also excludes younger men who died before they were able to accumulate the wealth necessary for inclusion in this study.

11. See Philip J. Greven, *Four Generations: Population, Land, and Family in Colonial Andover* (Ithaca, NY: Cornell University Press, 1970), 26–27, 108–11, 192–94; Susan Norton, "Population Growth in Colonial America: A Study of Ipswich, Mass.," *Population Studies*, XXV (1971), 433–52; John Demos, *A Little Commonwealth: Family Life in Plymouth Colony* (New York: Oxford University Press, 1970); idem, *Past, Present and Personal* (New York, 1986), 147–52; and Jackson T. Main, *Society and Economy in Colonial Connecticut* (Princeton, NJ: Princeton University Press, 1986), 10–12.

12. John J. McCusker and Russell R. Menard, *The Economy of Colonial British America, 1607–1789* (Chapel Hill: University of North Carolina

Press, 1985), 229; Stephanie Grauman Wolf, *Urban Village: Population, Community, and Family Structure in Germantown, Pennsylvania, 1683–1800* (Princeton, NJ: Princeton University Press, 1976), 282–85; and Billy G. Smith, "Death and Life in a Colonial Immigrant City: A Demographic Analysis of Philadelphia," *JEH*, 37 (1977), 863–89.

13. Trevor Burnard, " 'The Countrie Continues Sicklie': White Mortality in Jamaica, 1655–1780," *Social History of Medicine*, 12 (1999), 59–63.

14. T.H. Hollingsworth, "The Demography of the British Peerage," *Population Studies*, Supplement 18 (1964), 56; Lawrence Stone and Jeanne Fawtier Stone, *An Open Elite?: England, 1540–1880* (Oxford: Oxford University Press, 1984), 259–60; and E.A. Wrigley and R.S. Schofield, *The Population History of England, 1541–1871* (Cambridge, MA: Cambridge University Press, 1981), Table 7.21, 250.

15. Anita H. Rutman, "Still Planting the Seeds of Hope: The Recent Literature of the Early Chesapeake Region," *VMHB*, 95 (1987), 7.

16. Rutmans, " 'Now-Wives and Sons-in-Law'," 178; Menard and Walsh, "Death in the Chesapeake, 213; and Smith, "Mortality and Family in the Colonial Chesapeake," Table 3, 415.

17. Allan Kulikoff argues that life expectancy increased for men born between 1690 and 1729 with no further improvement in the colonial period. Yet, as Anita Rutman has pointed out, Kulikoff rests his argument entirely on selected genealogies that are heavily weighted in favor of those who survive. Kulikoff does not present his data supporting his claim in his book but only in his 1976 thesis. Kulikoff, *Tobacco and Slaves*, 61. Daniel S. Levy has also asserted that there was a substantial rise in life expectancy among native-born males in the colonial period in his analysis of Maryland legislators. His study is weakened because of the nature of his sample. Legislators did not enter the sample at birth but at date of entry into the legislature. Quite possibly, his study documents changes in the composition of the legislature rather than increasing life expectancy among elite Marylanders. Levy, "Life Expectancies in Colonial Maryland," 17–28. See also Rutman, "Still Planting the Seeds of Hope," 8.

18. David W. Jordan, "Political Stability and the Emergence of a Native Elite in Maryland," in Tate and Ammerman, *Chesapeake in the Seventeenth Century*, 247.

19. Ibid., 247.

20. Benjamin Franklin, "Observations Concerning the Increase of Mankind, Peopling of Countries, etc," in Leonard W. Labaree et al. (eds.), *Franklin Papers* (New Haven, CT: Yale University Press, 1959–), IV, 228.

21. Wrigley and Schofield, *Population History of England*, Table 7.28, 260; and Hollingsworth, "Demography of the British Peerage," 21.

22. Kulikoff notes that the deaths of women between the ages of 20 and 40 dramatically declined during the eighteenth century, leading to higher birthrates. Kulikoff, *Tobacco and Slaves*, 61.

23. The best discussion of the complexity of early Chesapeake family structures is Rutmans, " 'Now-Wives and Sons-in-Law.' "

24. Jim Potter, "Demographic Development and Family Structure," in Jack P. Greene and J.R. Pole (eds.), *Colonial British America* (Baltimore: Johns Hopkins University Press, 1984), 131.

25. Wrigley and Schofield, *Population History of England*, 255.

26. Hollingsworth, "Demography of the British Peerage," 21.

27. See Greven, *Four Generations*, 31–37; Demos, *A Little Commonwealth*; Daniel Scott Smith, "The Demographic History of Colonial New England,"

JEH, 32 (1972), 165–168; Kulikoff, *Tobacco and Slaves*, 55–59; Daniel Blake Smith, *Inside the Great House: Planter Family Life in the Eighteenth Century* (Ithaca, NY: Cornell University Press, 1980), 127–28; Lorena S. Walsh, "'Till Death Us Do Part': Marriage and Family in Seventeenth Century Chesapeake," in Tate and Ammerman, *Chesapeake in the Seventeenth Century*, 128, 150; and Rutmans, "'Now-Wives and Sons-in-Law'," 157–58.

28. Ibid.

29. Wrigley and Schofield, *Population History of England*, 255; and Hollingsworth, "Demography of the British Peerage," 10.

30. Smith, *Inside the Great House*, 79; Edmund S. Morgan, *American Slavery-American Freedom: The Ordeal of Colonial Virginia* (New York: W.W. Norton, 1975), 165–67; and Darrett B. Rutman and Anita H. Rutman, *A Place in Time: Middlesex County, Virginia, 1650–1750* (New York: W.W. Norton, 1984), 72. But, as Kathleen Brown notes, unlike other "archies," the influence of wealthy widows was not supported and perpetuated as normative by seventeenth-century ideologues. Brown, *Good Wives, Nasty Wenches, and Anxious Patriarchs*, 402n. For a comprehensive survey of widowhood in the seventeenth-century Chesapeake that modifies Morgan's idea of "widowarchy," see Terri Lynn Snyder, "'Rich Widows Are the Best Commodity This Country Affords': Gender Relations and the Rehabilitation of Patriarchy" (unpublished Ph.D., University of Iowa, 1992).

31. Walsh, "'Till Death Us Do Part'," 128; Morgan, *American Slavery, American Freedom*, 166; Russell R. Menard, "Economy and Society in Early Colonial Maryland" (unpublished Ph.D., University of Iowa, 1975), 193–95; and Lois Green Carr and Lorena S. Walsh, "The Planter's Wife: The Experience of White Women in Seventeenth Century Maryland," *WMQ*, 3d. ser., XXXIV (1977), 542–71.

32. Susan Socolow has found that the usual pattern for merchants in Buenos Aires during the eighteenth century was that local merchants would seek out promising immigrant merchants as husbands for their daughters. Socolow, *The Merchants of Buenos Aires, 1778–1810: Family and Commerce* (New York: Cambridge University Press, 1978), 36–39.

33. Paul G. Clemens, *The Atlantic Economy and Colonial Maryland's Eastern Shore: From Tobacco to Grain* (Ithaca, NY: Cornell University Press, 1980), 121–135.

34. See, for example, the concern felt by Governor Francis Nicholson on the difficulty of finding enough men of talent, experience, wealth, and education to fill political posts. Letter to Lords of Trade, November 15, 1694, C.O. 5/713, 111, no. 114, Public Record Office, London.

35. This theme is elaborated in Trevor Burnard, "A Tangled Cousinry? Associational Networks of the Maryland Elite, 1691–1776," *JSH*, LXI (1995), 17–44.

36. Kulikoff, *Tobacco and Slaves*, 253–55; and Peter Fontaine to John and Moses Fontaine, April 15, 1754, in James Fontaine, *Memoirs of a Huguenot Family*, translated and compiled by Ann Maury (New York: G.P. Putnam, 1853), 342.

37. I have defined cousin marriage very broadly, including marriages not just to first or second cousins but also to more distant blood kin. Genealogical information about the elite is patchy, and some marriages between blood relations may have been missed, but as marriages between blood relations were among the most likely records to be noted by historians and genealo-

gists, I doubt that the number of interkin marriages missed is large. The rate of cousin marriage found here is similar to that found among ante-bellum North Carolina planters in Censer, *North Carolina Planters and Their Children*, 84.

38. See the literature cited in Kulikoff, *Tobacco and Slaves*, 253, n. 87.
39. Smith, *Inside the Great House*, 21–22. See also Jan Lewis, *The Pursuit of Happiness: Family and Values in Jefferson's Virginia* (Cambridge: Cambridge University Press, 1983), 246; and Philip J. Greven, *The Protestant Temperament: Patterns of Childrearing, Religious Experience, and the Self in Early America* (New York: Alfred A. Knopf, 1977), Chapters VI and VII.
40. Kulikoff, *Tobacco and Slaves*, 7, 165–204; and Rhys Isaac, *The Transformation of Virginia, 1740–1790* (Chapel Hill: University of North Carolina Press, 1982), 39–42, 301–22.
41. Greven, *Four Generations*, 84–86, 89–90, 98–99.
42. Hollingsworth, "Demography of the British Peerage," 46; Philip Jenkins, *The Making of a Ruling Class: The Glamorgan Gentry, 1640–1790* (Cambridge: Cambridge University Press, 1983), 38–42.
43. We know more about the survival of sons than of daughters. Whereas at least 236 elite members are known to have left at least one surviving son, only 210 elite members are known to have left at least one daughter surviving into adulthood. Although colonial Americans recognized both matrilineal and patrilineal kin as part of their larger kin group, sons were more likely to be mentioned in public records. John E. Crowley, "The Importance of Kinship: Testamentary Evidence from South Carolina," *JIH*, XVI (Spring, 1986), 559–77.
44. For demographic differences between immigrants and the native born, see Levy, "Life Expectancies of Maryland Legislators," 17–28; Kulikoff, *Tobacco and Slaves*, 64–65; and Walsh and Menard, "Death in the Chesapeake," 214–19.
45. Menard and Walsh, "Demography of Somerset County," 32; Smith, "Mortality and Family," 413–14; and Kulikoff, *Tobacco and Slaves*, 61–62.
46. Smith, *Inside the Great House*, 28–33.
47. Walsh, " 'Till Death Us Do Part,' " 127–28.
48. Kulikoff, *Tobacco and Slaves*, 59–60.
49. Susan Klepp, "Revolutionary Bodies: Women and the Fertility Transition in the Mid-Atlantic Region, 1760–1820," *JAH*, 85 (1998), 910–45; and Jan Lewis and Kenneth Lockridge, " 'Sally Has Been Sick': Pregnancy and Family Limitation among Virginia Gentry Women, 1780–1830," *JSocH*, 22 (1988), 10. See also J. David Hacker, "Cultural Demography: New England Deaths and the Puritan Perception of Risk," *JIH*, 26 (1996), 367–92.
50. The literature on the landed classes and on the oligopolic political structure of eighteenth-century Britain is extensive. See, in particular, J.H. Plumb, *The Growth of Political Stability: England, 1675–1725* (London: Macmillan, 1967); John Cannon, *Aristocratic Century: The Peerage of Eighteenth Century England* (Cambridge: Cambridge University Press, 1984); J.C.D. Clark, *English Society, 1688–1832* (Cambridge: Cambridge University Press, 1986); Stones, *Open Elite*; Jenkins, *Making of a Ruling Class*; Christopher Clay, "Marriage, Inheritance, and the Rise of Large Estates in England, 1660–1815," *EHR*, 2d. Ser., XXI (1968), 503–18; H.J. Habbakuk, "The Rise and Fall of English Landed Families, 1600–1800," *Transactions of the Royal Historical Society*, 5th. Ser., XXIX (1979),

187–207, XXX (1980), 199–221, XXXI (1981), 195–217; and J.V. Beckett, *The Aristocracy in England, 1660–1914* (Oxford, 1986).

51. See Rutmans, " 'Now-Wives and Sons-in-Law" 153–82.

52. Peter Roebuck, *Yorkshire Baronets, 1640–1760* (Oxford: Oxford University Press, 1980), 93–102, 107–08, 133–37, 151–52, 257–60.

53. Burnard, "Tangled Cousinry," 19, 40–43; and Brown, *Good Wives, Nasty Wenches, and Anxious Patriarchs*, 184–5.

54. See, inter alia, Walsh, " 'Till Death Us Do Part' "; Russell R. Menard, "From Servant to Freeholder: Status Mobility and Property Accumulation in Seventeenth-Century Maryland," *WMQ*, 3d. Ser., XXX (1973), 37–64; Rutmans, " 'Now-Wives and Sons-in-Law' "; and Carr and Walsh, "Planter's Wife."

55. James Horn, *Adapting to a New World: English Society in the Seventeenth-Century Chesapeake* (Chapel Hill: University of North Carolina Press, 1994), 429.

56. Smith, *Inside the Great House*, 21; and Lewis, *Pursuit of Happiness*, 30.

57. See Andrew Tilghman to Richard Tilghman, 24 October 1697; J. Hollyday to Edward Lloyd, 7 June 1730; Leonard Hollyday to James Hollyday I, 25 July 1735; and Henry Hollyday I to his father, 10 December 1740. Hollyday Papers, Mss. 1317. MHS.

58. Ronald Hoffman, *Princes of Ireland, Planters of Maryland: A Carroll Saga, 1500–1782* (Chapel Hill: University of North Carolina Press, 2000). The correspondence can be sampled in Ronald Hoffman, Sally D. Mason, and Eleanor S. Darcy (eds.), *Dear Papa, Dear Charley* ... (forthcoming).

59. Letter from Richard Grafton to Mary Grafton (later Dulany), 3 September, 1737, Dulany Papers, Mss. 1919, MHS.

60. For the strength of emotion as a binding value after this period, see Melinda S. Buza, " 'Pledges of Our Love': Friendship, Love, and Marriage among the Virginia Gentry, 1800–1825," in Edward L. Ayers and John C. Willis (eds.), *The Edge of the South: Life in Nineteenth-Century Virginia* (Charlottesville: University Press of Virginia, 1991), 9–36.

61. Thomas Robins to James Hollyday II, 15 October 1757, Hollyday Papers, Mss., 1317, MHS.

62. Dr. Charles Carroll to Charles Carroll, Barrister, 15 February 1754, "Extracts from Papers of Dr. Charles Carroll," *MdHM*, XXVI (1931), 242–43.

63. Brown, *Good Wives, Nasty Wenches, and Anxious Patriarchs*, 319–66; Jack P. Greene, *The Diary of Colonel Landon Carter of Sabine Hall, 1752–1778*, 2 vols. (Charlottesville: University Press of Virginia, 1965); and Jan Lewis, "Domestic Tranquillity and the Management of Emotion among the Gentry of Pre-Revolutionary Virginia," *WMQ*, 3d. Ser., XXXIX (1982), 135–49.

64. Charles Carroll of Annapolis to Charles Carroll of Carrollton, 9 January, 1764, "Extracts from the Carroll Papers," *MdHM*, XII (1917), 26.

65. Stephen Bordley to John Bordley, 8 June 1745, Bordley Letterbooks, Mss. 64, MHS.

66. Bertram Wyatt-Brown, "The Ideal Typology and Antebellum Social History," *Societas*, V (1975), 5, 28.

CHAPTER 5

Arrows over Time

Elite Inheritance Practices

One of the most important acts in any colonial Marylander's life was the preparation of a last will and testament. The creation of a will had great significance both for the individual and for society. For the testator, a will allowed an individual to pass on accumulated wealth to the next generation. In a preindustrial, underinstitutionalized society, status and wealth were largely determined by what a person inherited. Most will makers faced a fundamental problem when composing their wills. Testators made wills for two reasons: to provide for their family and kin and to maintain the status and wealth of the family estate over time. Ensuring that one aim was achieved came at the expense of the other. This chapter will explore the ways in which wealthy Marylanders attempted to resolve this dilemma, bearing in mind that will-making strategies differed significantly depending on the wealth of the testator and the size, composition, and age structure of family and kin groups. I will show that wealthy Marylanders chose to provide for all their family members without sacrificing family position, managing to do so in part because they defined their families very narrowly to include only members of the immediate family and partly because growth and expansion allowed for division of estates without serious diminution of property. At the same time, they attempted to maintain control over their property and their families until death while encouraging children in particular to demonstrate independence of mind and character. Relatively early death meant that the contradictions between these two desires were not exposed in the colonial era.

The first issue for will makers was who was to have the executorship of his property. An executor was responsible for administering the estate after the testator's death: a position of considerable trust and authority. An executor not only had to be trustworthy but also had to be able to manage extensive properties, run businesses, and care for and control large numbers of dependent family members, servants, and slaves. When a wealthy Marylander decided on an executor, therefore, he was making an important statement about how he viewed the capabilities of significant people in his life. In the absence of other evidence, choices over executorship are some of the best indications that we have about how wealthy men ranked various family, kin, and nonkin. Indeed, the willingness of Maryland men to appoint their wives as executors in the mid-seventeenth century has been taken as signal evidence of the economic and social importance of white women in the early Chesapeake (Table 5.1).[1]

In the eighteenth century, wealthy Marylanders sometimes chose to entrust the administration of the estate to their widow.

Table 5.1 Types of Executor over Time by Percentage

	Pre-1726	1726–42	1743–59	1760+	Total
Number of sample	73	72	72	136	353
Single executor	64	54	69	50	58
Multiple executor	36	46	31	50	42
Wife only	40	32	43	27	38
Wife + others	14	24	24	18	20
Total wife	54	56	67	45	58
Sons only	16	11	18	21	17
Sons + others	12	14	14	15	14
Total sons	28	25	32	36	31
Friends only	10	11	8	13	11
Friends + others	5	7	15	10	10
Total friends	15	18	23	23	21

Source: Wills, MHR.

Just over a third of testators appointed their wife as sole executor. By mid-century, fewer wealthy Marylanders took that option.
The number of wives who were sole executors of elite estates
declined by nearly a third after 1759.[2] Wives were less necessary
as executors as family, kin, and friend networks increased in the
more settled eighteenth-century tidewater. Possibly, also, men
became less willing to allow women control over property. Daniel
Blake Smith suggests that as sex roles became more rigid and
estates larger and more complex, men increasingly turned to sons
and male friends to supervise the estate.[3] Nevertheless, three-
quarters of testators (declining to under 50 percent for testators
dying after 1759) allowed their wife some control, usually in
combination with male executors, over the administration of
their estates, reflecting the continuing importance of female presence in the lives of male relatives.[4]

Wealthy Marylanders also turned to sons and to friends to help
administer their estates. Nearly one-third appointed a son or sons
as executors and one in five chose a friend. Adult sons were the
preferred option. Four out of every five executors with adult sons
invited sons to exercise executorship. Few turned to kin outside
the immediate family. The relative infrequency of nonimmediate
kin being appointed executors suggests that within small rural
communities, where a high percentage of households must have
been interrelated, nonimmediate kin were appointed executors less
because of their blood relationship to the testator than because
they were friends and neighbors. It also suggests a narrow conception of family, a conception tied very closely to the nuclear rather
than to the extended family.[5]

Testators recognized that executorship was an important post
with important responsibilities, the dereliction of which could
easily waste the estate. Consequently, they increasingly appointed
more than one executor. Testators were reluctant, however, to
exclude immediate family members from playing some role in
executorship and almost never passed on executorship to professional administrators. Estate administration was as yet neither sys-
tematized nor professionally conducted, as happened elsewhere in
the colonies.[6] Moreover, wealthy Marylanders were willing to put
considerable trust in their wives' and sons' abilities to run their
business operations. Considering the potential for personal

aggrandizement that estate administration offered unscrupulous executors, this belief shows considerable faith in the family responsibilities of wives and sons (Table 5.2).[7]

Table 5.2 Testators without Wife or Children

Major Beneficiaries (N=22)	
Solely kin	64
Kin and nonkin	14
Solely nonkin	18
Charity	5

Source: Wills, MHR.

Ideally, a wealthy Marylander wanted at least one son alive at his death to pass the majority of his estate. Nevertheless, nearly a quarter of the elite died without any surviving sons, with 15 percent leaving neither sons nor daughters. Wealthy Marylanders who left no immediate family members had complete freedom both legally and morally when devising their estates. They could choose to enrich substantially some branches of their family at the expense of other kin, reward their friends, or endow charitable institutions. The various possibilities open to them allowed them some influence over the social and economic organization of the region—if, that is, they decided to exercise such influence. They indicated the relative importance they placed upon family, kin, and the maintenance of class relations by the manner in which they disposed of their estate. They also were able to indulge their personal preferences, rewarding those people of which they approved of while neglecting others. Richard Bennett, for example, who was probably the richest man in colonial Maryland and who died unmarried and without direct heirs in 1747, left the majority of his estate to his distant kinsman, Edward Lloyd III, at the expense of his other kinsfolk, solidifying the Lloyds' growing dominance in Talbot County. A number of very rich men left no wife or children, including Amos Garrett, the richest man in this study. The beneficiaries of their estates found their economic position considerably enhanced as a result of those legacies (Table 5.3).

Most will makers without immediate family went to considerable trouble when devising their estates. Only five testators had less than three beneficiaries and just two devised their entire estate

Table 5.3 Provision of Land for Wife over Time by Percentage

	Pre-1726	1726–42	1743–59	1760+	Total
Land outright	47	23	21	22	27
Land for life	24	30	41	26	30
Land for widowhood	2	5	4	15	8
Land until heirs are 21	0	9	4	4	4
Use of land	0	0	0	3	1
No land	28	33	31	30	30

Source: Wills, MHR.

to a single inheritor. A number of testators gave property to a large number of people or institutions. William Planner, for example, had 22 legatees, most of whom were given specific bequests such as livestock, land, slaves, forgiveness of debts, and cash. Most inheritors were left small bequests, but there usually were a number of major beneficiaries. Sometimes the estate was divided among several major beneficiaries. There were seven men who devised large portions of their estates to five or more inheritors, thereby lessening the effects of the distribution of the estate. Only two people in this sample owed their inclusion to large inheritances from men who were not their fathers. Stanley Robins, grandson of an elite member, amassed a personal fortune of £1,030 by the age of 25 as the major beneficiary of the estate of his uncle, William Robins. Amos Woodward was even more fortunate. As the nephew of Amos Garrett, he inherited £500 sterling (undeflated), along with six tracts of land and two lots in Annapolis. This legacy formed the basis of a substantial mercantile fortune of £3,606, much of which Woodward was able to pass on to his son, Henry.

Even if a wealthy Marylander had no children himself, he usually recognized some obligations to extended kin. Nephews and nieces were the most likely beneficiaries, with brothers, sisters, and mothers close behind. Joseph Hill, for instance, divided his estate 13 ways, with his brother and three nephews receiving most. But wealthy Marylanders seldom recognized ties of kinship outside the children of their siblings. Few testators—15 percent—gave substantial amounts of property to more distant kin. When they had no family or immediate kin, testators tended to bequeath property to friends, usually fellow wealthy gentlemen. John Chappell, for example, left a horse to Colonel William Holland, a legislator, and the residue of his estate to two daughters of elite member Gerrard Hopkins. George Robotham gave property not only to two sisters but also to Edward Lloyd II, John Pemberton, and Thomas Smithson, all members of the Talbot elite. Only one wealthy Marylander with complete freedom of testation gave large amounts to charity. Benedict Leonard Calvert bequeathed one-third of his personal estate to the Free School in Annapolis and another one-third to St Anne's Vestry. As the son and brother of the proprietor and governor of the province, he had a vested interest in supporting provincial institutions. As a son of a peer, he was possibly motivated by feelings of *noblesse oblige* in ways not shared by Marylanders of lower social status.[8] Choices made by other will makers with free testation indicate that wealthy Marylanders believed that their principal obligations were to their collateral kin and secondarily to wealthy friends. They placed little emphasis on charitable giving or on efforts to alter or reinforce the social structure. Inheritance followed an orderly pattern of succession: first, children and their children; then siblings and their children; then other kin; and, finally and least importantly, nonfamily.

One person who had to be provided for in most wills and who was not in this path of succession was the widow: over two-thirds of testators noted a wife still living in their wills. Husbands indicated through their provision for their widows how much economic control over property they were willing to relinquish to their wives and sometimes described the degree of affection or otherwise they had for their spouse. But wealthy Marylanders had to balance the needs of their widow with other members of their families: fewer than 10 percent of testators had no immediate family except for their wives. Consequently, widows' portions must be evaluated in terms of the family situation of the testator: how many children, especially sons, there were; whether there were underage children; and whether the testator or his wife had kin nearby who could supplement the husband's support for his widow.

Widows did not play as pivotal a role in the eighteenth-century elite family as they had done in Maryland society in the mid-seventeenth century.[9] Few wealthy Marylanders were willing to place all of their property in the hands of their wives to use and devise as they saw fit, even when they had no surviving children. Just one testator bequeathed all his land and property to his wife outright. Tamerlaine Davis left "to my dear wife Hannah all my estate for her and her heirs for ever,"[10] naming her in addition sole executor. Five testators left their widow a life estate in all of their property. Vachel Denton, for instance, made his wife sole executor of his estate and gave her all his real and personal fortune but only for her lifetime, after which it was to descend to his niece and god-daughter Ann Hammond, wife of Philip Hammond, Speaker of the House. In such a way, Denton affirmed his belief that his wife could manage his property without wasting it while retaining his control over the disposal of his estate (Table 5.4).

Nevertheless, the majority of testators with wives but no children were prepared to give their widow some voice in the division of marital property. Over half gave outright gifts of land to their widow with two-thirds bequeathing personal property to their wife without any conditions attached to the gift. Yet the more significant statistic is the percentage of testators who placed restrictions on their widows' enjoyment of their estate. Overall, 38 percent bequeathed land to their wives but did not allow them any power of disposal, while one-quarter placed restrictions on gifts of personal estate. We should expect that when there were no direct heirs widows would be likely to get at least one-third and usually more of the husband's property—that, after all, was what widows were entitled to by law.[11] The frequency of restrictions on wife's gifts by childless testators suggests that wealthy Marylanders were unwilling to give their spouses absolute control over their property

Table 5.4 Comparison of Provisions for Daughters by Percentage

	Heiresses	Unmarried Daughters	Married Daughters
Nothing	13	2	32
Minor bequests	10	44	58
Major bequests	55	54	10
All estate	23	0	0
Receiving land	81	35	20
Receiving slaves	50	44	36
Receiving money	16	28	16

Source: Wills, MHR.

and the significant power within the family that such control allowed. Granting a life estate to the greater part of their property, which allowed widows use of the property while they lived or until they remarried, but which did not allow them to alienate property from the family estate, was an effective strategy to circumvent the strictures of Maryland inheritance law. The widow had the use of more than the law required and was hence unlikely to insist on her rights under law, while the testator was able to ensure the successful transfer of property to his own kin.[12]

Presumably this policy was intended to prevent a wife's remarrying and giving her second husband the freedom to dispose of the first husband's property. Only four widows of wealthy will makers without children are known to have remarried. Three of these inherited substantial property. Significantly, all three widows with large estates were the widows of testators who died in the first years of the eighteenth century. In the frontier conditions of the seventeenth century where mortality rates were extraordinarily high, marriage to a widow was a common route to wealth. The marriage of Henrietta Maria Bennett, the widow of the prominent merchant and legislator Richard Bennett, to Philemon Lloyd, for instance, was the single most important event, along with the inheritance by the Lloyds of the estate of Bennett's stepson in 1749, in the rise of the Lloyds to prominence in Talbot County. Likewise, in Somerset County, the marriage of the widow of the wealthy merchant-planter Francis Jenkins to Reverend John Henry was the basis of the Henrys' fortune. This path to wealth seems to have been cut off as the eighteenth century progressed. The widow of Stephen Onion, from Baltimore County, was the only widow of the 27 childless testators dying after 1710 to remarry, and she took very little of Onion's estate with her for the use of her second husband. Although she had control over one-half of her husband's personal estate, she retained management and power over the other half of his personal property and over all real estate only until Onion's nephew was of age. In this way, Onion was able to pass on his estate largely intact to his designated heir. A side effect of this strategy was to reduce the attractiveness of his widow—the wife of a very wealthy man who left over 10,000 acres and a total estate value (TEV) of £4,228—to potential fortune-seekers.

Wealthy Marylanders had no single standard formula for providing for wives. Many gave to their widows more than the law required, but a large number also gave less. Altogether, wealthy Marylanders used 26 different methods of property disposal to provide for their wives, ranging from nothing at all to the unrestricted bequest of the entirety of the estate. The most common form of bequest was an outright gift of land and a portion of the testator's personal property, but only one in five testators followed this pattern. Other will makers left their widows personal property outright with a life estate in land. A third strategy was to give a wife no land at all but only personal property. The remaining will makers left property to their wives in a variety of forms. Thomas Chamberlaine, for example, left his widow over one-half of his personal estate and "the profits and use of my plantation for five years after my death."[13] Dr. Samuel Chew, on the other hand, gave his wife a life estate in both his real and personal property with the reversion to his four children on her death. A number of testators made their bequests conditional on their wife not remarrying. Henry Waggaman bequeathed considerable personal and real property to his wife but retained the right of disposal over his household furniture, chaise, and dwelling plantation with its livestock and agricultural implements. Some testators allowed their wife control over their property only while their children were minors. Feddeman Rolle gave no outright gifts to his wife but just a right to the use of his dwelling house. Another option, employed by 17 men, was not to provide for their wife through their will at all. Possibly, these widows were provided for by arrangements made in their husbands' lifetimes, but their omission from wills does suggest a willingness by testators to violate legal rules regarding widow's rights and possibly an acceptance by wives of various ways of being provided for outside inheritance. The diversity of practice, as well as in law, in regard to what property women received and in what form makes it unwise to make sweeping generalizations about changing trends in female property holding.[14]

The reluctance of wealthy men to allow wives control over the disposal of land offers convincing testimony to their declining power within the family. Wealthy men could usually allocate land to their widow without substantially reducing their heirs' inheritances. Yet comparatively few men—15 of 83 men with at least one adult son—were prepared to do this. If testators did give land to their widows, they increasingly made it a conditional gift, retaining control over who eventually would receive fee simple in their real property. A common strategy was to leave wives a life estate in land (usually the dwelling plantation) with the reversion to children or other heirs. Gifts of land to wives became more restrictive over time, possibly because the value of land increased dramatically. A testator dying after 1759 was twice as likely to give his wife land only while she remained a widow or to the time of their children's minorities compared to earlier testators. By the mid-eighteenth century, a widow had a good chance of having adult children or kin in the region who could care for her after her husband's death. Consequently, the priorities of a wealthy testator shifted from preventing his wife from suffering deprivation to planning the successful transfer of property largely intact to the next generation. To succeed in this latter objective, a testator sought to minimize the possibility of a widow alienating property from his heirs (Tables 5.5, 5.6, and 5.7).

The position of daughters in wills was somewhat analogous to that of their mothers. Testators were concerned to protect both their daughters' and their widows' future while not allowing their

Table 5.5 Provision for Unmarried Daughters When Surviving Sons by Percentage

	Pre-1726 (N=25)	1726–42 (N=23)	1743–59 (N=41)	1760+ (N=62)	Total (N=151)
Land	56	57	22	27	35
Slaves	20	30	37	65	44
Money	24	22	29	31	28
Land + slaves	0	17	7	13	10
Nothing	8	0	0	2	2

Source: Wills, MHR.

Table 5.6 Provision for Married Daughters (N = 106)

	%
Nothing or token bequest	32
Land	20
Land + personal estate	15
Personal estate only	33

Source: Wills, MHR.

Table 5.7 Provision for Adult Sons over Time

Nature of Bequest	Pre-1726 (N=23)	1726–42 (N=22)	1743–59 (N=36)	1760+ (N=55)	Total (N=136)
Token	13	18	11	11	13
Reduced	22	9	22	31	22
Token or reduced	35	27	33	42	35
Substantial	65	73	67	58	64

Source: Wills, MHR.

sons' inheritances to be reduced precariously. Yet a daughter's relationship to her father was different from a wife's relationship to her husband. Testators felt a strong obligation to ensure their daughters' welfare—at least until they were married—and in particular wished to make their daughters attractive prospects for potential husbands. A suitable marriage would not only move responsibility for support of the daughter elsewhere but could cement friendships and alliances between different families. Daughters' portions, therefore, could be very important in improving the position of a family in Chesapeake society. A superfluity of daughters, however, could be a burden on an estate, especially if some daughters remained unmarried and in need of support from other siblings. Provisions for daughters in wills varied from estate to estate mainly according to the status that the daughter held within the family. Daughters fall into three categories: heiresses (daughters without male siblings), unmarried daughters living at home, usually under 18 years of age, and married daughters dwelling in their husbands' households.

As scholars of the British aristocracy and gentry in the seventeenth and eighteenth centuries have shown, the failure of a family to produce male heirs could have important consequences.[15] They have characterized the early eighteenth century as a period of demographic crisis for the landed elite in Britain, with over half of owners of large landed estates dying without surviving sons.[16] Some historians have speculated that the crisis helped to concentrate land and wealth in the hands of larger magnates: at the very least, it led to a dramatic increase in the number of women who had control over substantial amounts of property and gave great opportunity to surviving sons of good families to make highly advantageous marriages. There was no similar "age of heiresses" in colonial Maryland: fewer than one in ten testators left only daughters. To make matters worse for fortune seekers, four testators were forced to divide their estate among four or more heiresses, and Matthew Hawkins and Edward Oldham had six heiresses each. Only 19 testators left a sole heiress.

Nevertheless, an heiress, if one was lucky enough to find one, was quite a catch. In the majority of cases, a wealthy man without sons preferred to leave his estate to his wife and daughter rather than to collateral or affinal kin. Only a quarter of men with daughters but no sons left substantial portions of their estates to others besides their wives and daughters, with six of these testators bypassing their married daughters to bestow property on their grandchildren. Robert Smith was the only man who gave much of his estate to collateral kin at the expense of his heiress.

Unsurprisingly, heiresses were able to marry wealthy Marylanders or the sons of wealthy Marylanders. The daughters of Robert Grundy were typical. The eldest, Anne, married James Lloyd I, with the younger, Deborah, marrying another wealthy man, John Pemberton I. Both sons-in-law received considerable benefits from their marriages, not only from the portions that their wives brought with them into the marriages but from sizable bequests left to them from their fathers-in-law. The matches suited all parties. As the children of prominent merchant-planters in Talbot County, Lloyd and Pemberton had certain advantages when pressing their claims to the Grundy sisters. In turn, they profited from the large infusion of property that the two heiresses brought into their marriages.

Most daughters of wealthy men, however, were not heiresses. How did a father provide for them? First, and most importantly, a father needed to give his daughters suitable dowries for their marriages or for their support if they remained unmarried. Second, he had to decide whether to treat all of his children equally or favor one or all sons over daughters. Third, he wanted to protect his daughter from the possible misuse of her property by her husband. The crucial event in bringing about a consideration and a resolution of these issues was marriage. On her marriage, a woman left one economic unit to join another household into which she was expected to contribute property. At this point, she relinquished managerial control over her estate in favor of her husband. Testators recognized this and dealt differently with daughters depending on whether they were married or not.

Unmarried daughters were provided for by will rather than by marriage settlement or inter vivos gifts at date of marriage. These took a variety of forms: gifts of land, slaves, money, items of personal estate, or a combination of types of property. Unmarried daughters received land surprisingly often: over one-third of men with unmarried daughters and sons gave land to each, even if generally daughters received less land than did their brothers. Edward Talbot, for example, divided his land between his two sons and single daughter with the sons receiving over 1,000 acres each and the daughter 500 acres. Occasionally, however, testators favored daughters equally with sons in regard to land. John Cromwell divided the entirety of his estate equally between all of his children. George Robins was the sole will maker to leave land to his daughters without providing in like manner for his son. Because Robins was one of the wealthiest men in this sample with a TEV of £10,605 and 7,972 acres, it seems unlikely that his son was left landless. He was probably provided for in a separate deed. Over time, unmarried daughters became less likely to receive land, reflecting probably less a change in ideology than increasing pressure on land and also larger elite families. Whereas over half of testators who died before 1742 left land to unmarried daughters, only one-quarter of those who died after that date did so.

Instead of land, daughters were often given slaves. Over time, bequeathing slaves to unmarried daughters became a common elite strategy, with at least two-thirds of testators who died after 1759 following this practice.[17] Because of their productive worth, reproductive potential, and high cost of purchase, slaves were ideal bequests for unmarried daughters. For most well-born Marylanders, the key to economic success was less likely to be the acquisition of additional increments of land than the input of more bonded labor to improve and work the land they already had. Consequently, many men who already had sufficient land sought wives who could bring the necessary labor to work that land with them into their marriages. Testators seem to have made a conscious choice to favor daughters over sons when allocating slaves, probably to compensate for their tendency not to leave land to daughters, especially after mid-century. Just 37 percent of testators dying after 1759 with sons left slaves to their male descendants.

Receiving slaves as part of female inheritances had both advantages and disadvantages. The monetary value of slaves usually was less than the value of a gift of land, and slaves could always die before their value had been realized. As the eighteenth century progressed, however, slave mortality rates declined and slave owners were able to profit not only from their increased longevity but also from slaves' reproductive potential.[18] For women in particular, slaves could be a very valuable dowry. When added to their husband's property, slaves may have substantially increased a plantation's slave population, not only multiplying personal wealth but also allowing more real estate to be worked.[19] In addition, slaves were a more liquid form of capital than land and hence more desirable in the Chesapeake plantation economy where capital was in short supply. Monetary bequests, which were quite common gifts to daughters, although far less so than in the Caribbean, may also have been given for this reason.[20]

Legally, marriage was an event that removed responsibility for and control over a woman from a father to a husband. Historians have assumed that at the date of marriage a father gave his daughter her inheritance in the form of a dowry and relinquished any real economic control over her future. Later gifts in the father's will to the married daughter, therefore, would be minimal both because the daughter had already been provided for and also because of her position as *feme covert* with her property automatically under the control of her husband. If a father wished to bequeath property to a married daughter, he did so with the knowledge that his son-in-law had extensive rights in that property. Nearly one-third of testators with married daughters either excluded their daughters from the will or, as Caleb Dorsey I stated, gave them "5/- and nothing else."[21] The rest left married daughters sizable portions. Most commonly, these bequests took the form of slaves, cash portions, or a share of the residue. Occasionally, however, testators left land to their married daughters. Large landowners such as Richard Snowden, Charles Ridgely, and John Ridgely had sufficient land not only to provide for a daughter's dowry but also to divide among all of their children at their death. Others, such as Jeffrey Long, who had only 771 acres, chose to bequeath land and personal property to their daughters not at the date of marriage but only after their own death. Clearly, many testators were unwilling to abandon some sort of economic power over their daughters even after their daughters had left their households to join the households of others. Reserving a child's inheritance until well after marriage was a means of ensuring a measure of power over their children even after they had become adults. Alternatively, fathers may have had considerable confidence in the ability of their daughters and sons-in-law to secure a competency by themselves alone.

Testators felt a duty toward daughters but an obligation toward sons. Through sons, wealth descended to future generations. The provisions wealthy testators made for sons were therefore crucially important. What we need to know is whether all sons received land and when they received that land and other property. Determining these issues allows us to answer two major questions: were sons able to replicate their fathers' position in society, and were they able to achieve a degree of independence from their fathers after they attained adulthood? The inheritance practices of the wealthy in Maryland diverged from those followed by the wealthy and well born in Britain. In Britain, the landed classes maintained their social and economic authority over several centuries by adopting a system of primogeniture and entail. The device of the strict settlement that provided continuity over generations for the British landed gentry had legal sanction in Maryland but was generally abandoned in favor of other testamentary practices.[22] Wealthy Marylanders usually favored some form of partible inheritance with few restrictions placed on the transfer of gifts over succeeding generations (Table 5.8).[23]

Table 5.8 References to Kin and Friends over Time

	Pre-1726 (N=73)	1726–42 (N=72)	1743–59 (N=72)	1760+ (N=136)	Total (N=353)
No references	40	43	69	63	56
References	60	57	31	37	45
Friends	34	19	18	14	20
Near kin	30	21	11	15	18
Niece/nephew	10	7	14	10	11
Distant kin	23	17	10	5	12
Affinal kin	12	10	7	5	8

Source: Wills, MHR.

Most wealthy Marylanders had sufficient land to provide for all of their sons. Very few sons—56 underage sons of 39 decedents—were left without land, and at least two of these decedents probably gave land to their sons in a separate deed. Two other sons were not allotted land because their fathers deemed them incapable of managing their own affairs. The eldest son of Richard Cromwell was non compos mentis, while the son of Henry Hill I was so heavily in debt that Hill instructed his executors to sell his land in order to pay off his debts. Just one testator, aware that he did not have sufficient land to divide equally among his sons, ordered his land to be sold and the profits divided. Barnet Holtzinger instructed his executor to sell all of his lands and then give each of his three sons and two daughters £200 (undeflated) and one-fifth of the residue. A more common strategy was to leave no land to a son but to make bequests of land to an elder son conditional on the elder son giving the second son a portion of his inheritance. But only 22 testators were placed in the difficult position of favoring some sons with land at the expense of other sons. In general, Chesapeake planters tried to keep intact one property as the major family farm, but permitted younger sons to take up new farms created around what Carole Shammas has called the family firm.[24]

James Lloyd II faced the situation head on. He stated that "since I have five sons and three daughters and cannot provide land for more than four of my sons . . . if any son dies [his land] goes to my youngest son Frisby."[25] Few testators were so forthright about their predicament, but several testators were in the same situation as Lloyd after 1760. Generally this problem affected only men with large families and limited land. Nevertheless, Lloyd's difficult decision was a portent of what was to come after the Revolution when the combination of partible inheritance and declining prices for agricultural produce severely reduced the value of a gentleman's patrimony.[26]

One question we need to concern ourselves with is when sons were able to take possession of their inheritances. Historians have suggested that New England and the Chesapeake differed in the amount of economic independence fathers allowed their sons while they were still alive. In New England, where most sons reached adulthood while their fathers were still alive, many fathers exercised considerable authority over their sons, not allowing them to become fully independent economically until well after marriage and often not until after the father's death.[27]

In the Chesapeake, it has been argued, a quite different pattern emerged. The extreme demographic disruptions of the seventeenth-century Chesapeake made it highly likely that children would be orphaned at a young age and that they would enter into their inheritances well before the age of majority.[28] Economic independence from parental control was achieved at a comparatively young age, a fact parents realized and encouraged. Thus, Chesapeake parents fostered independence in their children and were willing to let them marry at a young age and enter into their inheritances as soon as they reached adulthood.[29]

How willing were wealthy Marylanders to transfer control over their property to their sons as soon as their sons passed the age of majority? Many had no choice in deciding when their children would enter into their inheritances, because they died before their children were of age. But 136 testators died leaving adult sons. In their bequests to these sons, we can see how much economic and social independence wealthy Maryland planters and merchants were prepared to give to their adult sons. We have no way of determining the precise extent of a father's generosity to a son while both were alive because deeds of gift were seldom recorded through the courts. We do have some indication, however, of how much a father provided for a son after that son reached adulthood. A testator would often give his son "the land he already lives on" or mention that the son was receiving less than his due because he had already received property. When an adult son received only a token bequest or a gift substantially less than what underage sons received, he had probably already been given property while his father was alive. When there was little difference in the portions that underage and of-age sons received, however, the father probably held back from giving his son the majority of his inheritance as soon as he either attained the age of 21 or married.

Nearly 64 percent of testators left adult sons substantial inheritances. A number of wealthy men, of course, were prepared to allow their sons an independent existence, and in a few cases adult sons had attained considerable wealth by the time of their father's death. Thomas Chamberlaine and John Ridgely, for instance, had acquired estates large enough to qualify for inclusion in this study while their fathers were still alive. Yet they seem to have been exceptional. Most testators retained a substantial say in their sons' future by not willing them property until after their own death. Chesapeake planters, if they lived long enough to see their sons reach adulthood, wished to retain paternal power and authority just as eagerly as their counterparts in New England. This unwillingness to relinquish control over property demonstrates that a professed desire by parents for children to be independent as soon as possible and an unwillingness to lose any of one's own independence created tensions. Literature on the relationships between adult sons and their fathers suggests that there was often considerable intergenerational conflict between fathers and sons. The Virginia planter Landon Carter's stormy relationship with his son may not have been unusual.[30] Their disputes illustrate the difficulties both fathers and sons had in asserting but also maintaining independence. Relationships between fathers and sons were complicated even more by fathers' commitment to being both stern patriarchs and also affectionate fathers. As Kathleen Brown argues about Carter and William Byrd, each failed to achieve the paternal relationship they most desired, being "unable to compel unquestioned obedience from children, yet only partially embedded in the discourse of affectionate family relations."[31]

Was there in addition intragenerational conflict between brothers because fathers treated some more favorably than others? In only 22 cases was a testator forced to choose which sons would receive land and which would not. But wealthy Marylanders did not uniformly treat sons equally. At least a third of testators leaving two or more sons gave their eldest son a larger portion than they gave to other sons. A common pattern was to leave the dwelling plantation to the eldest son with smaller and less valuable tracts of land to younger sons. Often, however, there were restrictions placed on the gift of land to the eldest son that did not apply to other children's' inheritances. The eldest son of Thomas Gassaway, for example, received the dwelling plantation of over 800 acres while his two brothers received 500 and 250 acres, respectively, but was unable to enter into that property in his own right until after the death of his mother. By contrast, his two brothers held their land in fee simple as soon as they reached the age of 21. Wealthy testators often may have favored their eldest son over other children, but this favoritism was seldom pronounced. Certainly the plight of younger sons in Maryland was in no ways similar to the situation of younger sons of gentry in Britain who were sometimes left destitute at the expense of the elder son.[32]

The principal concern of testators when making out a will was for their immediate family. Wealthy Marylanders, however, were not just heads of households. They had duties and responsibilities toward kin, friends, neighbors, servants, and slaves. They were important members of their local communities as vestrymen and J.P.s and as officers in the local militia. When making their wills, they had an opportunity, if they wished, to acknowledge their wider responsibilities. Wills were in effect self-conducted surveys of the relative importance of different relations to the testator.[33] We should be careful, however, not to judge the importance of kinship relations from wills alone. As David Cressy notes, wills were seldom meant to be a complete "rollcall" of relations and an absence of legacies to cousins or nephews does not mean that they were necessarily insignificant in other aspects of a person's life. Nevertheless, wills do provide evidence about the importance of kin that is unavailable in other documents. A willingness to leave property to kin is *prima facie* evidence of their significance to the testator.[34]

More often than not, wealthy Marylanders did not leave bequests to anyone outside of their immediate family circle. Over half of testators did not mention either extended kin or friends in their wills. The exclusion of all except immediate family members increased over time, with two-thirds of men dying after 1742 confining their bequests to their immediate family. This change could be seen as evidence of a deemphasizing of nonnuclear family relationships over time, as several historians have argued occurred in the mid-eighteenth-century Chesapeake. Increasingly, according to this view, planters turned inward, devaluating the importance of wider kin and friends to focus on the warm and loving bonds they were cultivating with their wives and children. Such shifts, it has been argued, had important social consequences. Jan Lewis argues that increasing "privatization" and affirmation of the importance of a more intimate, sentimental family life was a factor in the withdrawal of many wealthy Virginians from participation in public affairs.[35]

Yet kinship ties outside the nuclear family were never very

important in the Chesapeake.[36] The relative frequency of references to kin and friends by testators dying before 1726 does not indicate a greater recognition of kin in the late seventeenth and early eighteenth centuries, but conversely reflects the exigencies of family life in a frontier society characterized by remarkably fragile demography. Though difficult to prove, it is possible that the development of more extensive kin networks over time allowed testators to feel less need to acknowledge nonimmediate kin or friends in a will. They knew that they now had numerous people on whom they could depend to protect the interests of their wives and children. The expansion of social universes, composed of friends, neighbors, and kin, that occurred in the eighteenth century, enabling Creoles to be more selective about how they created personal ties in the community, did not lead to a reduction in the importance of kin and friends. The steady growth of population, the development of institutions such as taverns and social clubs that fostered sociability, the increasing social maturity of colonial society, the expansion of the public sphere, and the development of ever more complex social, familial, economic, and political networks, especially after 1750, make it highly unlikely that wealthy Marylanders retreated into domesticity. Instead, wealthy gentlemen sought out people with whom they may not have shared a common genealogy but with whom they shared common values, noticeably an aspiration toward gentility and respectability.[37] The reduction in references to nonimmediate family members shows the maturation of family structures over the century and a movement away from the "irreducible imprecision in family language" of William Byrd's correspondence and diaries to a recognition of the primacy of the nuclear family unit.[38]

But although imprecision in regard to the definition of kin declined, it by no means disappeared, even as the population swelled and most native-born men and women grew up within extensive kin networks. The provisions of wills are evidence of the continuing low importance that colonial Marylanders attached to kin who were not immediate family and their indifference to degrees of kinship. When testators assigned responsibilities for their families' interests, they just as frequently gave them to nonkin as they did to extended kin. Moreover, wealthy Marylanders were little bothered by hierarchies of kinship and blurred ascribed status. Wealthy Marylanders did not distinguish between paternal and maternal relatives or even between affinal and consanguineal kin, permitting nonkin to have at least a similar status and often a more privileged relationship to them than nonimmediate blood relatives. None of this is surprising in a kinship system that was cognatic (recognizing descent from both men and women). Yet it does undercut depictions of a society increasingly divided and determined by kinship ties. Outside the immediate family, relations with kin and friends were comparable, being, as Crowley argues for South Carolina, associations of choice that depended on reciprocal loyalty and friendship rather than blood.[39] Native-born Marylanders could choose between a number of categories of relationship when deciding with whom to associate. Kin were not necessarily at the head of the list.

Neither did their loyalties naturally extend from the immediate family toward the community. If evidence from wills is an accurate indication, wealthy Marylanders felt little responsibility to the larger community. Their charitable giving was almost negligible. Just 28 testators made bequests to charity, of which 10 were sizable gifts. One explanation for this lack of giving is that most felt their primary obligation was toward their wife and children. Another is that they felt they contributed in other ways, notably in the public sphere. But a noticeable decline in charitable giving over time does cast doubt on the elite's self-proclaimed devotion to the public weal. Their devotion to the priority of immediate family interests over community concerns and their insistence that property be kept under family control are obvious when colonial wealthy Marylanders are compared to wealthy urban merchants in Baltimore in the early republic. Much less devoted to keeping existing estates intact and more egalitarian in their treatment of wives and children, these bourgeois merchants were considerably more generous in their bequests to persons and community institutions beyond immediate or extended kin.[40]

The few gifts that wealthy Marylanders did make were of two kinds: bequests of a religious nature and gifts to the poor of the local area. William Cole, for example, left £10 sterling to the Quakers, while Robert King left 20/- to Rev. John Hamilton of Somerset. An alternative to a monetary bequest was land. Robert King's son Nehemiah not only left £6 per annum (undeflated) for the support of the local Presbyterian minister but also specified that £200 (undeflated) should be given for the building of a meeting house in Queen Anne's. Other gifts were designed to alleviate the sufferings of the poor. There were 13 testators who gave bequests for the use of the poor. Usually wealthy men concentrated on helping the "deserving" poor in their own neighborhood. Thomas Chamberlaine summed up attitudes about who deserved help when he bequeathed "£15 to the poor, persons of honest repute, preferring such as live in this neighborhood and have many children."[41] Wealthy Marylanders were particularly ungenerous in respect to education. Only two wealthy men gave part of their property for educational purposes. Admittedly the gifts of these two testators were considerable. Yet the commitment of wealthy Marylanders to local education was minimal, despite repeated injunctions by burgesses in the Maryland Assembly that the government should "promote the practice of piety and worship of allmighty God by Erecting Churches, Schools and nurserys of learning both for reforming of manners and for the Education of youth."[42]

Testators made wills for two principal reasons. First, they wished to provide for each individual member of their family. They wanted to protect their wives in their widowhood and prevent them from becoming impoverished; they tried to provide adequate dowries for their daughters so that they would be attractive to future husbands; and they attempted to ensure that their sons could set up a household and become prosperous members of the community. Second, they wished to perpetuate both the family name and the social and economic position of the representatives of that family. More specifically, they endeavored to ensure that some male representative or representatives of their family would be able to maintain the same position within society that they held. In this way personal glory could be passed on to future generations and a dynasty perpetuated or established. These two aims conflicted. To provide for all members of his family, a testator was forced to divide his property into several smaller parts. If a testator had a number of children, the division of this property—unless he was exceptionally wealthy—reduced his heirs' patrimony significantly.

The British gentry and aristocracy solved this dilemma by adopting a strict system of primogeniture and entail. Virginians adopted a modified system of entail that made it difficult to alienate the core family property, although continual acquisitions of new land mitigated the effects of such inheritance restrictions.[43] This system sacrificed the claims of younger children on the altar of family continuity. Wealthy men in Maryland preferred instead to divide up property, more or less equally, between all surviving sons, with some land occasionally going to daughters. How effectively, then, were Maryland testators able to perpetuate their family position, at least into the next generation?

To answer this question, we need to compare the number of sons of wealthy men who managed to become wealthy themselves to the number whose circumstances were reduced compared to their fathers. I have defined as wealthy all sons who left over £650 at death or who were legislators. Both political authority and wealth were vital indicators of status and showed to what extent wealthy Marylanders were able to maintain their position in society over several generations during the eighteenth century. We should bear in mind, however, that we are more likely to have information concerning sons of wealthy Marylanders who prospered than about sons who did not and more able to know about those who remained in Maryland than about those who moved out of the state.[44] Consequently our analysis is likely to overemphasize the successes at the expense of the failures, the stay at homes against the migrants. Moreover, we have more information about the richer, more established, and more prominent families than about less wealthy families. We can estimate the economic position of all seven sons of third-generation elite member Caleb Dorsey I, for example, six of whom were wealthy enough to be included in this sample, but we know nothing about the status of new elite member Jacob Macceney's four sons (Table 5.9).

We have information about the social or economic position of 407 sons of 230 wealthy Marylanders, or over half of the 789 sons of elite members. Of these, 252 attained wealth or high political office. Calculated another way, 70 percent of wealthy Marylanders who left sons whose economic position is known left at least one son who did well economically or politically. These figures did not vary greatly over time, although the pressure of population on land after mid-century led to a slight decrease in the percentages of sons of elite members in the last cohort doing well. Those sons who did slip in status did not plummet into poverty but entered

Table 5.9 Economic Position of Sons of the Elite

| | Father's Death | | | | | |
	Pre-1708	1709–25	1726–42	1743–59	1760+	Total
Number of sons	38	74	102	75	98	407
Elite	47	73	64	60	60	62
TEV £401–650 (%)	8	8	8	19	14	12
TEV £226–400 (%)	24	8	13	9	12	12
TEV £101–225 (%)	13	8	10	9	8	10
TEV under £100 (%)	8	3	5	3	5	4

Source: Inventories and Accounts, Inventories, MHR.

what we might term shabby gentility. £225 was about the minimum level of personal wealth required for slave ownership. Men with less than that amount of personal wealth lived in somewhat straitened circumstances. Personal wealth of less than £100 meant poverty. Not many sons fell below the line separating the landholder/slave owner class from the rest of Chesapeake society and even fewer could be classified as being poor. Fewer than 15 percent left personal wealth of less than £225 and 4 percent left personal effects under £100.

An important caveat must be added to this description of a wealthy group successfully reproducing itself over following generations. Although many sons of wealthy Marylanders also became rich, only 23 percent used their inheritances to build fortunes larger than their fathers. One would expect that a native-born son of good family who inherited an established plantation and considerable personal effects would be able, with but a little application, to improve substantially upon his father's wealth and social position. Few did. Certainly, the Maryland elite did not follow the practice of the English landed classes and increase the wealth and authority of one stem of the family at the expense of cadet branches. Instead, they fragmented their estates to the extent that it was an achievement, even in a growing economy, for their children to do more than attain the status and wealth of their father and very difficult for heirs to surpass their parents' social and economic position. Dynastic aggrandizement, however, was possible and led to great success. The two wealthiest men in colonial Maryland in the revolutionary era—Charles Carroll of Carrollton and Edward Lloyd IV of Talbot County—owed much of their exceptional wealth to their families' decision to channel the majority of their estate to a principal heir at the expense of other members of the family.

Such conscious empire building was rare and was characteristic of only the very richest families in Maryland. Most wealthy Marylanders leaned toward providing for all of their family rather than toward the consolidation of family wealth in one person. The opportunities for moneymaking that were present in a developing society convinced them that it was possible for all of their sons to achieve a gentleman's competency. They were justified in this belief by the numbers of their sons who became well-off themselves. In an expanding economy, wealthy Marylanders could concentrate on increasing the size of their family networks rather than ensuring that their family name and prestige would survive. In other words, the family policy of wealthy Marylanders was to broaden rather than deepen their lineage.

The unwillingness of wealthy Marylanders to found dynasties focused around a single wealthy family head does not mean that they had no conception of what the future of individual members of their families should be and that they did not distinguish between different types of relations. An analysis of wealthy men's wills makes it clear that there was a clear hierarchy of kinship within rich families. A wealthy man felt an overwhelming obligation toward his immediate family, especially to his sons. He recognized his ties to consanguineal kin, although he placed their demands on him well below those of his wife and children. He made little acknowledgment, however, of any duties toward affinal kin or toward his friends. Blood, and close blood at that, was the tie that bound, and testators endeavored to transmit as much property to close blood relatives as they could. Moreover, they attempted to concentrate the disposition of property in the person of the father rather than the mother. Wealthy Marylanders valued highly the wealth and power they had acquired over their lifetimes and did not easily relinquish their authority. They tried to retain substantial economic control over their adult children and withheld inheritances until after their own deaths. The desire to set up their children in independent lives was mitigated by their fear of becoming dependent on their children for support and their reluctance to give up the slaves and broad acres that were the basis of their status within the community. Continuing high mortality meant that the inherent tensions between encouraging children to be independent and withholding the means by which independence could be attained were not fully faced by wealthy Marylanders in the colonial period.

NOTES

1. Lois Green Carr and Lorena S. Walsh, "The Planter's Wife: The Experience of White Women in Seventeenth Century Maryland," *WMQ*, 3d. Ser., XXXIV (1977), 542–71.
2. A similar decline occurred in colonial New York City. David Narrett, *Inheritance and Family Life in Colonial New York City* (Ithaca, NY: Cornell University Press, 1992), 106–9.
3. Daniel Blake Smith, *Inside the Great House: Planter Family Life in the Eighteenth Century* (Ithaca, NY: Cornell University Press, 1980), 238.
4. Kathleen Brown, *Good Wives, Nasty Wenches, and Anxious Patriarchs: Gender, Race, and Power in Colonial Virginia* (Chapel Hill: University of North Carolina Press, 1996), 335.
5. For the great importance of neighbors in the early Chesapeake, see Lorena S. Walsh, "Community Networks in the Early Chesapeake," in Lois Green Carr, Philip D. Morgan, and Jean B. Russo (eds.), *Colonial Chesapeake Society* (Chapel Hill: University of North Carolina Press, 1989), 200–41.
6. John E. Crowley suggests that in South Carolina it was possible to earn a livelihood from the administration of estates combined with other activities. Crowley, "The Importance of Kinship: Testamentary Evidence from South Carolina," *JIH*, XVI (1986), 568.
7. Charles Carroll of Annapolis, for instance, was accused of amassing much of his fortune through the careful mismanagement of other people's estates. See Mary Florence Reynolds, "Charles Carroll of Annapolis: Colonial Capitalist" (unpublished M.A. thesis, The Johns Hopkins University, 1971). For a different account of Carroll's executorships, see Ronald Hoffman, *Princes of Ireland, Planters of Maryland: A Carroll Saga, 1500–1782* (Chapel Hill: University of North Carolina Press, 2000), 123–30.
8. For Calvert, see Anne Elizabeth Yentsch, *A Chesapeake Family and Their Slaves: A Study in Historical Archaeology* (Cambridge: Cambridge University Press, 1994), 72–94. Most of Calvert's estate, which he thought of the order of £10,000, was held in Britain and was given to his youngest brother. Ibid, 93.
9. James Horn, *Adapting to a New World: English Society in the Seventeenth-Century Chesapeake* (Chapel Hill: University of North Carolina Press, 1994), 431.
10. Wills (1735) 21/433.
11. In England, widows were entitled by common law to a dower estate of one-half of all property if the marriage was childless. See William Blackstone, *Commentaries on English Law*, 4 vols. (London, 1765–1769), ii, 129,139.
12. Merchants and wealthy professionals in New York City also adopted legal stratagems that explicitly circumvented widows' dower rights while providing generously for widows. Narrett, *Inheritance and Family Life in Colonial New York City*, 103–4.
13. Original Wills, Talbot County (1764), Box 6, 14 *MHR*.
14. Mary Lynn Salmon, *Women and the Law of Property in Early America* (Chapel Hill: University of North Carolina Press, 1986), Chapter 1.

15. See Lawrence Stone and Jeanne Fawtier Stone, *An Open Elite?: England 1540–1880* (Oxford: Oxford University Press, 1984), 100–103; Randolph Trumbach, *The Rise of the Egalitarian Family: Aristocratic Kinship and Domestic Relations in Eighteenth Century England* (New York: Academic Press, 1978); Philip Jenkins, *The Making of a Ruling Class: The Glamorgan Gentry, 1640–1790* (Cambridge: Cambridge University Press, 1983), 38–42; and Christopher Clay, "Property Settlements, Financial Provision for the Family and the Sale of Land by the Greater Landowners, 1660–1790," *Journal of British Studies*, 21 (1981), 32–34.

16. Stones, *An Open Elite?*, 101.

17. A number of men did not leave bequests of slaves to their daughters but included slaves in the residue of their estate, in which daughters often received a share.

18. Allan Kulikoff, "A 'Prolifick' People: Black Population Growth in the Chesapeake Colonies," *Southern Studies*, XVI (1977), 391–428.

19. Jean Butenhoff Lee, "Land and Labor: Parental Bequest Practices in Charles County, Maryland, 1732–83," in Ronald Hoffman and Peter J. Albert (eds.), *Women in the Age of the American Revolution* (Charlottesville: University Press of Virginia, 1989), 306–41.

20. Employed as an inheritance strategy by 42 testators (28 percent). For cash bequests to daughters in the Caribbean, see Trevor Burnard, "Family Continuity and Female Independence in Jamaica, 1665–1734," *Continuity and Change*, 7 (1992), 191–93.

21. Wills (1742), 23/239.

22. C. Ray Keim, "Primogeniture and Entail in Colonial Virginia," *WMQ*, 3d. Ser., XXV (1968), 545–86; Bernard Bailyn, "Politics and Social Structure in Virginia," in James Morton Smith (ed.), *Seventeenth Century America* (Chapel Hill: University of North Carolina Press, 1959), 90–115; and Lois Green Carr, "Inheritance in the Colonial Chesapeake," in Hoffman and Albert (eds.), *Women in the Age of the American Revolution*, n.3.

23. Only three elite members entailed their land explicitly in their wills. Holly Brewer suggests that in Virginia, entail was much more significant than C. Ray Keim had thought, with up to 78 percent of land entailed. The work that Brewer has done for Virginia has not been done for Maryland. Brewer, "Entailing Aristocracy in Colonial Virginia: 'Ancient Feudal Restraints' and Revolutionary Reform," *WMQ*, 3d Ser., LIV (1997), 307–46.

24. Lois Carr states that liquidation of estates, followed by distribution of profits to the children, was rare. Carr, "Inheritance in the Colonial Chesapeake," 169. Carole Shammas argues that liquidation of estates benefited wives, younger sons, and daughters but I believe she underestimates the disadvantages of cash portions, especially for dependent women. Cash was much more easily alienated than were fixed assets. Carole Shammas, "Early American Women and Control over Capital," in Hoffman and Albert (eds.), *Women in the Age of the American Revolution*, 146, 149; Burnard, "Family Continuity and Female Independence in Jamaica," 192–93.

25. Wills (1768), 36/346.

26. For the decline of the plantation economy in Maryland after 1790, see Bayly Ellen Marks, "Economics and Society in a Staple Plantation System, St. Mary's County, Maryland, 1790–1840," (unpublished Ph.D., 1979); and Steve Sarson, "Landlessness and Tenancy in Early National Prince George's County, Maryland," *WMQ*, 3d. Ser., LVII (2000), 569–98.

27. See Philip J. Greven, *The Protestant Temperament: Patterns of Childrearing, Religious Experience and the Self in Early America* (New York:

Alfred A. Knopf, 1977), Chapters 4, 6, 8, 9. and also idem, *Four Generations: Population, Land, and Family in Colonial Andover, Massachusetts* (Ithaca, NY: Cornell University Press, 1970).

28. See Lorena S. Walsh, "'Till Death Us Do Part,'" 126–52; and Darrett B. and Anita H. Rutman, "'Now-Wives and Sons-in-Law': Parental Death in a Seventeenth Century Virginia County," in Tate and Ammerman, *The Chesapeake in the Seventeenth Century*, 153–82.

29. See Smith, *Inside the Great House*; and Greven, *Protestant Temperament*, 284–86, 320–22.

30. Jack P. Greene (ed.), *The Diary of Colonel Landon Carter of Sabine Hall, 1752–1778* (Charlottesville: University Press of Virginia, 1965), 2 vols.

31. Brown, *Good Wives, Nasty Wenches, and Anxious Patriarchs*, 346–47.

32. Joan Thirsk, "Younger Sons in the Seventeenth Century," *History*, LIV (1969), 358–77.

33. Crowley, "The Importance of Kinship," 565.

34. Kinship involved a range of possibilities rather than a set of concrete obligations. David Cressy, "Kinship in Early Modern Europe," *Past and Present*, 113 (1986), 59.

35. Smith, *Inside the Great House*; Jan Lewis, *The Pursuit of Happiness: Family and Values in Jefferson's Virginia* (New York: Cambridge University Press, 1983).

36. Michael Zuckerman, "William Byrd's Family," *Perspectives in American History*, XII (1979), 253–311.

37. Trevor Burnard, "A Tangled Cousinry? Associational Networks of the Maryland Elite, 1691–1776," *JSH*, LXI (1995), 19.

38. Zuckerman, "William Byrd's Family."

39. John E. Crowley, "The Importance of Kinship: Testamentary Evidence from South Carolina," *JIH*, XVI (1986), 577. See also Trumbach, *The Rise of the Egalitarian Family* (New York, 1978), 13–17; and Eric Wolf, "Kinship, Friendship and Patron-Client Relations in Complex Societies," in Michael Banton (ed.), *The Social Anthropology of Complex Societies* (London: Tavistock, 1966), 1–22.

40. Charles G. Steffen, "Gentry and Bourgeois: Patterns of Merchant Investment in Baltimore County, Maryland, 1658 to 1776," *JSocH*, XX (1987), 540–42.

41. Original Wills, Talbot County (1764), Box 6, 14.

42. *AM*, XXII, 20 October 1698, 201.

43. Brewer notes that one effect of entail was to give eldest sons considerable power over fathers, as they could not be easily disinherited, possibly accounting for the greater extent of father-son conflict among the greater gentry in Virginia than Maryland. Brewer, "Entailing Aristocracy," 344.

44. There is, of course, always the exception that proves the rule. The most prominent of all the sons of the Maryland elite in the colonial period was undoubtedly Robert Morris, the financier, who made his career in Philadelphia. A number of the sons of the Maryland elite, including Chews, Dickinsons, and Galloways, moved to Philadelphia and became important members of the elite in that city.

CHAPTER 6

The Rule of Gentlemen
Elite Political Involvement

Certain facts about the political process and wealthy Marylanders' role in politics in late seventeenth- and eighteenth-century Maryland are clear. First, after considerable political and social unrest in the years immediately following European colonization, Maryland became a remarkably settled polity after 1660 and remained so until the turmoils of the Revolutionary era.[1] On the surface, serious disputes between the proprietary government and local politicians and rampant factionalism within the legislature made Maryland dangerously volatile throughout the colonial period. But these apparent frictions obscure the fundamental settledness of colonial Maryland's social and political institutions. Unlike their neighbors in Virginia, Maryland's political leaders never faced a serious challenge from below motivated by social concerns.[2]

The only major political upheaval, the "revolution of government" that overturned proprietary rule in 1689, was not a social revolution led by disappointed sectors of the community against established leaders. Rather, it entailed a change in political leadership and barely affected the underlying social structures and political authority in the colony. Local government and customary social relationships were largely undisturbed.[3] In the eighteenth century, Maryland's political life was remarkably tranquil. No event upset the existing social fabric in the colony. Certainly, conflicts over political measures occurred, but such conflicts never generated widespread violence or upheaval.

The few conflicts that there were did not result in challenges to the legitimacy of established authority. Although such authority was always fragile and was conditional on the continuing consent of a not especially deferential populace, the political dominance of the province's leaders was accepted so long as the delicate balance of existing social relations was maintained. Politicians did this by adopting a posture of "minimal retribution, moderation, and accommodation."[4] It was only when divisions opened up within the ranks of the political elite, as occurred during the American Revolution, notably on the Eastern Shore, that the reciprocal understandings between wealthy men and lesser planters became frayed. When the most enthusiastic revolutionaries disrupted established relationships and too zealously intruded in the affairs of planters already feeling social and economic strain, some degree of political dissent and class antagonism developed.[5]

Wealth rather than political prominence is the determining quality for inclusion in my elite sample. We should note, therefore, that Maryland's economic elite was not the same group of men as Maryland's political elite. Although there was a clear link between wealth and political office, the fit was not perfect. A few political leaders, especially before 1720, were not wealthy; a larger number of wealthy men, especially after mid-century, were not involved in public affairs. I want to examine the extent to which Maryland's economic and political elites overlapped and to assess to what degree the economic and political elites were synonymous. To do this, I have examined Maryland's political elite in two ways. First, I have isolated all members of the Governor's Council and all members of the Assembly from the four counties studied here who died between 1691 and 1776. Second, I have examined all members of the legislature in a single session at 20-year intervals— 1690, 1710, 1730, and 1750.[6] These two samples of legislators have been compared to the main sample of wealthy Marylanders in order to determine the following questions: What were the links between wealth and political office? Were other factors such as kinship more politically significant than wealth? In what ways was the political elite different from the economic elite? What differences were there between wealthy men in politics and wealthy men not in the public sphere?

I also explore in this chapter how the political elite of Maryland managed to retain its authority over a very long period of time. Generally, historians have explained the remarkable acquiescence of a large electorate devoted to maintaining individual independence to a mixture of "deference and patronage politics."[7] Does deference—defined by J.G.A. Pocock as the nonelite recognizing, without too much resentment, that elites were superior to themselves and considering elite leadership as normal and natural—explain the limited challenges to elite that emanated from below?[8] Did patron/client relations work to elide potential class and social differences between the politically engaged and the politically quiescent? My contention is that deference and patronage politics were necessary but not sufficient reasons for a close equation in the prerevolutionary eighteenth century between the upper class of wealth and the political elite.[9] Wealthy Marylanders maintained their power primarily because they remained accessible to community influence and because they reflected rather than contradicted community opinion.

Wealthy merchants and planters were at the apex of Chesapeake society and dominated politics in the province. The connection between wealth and political office was less evident in the seventeenth century, not so much because colonists did not consider the link between economic and political power unimportant—after 1660 "the social order began to reflect both the assumptions and material reality that underpinned social hierarchy in England"—but because continuing demographic disaster led to rapid turnover, especially before the 1670s, and the newness of society in the region meant that few fortunes of any considerable size had been created. Consequently, the elite was more open than it was to be later on to recent immigrants with few connections and relatively poor men.[10]

The comparative poverty of many seventeenth-century legislators was one reason, seventeenth-century governors believed, why political leadership in the province was so poor. Most men with either education or wealth were coopted into holding office. Consequently, as Governor Francis Nicholson complained, the quality of colonial politicians was low: "Severall of the principal Inhabitants of this province are not qualified to serve his Majesty in any Imployment, which makes it difficult for me to supply them with good men."[11] Nicholson had in mind men such as Colonel John

Coode, one of the leaders of the 1689 Revolution and a scion of a prominent English family. Coode distinguished himself in politics by a total inability to work cooperatively with any government for any appreciable length of time.[12] The exclusion after 1690 from political office of the small but highly visible and rich Catholic elite that had formerly monopolized provincial office highlighted the deficiencies of leaders such as Coode. Nicholson's inability to appoint to office the talented, influential, and rich Charles Carroll the Settler, who described the Protestant rebellion's leaders as "profligate wretches and men of scandalous lives," was especially galling.[13]

Matters improved in the eighteenth century. As early as 1710, over three-quarters of provincial legislators were wealthy men. In the 1730 legislature, the percentage of legislators who left estates over £650 was nearly 85 percent, increasing to over 90 percent by the 1750 legislature. The premier political body in the province—the Governor's Council—was the preserve of the very wealthy, especially in the eighteenth century. Just two councilors who served after 1720 left estates of less than £650. The average councilor tended to be very rich: over half of eighteenth-century councilors left estates greater than £2,500. Provincial assemblymen also tended to be wealthy, although this varied from county to county and over time. Taking the four counties in this study, 65 percent of post-1692 assemblymen estates were worth more than £650. In the decade before the Revolution, virtually every legislator qualified for membership in this sample. Wealthy legislators were common in each county except the poorest, Somerset, where just under half of all legislators owned estates valued at more than £650. Even there, the great majority of poor assemblymen served in the late seventeenth century or early eighteenth century. Just three of the eighteen assemblymen from Somerset who died after 1742 left estates less than £650. Those assemblymen who were not wealthy enough to make it into this elite sample were seldom destitute: less than one in six legislators, all serving before 1725, left estates smaller than £250. None of these relatively poor legislators was politically prominent.

Was the legislature also the preserve of the well born? Did the Maryland legislature increasingly become a closed shop, occupied by the descendants and close connections of former legislators and closed to new wealth and new men? The common wisdom is that the Maryland political elite had become a "tangled cousinry" by the early eighteenth century, dominated by long-serving legislators who were all related to each other. Certainly, kinship links between legislators became more frequent between the Revolution of 1692 and the 1770s. In conservative Talbot County, long-serving assemblymen from a small number of heavily interconnected powerful planter families did form a "tangled cousinry." Members of the Lloyd, Goldsborough, and Tilghman families were present every year in the Maryland legislature in the eighteenth century. Nevertheless, increasing kinship links and ancestral connections were largely the result of social development. Only a small percentage of the total population in the late seventeenth century had sufficient assets to make them likely candidates for high office: 314 men dying before 1726 who left probated estates over £225 and 165 who left total estate values (TEVs) over £400. This small group formed the core constituency from which provincial legislators were chosen. A considerable proportion of that group married within the group, given the propensity of like to mix with like. Over time, kinship links between the politically eligible increased, more as a function of time and from close proximity than from purposeful design. Similarly, as colonial society matured and the number of men who had served in the Maryland legislature multiplied, a greater number of men were descended from legislators. Maryland was a sparsely populated, predominantly rural society with considerable social divisions and a commitment to hierarchical power structures. It was inevitable in such a small-scale society that a large percentage of political figures would be connected to each other.

Nevertheless, the kinship and ancestral links between legislators by mid-century were impressive and point to a legislative body that had many common interests. In contrast to the seventeenth-century legislature, which was dominated by short-serving immigrant small planters only recently established in the province, the eighteenth-century legislature was a unified body, connected in numerous ways, especially by kinship ties. In 1750 at least seven legislators had familial connections with seven or more legislators each. Edward Lloyd III, a very wealthy councilor from Talbot County and the leading representative of the most prominent family in the province, was related to no less than eleven other legislators in a legislature of seventy members. In the 1750s, eight of nine legislators in Talbot County were connected to another legislator, with Edward Oldham related to three legislators, and brothers-in-law Samuel Chamberlaine, Edward Lloyd III, and William Goldsborough served in the Upper House.

Increased interconnections between legislators accelerated over time. In the 1690 legislature, most assemblymen were isolated individuals, seldom connected by kinship to previous or to current legislators. The Maryland legislature was a legislature dominated by immigrants, with just four native-born legislators. Some of these immigrants had solidified their position within Maryland society by marrying the widow or daughter of a previous legislator. Thus, half of all legislators were allied by marriage to families with some political experience in Maryland. Still, these links did not translate into significant interconnections within the legislature. Four in five men were not related to other legislators. Only three sets of relationships were very close: James Keech and John Courts were brothers-in-law, John Brooke was the stepfather of Henry Trippe, and Brooke was also the son-in-law of Thomas Cooke. With the possible exception of St. Mary's County, where three of the four assemblymen were linked by kin ties, no core group of closely connected men, tied by history and family to the traditions of the legislature, existed. Despite the changes wrought by the Revolution of 1689, the provincial assembly continued to resemble seventeenth-century assemblies.

Matters had changed by 1710. Although the Assembly still experienced considerable turnover of members, with nearly 60 percent of members having held their seats for less than 5 years, a solid cadre of long-serving legislators had emerged, especially in the Council. The longest serving councilor, Francis Jenkins from Somerset County, had been in office since 1689, eight other councilors and seven assemblymen had served for more than 10 years, and a further fifteen legislators, two in the Council and thirteen in the Assembly, had served between 5 and 10 years. These long-serving men were the founders of Maryland's emerging political elite, which was to dominate politics in Maryland for the remainder of the colonial period. During this session of the legislature many of the fundamental features of eighteenth-century political life in the colony, notably a firm insistence on the authority of the Lower House, were first securely established.[14]

The composition of the legislature had changed significantly since 1690. For the first time, immigrants were outnumbered by the native born. One in five legislators and 42 percent of the native born were sons of legislators. Moreover, a third of legislators had married daughters of legislators. These descendants of seventeenth-century politicians were already imbued with the traditions of the legislature. They assiduously and aggressively asserted their rights and privileges, much to the chagrin of Maryland's governors. Nevertheless, the legislature still contained a considerable number of immigrants and men who were the first men in their families to be elected or appointed to provincial office. Many of these unconnected men served just one or two terms, but the unconnected included some of Maryland's political leaders, such as William Holland, a 10-year veteran of the Council, and the most powerful man in the Assembly, the speaker, Thomas Smithson, from Talbot County. Talented and ambitious men from humble backgrounds still had a place in Maryland politics.

Not surprisingly, given the increase in native-born descendants of legislators in the 1710 Assembly, the number of connections between assemblymen in 1710 was greater than in 1690. By 1710, there were seventeen different kin connections in the legislature, involving twenty-three legislators of whom five were councilors. These included nine close connections such as brothers or brothers-in-law (eight examples) and a father and son combination. Nevertheless, nearly two-thirds of legislators were not related to any other legislator. Thomas Greenfield in the Council, his son in the Assembly, Thomas Trueman Greenfield, and Thomas Trueman Greenfield's father-in-law Walter Smith formed the only family bloc of any importance.

The trends apparent in the 1710 legislature had intensified by 1730 and were dominant by 1750. Length of service increased, as did the proportion of legislators who had been in political office for a long time.[15] Just like the economic elite, Maryland's political elite was increasingly native born and interconnected through familial and other links. By mid-century, the jibe that the leading men of the province were all part of a complicated "tangled cousinry" contained some truth. Nevertheless, the Maryland legislature was not a closed shop. Even though it became more difficult for unconnected men to gain office than it had been in the seventeenth century, men with talent and ambition in the eighteenth century were always able to force their way into the legislature, provided, of course, that they had the means to fulfill their obligations. Daniel Dulany, Sr. and Samuel Chamberlaine were two examples of talented outsiders who became prominent insiders. The legislature became a much more cohesive and integrated body as the century progressed. Yet it retained sufficient fluidity in membership to prevent a discontented group of frustrated office-seekers emerging. This combination of cohesiveness and fluidity helps to account for the extraordinary success of Maryland's political elite in the eighteenth century in solidifying and augmenting its authority in society without provoking dissension either from discontented wealthy men excluded from office or from the ranks of the politically disenfranchised.

Both in 1730 and in 1750 men who had been in office for many years dominated the Maryland legislature. Longevity of service was especially evident in the Council. In 1730, councilors had been in office for an average of over 19 years, with five councilors having been either in the Assembly or the Council for more than 20 years. Just one councilor had been in office in 1730 for less than 5 years and he was a member of the proprietary family. Of eleven councilors, eight had been in office since the royal period of representative government in Maryland had started in 1715. Both John Hall and Richard Tilghman could date their legislative service from the last decade of the seventeenth century.

The Council of 1730 was exceptionally long serving, but longevity of office continued to be a feature of Maryland political life until the Revolutionary era. The Council of 1750 included four men who had been in provincial office for over 20 years, with Benjamin Tasker having been in office for 34 years and in the Council since 1722. Tasker, the president of the Council and the leading local politician in the province, was to remain a councilor until his death in 1768, serving in that position for 47 years. Tasker, and his fellow councilors, Edmund Jenings, Daniel Dulany, and Samuel Chamberlaine, had all served in the 1730 Assembly and had been important in public affairs ever since. Significantly, the Council of 1750 was more firmly rooted in Maryland and in the representative traditions of Maryland than the Council of 20 years previously with six of the eleven councilors in 1750 being sons of legislators as compared to three in 1730.

Members of the Assembly could not boast the impressive pedigrees and lengthy service of their superiors in the Council but longevity of service had increased in that body as well. By 1730, the average assemblyman had been in office for 7.6 years, with nearly as many having held office for more than ten years as for less than 5 years. No one could match the 36 years in office of councilor John Hall, but John Mackall of Calvert County and Thomas Trueman Greenfield of St Mary's had both been assemblymen for more than 20 years. Longevity of service in the Assembly had decreased a little by 1750, to an average of 6.8 years for each assemblyman, but the Assembly continued to contain a number of long-serving assemblymen. The Assemblies of both 1730 and 1750, therefore, contained a substantial body of politically experienced men long conversant with political matters and devoted to upholding the rights and privileges of the colonial legislature.

Many legislators were firmly attached to the Maryland legislature not only by virtue of long attendance but also through their connections to both present and past legislators. Legislators who had arrived as immigrants in Maryland did not disappear from either the Council or Assembly but they accounted for less than 20 percent of the legislature after 1710. The typical legislator was native born, the descendant of settlers who had arrived in Maryland in the second half of the seventeenth century, and was related either by descent or marriage to previous legislators. The Assembly was not quite an hereditary body but by 1750 a small majority of native-born legislators were the sons of legislators with nearly 40 percent of the native-born and 30 percent of all legislators having married the daughter or widow of a legislator. Several men came from what were effectively political families, with multiple connections to previous legislators both by descent and by marriage. In the 1730 legislature, for example, John Rousby, a councilor from Calvert County, was the son of a legislator, the maternal grandson of a legislator, married the daughter of a legislator, and had both an uncle and a brother-in-law who had held political office. By 1750, the political connections of the most well-connected legislators were especially dense. Edward Lloyd III was the son, grandson, and great grandson of legislators, with six uncles as legislators even before he multiplied his political kinship network by marrying the daughter of the equally well-connected John Rousby. No one could match Lloyd's political pedigree but Benjamin Mackall, Jr., John Addison, and Nathaniel Wright each had at least five uncles who had been legislators prior to their own entry into politics. The 1750 legislature was full of men whose personal history was intimately tied to the history of representative government in the province.

Eighteenth-century legislators became ever more closely tied by kinship and marriage ties, with two-thirds of legislators linked in the 1750 legislature. Councilors were especially well connected: seven of the ten councilors whose power base was in Maryland were connected by kinship or marriage to two or more sitting legislators. The councilors were themselves related in a myriad of ways. Benjamin Tasker married one daughter to the governor, Samuel Ogle, married another to Daniel Dulany's eldest son, and had a niece who married George Plater. Dulany was related through his wife to both Edward Lloyd III and Samuel Chamberlaine while Plater had connections not only with Tasker but also with Lloyd and with Benedict Calvert. These connections gave them an enormous advantage other over politicians in formulating policy in either the Council or the Assembly. But other men could also hope for support from relatives in the legislature, with 44 percent of legislators in the 1750 Assembly linked to three or more fellow legislators. A substantial rump within the Maryland legislature by 1750 could see political life in the province as an expansion into the public sphere of their connections in private life.

Nevertheless, the impressive links that had developed between legislators did not mean that the mid-eighteenth-century Maryland legislature was dominated by family groupings. Closeness by blood did not necessarily mean closeness of interest. Not all relatives were close friends. Eighteenth-century Maryland gentlemen were not especially clannish, as previous chapters have detailed. Devoted to their immediate families, wealthy Marylanders felt little connection with more distant kin, preferring usually to associate with friends and business associates rather than with relatives.[16] Some of the fiercest political disputes in the colonial era were fought between men who were related. The intensified attacks upon Roman Catholics that disfigured Maryland politics in the 1750s were chiefly propounded by Dr. Charles Carroll, a kinsman of Charles Carroll of Annapolis, who had converted to Anglicanism. Dr. Carroll was partly motivated by spite against Charles Carroll of Annapolis, having been involved in a lengthy and bitter dispute over Dr. Carroll's appropriation of bequests from Charles Carroll of Annapolis's cousin. Dr. Carroll wanted to lay "a great Man by his Heels." But the confrontation was more than just a personal feud. It involved ideological antagonisms as well, between wealthy men anxious to retain their property and Protestants alarmed since the Jacobite rebellion of 1745 about what they considered to be the dangerous growth of "Popery" in the province.[17]

Moreover, opportunity always existed in Maryland for ambitious and talented outsiders to become prominent political leaders. Two of the longest serving Maryland councilors, Daniel Dulany and Samuel Chamberlaine, had arrived in Maryland as immigrants but managed to attain office with relative ease. Dulany, an Irish indentured servant who arrived in Maryland in 1703, and served as a law clerk in the office of councilor George Plater, had prospered so well as a lawyer and merchant-planter that he became an assemblyman at age 37. His legal and oratorical skills enabled him to become the leading representative of the country party and Speaker of the House. By his death in 1753 Dulany was extremely well connected. He had married into three of the most prominent political families in the province, culminating with a marriage, his third, to the daughter of Philemon Lloyd. Significantly, Dulany's connections to other legislators occurred well after he had established himself as a leading politician in the province. Most of his success was due to his own efforts and character rather than to his powerful friends and relatives.[18]

Samuel Chamberlaine was another powerful eighteenth-century legislator, a member of the council for nearly 30 years, who arrived in the colony as an immigrant. Better connected than Dulany on arrival (Chamberlaine was the son of a Liverpool merchant involved in trade to Talbot County), he increased his advantages by marrying 2 years after arrival the heiress daughter of Robert Ungle and then, soon after entering the Assembly for the first time, Henrietta Maria Lloyd, the daughter of James Lloyd. Chamberlaine quickly associated himself with the leading family in Talbot County and soon became a major power broker in the county and province. All three of his sons married into prominent Talbot County families, with two becoming assemblymen.

Few immigrants did as well as Dulany and Chamberlaine, either economically or politically. But each legislature was a mixture of the long serving, the well connected, and new faces. In the 1690 legislature, newcomers comprised a majority of the Assembly. In some counties, such as Somerset County, the whole county representation was new. None of the Somerset assemblymen—Francis Jenkins, David Browne, Robert King, or Samuel Hopkins—had represented the county before and none was related to any previous legislators. Lack of connections did not stop Browne and Jenkins from becoming councilors and King and Hopkins left children who also became legislators. The 1690 legislature was unusual insofar as it was the first legislature after the Revolution of 1689 and it is not surprising that there were few familiar names among the new assemblymen. But fresh names continued to appear in the Assembly throughout the eighteenth century. In 1710, one-third of legislators were not connected to previous legislators, including John Mackall from Calvert County, an assemblyman from 1704 to his death in 1739, Speaker from 1724 to 1735 and again from 1738 to 1739, and progenitor of a formidable political dynasty. The percentage of unconnected assemblyman had declined to 20 percent by the Assembly of 1730 and to 16 percent by 1750, but new men still appeared, such as Robert Gordon, an immigrant to Maryland from Scotland in 1719 and a wealthy Annapolis merchant. He represented his adopted town from 1725 until his death in 1753. The Assembly never quite became a self-perpetuating club, closed to outsiders.

Wealthy Marylanders with political experience formed a distinct subset of the economic elite. Nearly 60 percent of the elite did not participate in either provincial politics or in any of the higher offices of local government, such as being justices of the peace (J.P.s), sheriffs, or militia officers. Nonparticipants increased substantially over time, from 36 percent of testators dying before 1708 (half of whom were Catholics or Quakers and thus excluded from office) to three-quarters dying after 1759. One explanation for increased nonparticipation is logistical. By the mid-eighteenth century, many more men were qualified to enter politics than there were posts available. Each county had only four seats allotted to it in the legislature,[19] a limited number of J.P.s, and one person appointed sheriff. Moreover, these positions became vacant less frequently, especially between 1720 and 1760 when the length of service of both J.P.s and legislators increased. Wealthy legislators dying between 1743 and 1759 (generally entering the Assembly between 1720 and 1750) averaged 12 years in the legislature compared to 7 years for those dying before 1743, and several served for over 20 years. In Talbot County, to take one county distinguished by long-serving assemblymen, only 13 new men entered the Assembly between 1730 and 1760, an average of one new man every 2.3 years. Longer service inevitably reduced opportunities for other elite members to take up positions.

As the potential pool of qualified applicants for political office grew with the steady increase in elite numbers, the composition of the political group within the elite took on specific characteristics differentiating them from the elite as a whole. These characteristics varied from office to office. Wealthy Marylanders who became councilors, for example, were drawn from the highest reaches of Maryland society. They included the richest and most talented men in the colony—Thomas Bordley, Levin Gale, Daniel Dulany, Edward Lloyd II, and Edward Lloyd III. Each of these men entered local and provincial politics early (the two Lloyds became councilors at the ages of 31 and 33, respectively) and died with large estates. The average estate of the ten elite members dying after 1726 who were councilors was £7,181, nearly four times as much as the average elite estate. Mostly native-born members of already prominent political families, they were political high-fliers and integrated into the broader Atlantic economy as large-scale merchant planters. The small number of wealthy Marylanders fortunate enough to secure a provincial sinecure such as provincial justiceships, or major proprietary offices such as commissary general, attorney general, or colonial governorship, resembled councilors in wealth and in political and social prominence (Table 6.1).

Legislators were poorer and less well connected than councilors. Still, the 91 members of the elite sample who became legislators left estates 56 percent greater than the average elite estate. They

Table 6.1 Provincial Officeholding

	Pre-1726	1726–42	1743–59	1760+	Total
	Numbers of elite holding office				
Upper House	13	4	2	4	23
Lower House	38	15	18	20	91
J.P.s	41	17	23	28	109
	Percentage of elite holding office				
Upper House	13	5	2	2	5
Lower House	39	17	18	11	20
J.P.	42	20	23	16	24
	Average TEV				
Upper House	£2,504	5,159	8,389	8,599	4,538
Lower House	£1,908	4,871	2,493	3,839	2,936
J.P.s	£1,843	3,967	1,577	2,108	2,186
	Average length of service: years				
Upper House	8	16	9	22	12
Lower House	7	11	12	6	8
J.P.s	10	13	9	10	10
	Average age at first entry				
Upper House	47	40	46	42	45
Lower House	39	39	39	40	39
J.P.s	34	34	35	35	34

Source: County Records, *MHR*; Papenfuse et al., *Biographical Dictionary.*

were also more likely to be native born, more likely to be merchant planters or lawyers, and over a third more likely to be children of wealthy men. Those who entered politics before age 30 (the average age of entry being 39) were most likely to be wealthy native-born descendants of elite fathers. Because they entered politics young and because of their high position within Maryland society, they tended to serve long periods in the legislature (two-thirds were legislators for more than 10 years) and obtained important political posts. Most served a political apprenticeship as a J.P. before entering the House, although over time the more cosmopolitan gentlemen, such as Edward Lloyd III and Levin Gale, bypassed such an apprenticeship to start politics in the House itself. The characteristics of the 109 men who were J.P.s and the 89 men who served as militia officers resembled those of men entering the Assembly, except that their wealth closely approximated that of the average elite member.

Comparing the political elite to the economic elite shows that the two were not conterminous. Wealth was necessary but not sufficient to become a political leader. Long-term residence, connections to previous generations who had served the public in office, and attachment to the landed interest of the province either eased the path to office or else convinced wealthy gentlemen that they owed a duty to their fellow countrymen and that they should offer themselves for office. But if the two elites were not conterminous, they were hardly functionally distinct either. The characteristics that distinguished the economic elite were those that marked the political elite, notably appreciable wealth, long-term commitment to both the province and to the planting interest, and a shared devotion to gentility as a principal social value. The political elite may have been open to newcomers but the door was hardly wide open to all and certainly was not open to anyone who did not demonstrate that he was a gentleman. If Maryland's political establishment was not quite the "Tangled Cousinry" of popular legend, it was no meritocracy either. Gentlemen dominated, as gentlemen thought was right and proper.

The question we have to ask is why gentlemanly rule was so universal, even in an age when the importance of social and political hierarchy was so widely accepted. We need to explain why within a relatively broad franchise gentlemen were usually chosen or appointed to fill political offices of any importance. This question has been, of course, one widely examined by historians. The classic account of the operation of Chesapeake politics remains Sydnor's *Gentlemen Freeholders*. Sydnor describes how wealthy planters were able to maintain control over politics by a combination of ostentatious hospitality at election time, which encouraged the common voter to believe he was the gentleman's equal, and mutual assumptions by both gentlemen and ordinary planters that the gentleman's social superiority gave him a natural right to hold real power. Because the voter was confident that the gentleman he voted for would support and protect his interests and because he agreed to a hierarchical ordering of society in which men of wealth and status were the natural leaders, he abrogated his chances for political participation.[20]

Chesapeake politics, and by implication Chesapeake society, were, according to this interpretation, deferential in nature. The essential characteristic of a deferential society is the voluntary acceptance of a leadership elite by persons not belonging to that elite.[21] Nonelite members did not give up their political voice altogether. In theory, they were supposed to be able to identify the politically capable members of the elite and to display an intelligent critical attitude to their natural leaders.[22] Nevertheless, elite and nonelite alike assumed that nonelites were precluded from leadership positions by reason of their inferior wealth and training. Historians have found elements of deference in Chesapeake society from the beginnings of settlement. They have argued that by the mid-eighteenth century deference had become an essential ingredient in the smooth operation of society and in justifying unequal social relationships between rich and poor, free and unfree. Rhys Isaac, for example, emphasizes the institutionalization of gentry domination in hierarchical religious and governmental structures and examines the ways in which the gentry subtly used display and symbolism to reinforce their authority. Moreover, power over sources of credit and other forms of social and economic control supposedly enhanced the gentry's ability to secure deferential compliance to their authority.[23]

Other historians have followed Edmund Morgan in tracing the establishment of political stability and the dominance of gentry power to the imperatives forced on whites by the growth of black chattel slavery. The presence of large numbers of dependent black slaves established a consensus of identity among whites, allowing whites to define themselves increasingly in caste rather than class terms.[24] Poor whites, therefore, accepted the social and political domination of rich slaveholders in order to differentiate themselves from the unfree blacks and, most importantly, to protect themselves from possible black resistance to white rule. Owners of large numbers of slaves promised that they would control their own slaves and the importance of securing that control for social order persuaded nonslaveholders to acquiesce to their authority. Stephanie McCurry adds a different gloss to this interpretation by arguing that large planters and yeomen were linked together by a common identity as masters and heads of households. They formed a propertied and enfranchised minority bound by a common set of assumptions about manly independence, wifely submission, and enslaved dependence. That common identity, McCurry argues, committed both planters and yeomen to "independence and the public assertion of their social and political rights even as it wedded them to the relations of power and domestic dependency that supported it." Yeomen deferred in order to protect their own privileged position as masters within their own small households.[25]

These interpretations of political behavior in the colonial Chesapeake stress the central importance of a keenly self-conscious gentry group and make several assumptions about yeoman political conduct that are essential preconditions for gentry hegemony. For what Fischer calls the "Anglican idea of Hegemonic Liberty" to prevail—a hierarchical, inegalitarian system of government in which freedom was conceived as the power to rule, and not be overruled by others—the acquiescence of yeoman to the authority of wealthier men was necessary.[26] That political support, it is argued, was easily bought. Ordinary planters and property holders, fiercely independent, committed to liberty but apathetic in politics and naturally deferential, accepted wealthy men's views that those with superior wealth, education, and ancestry ought to be allowed to govern as long as they did so with due regard to the dictates of duty. Rulers ensured the continued support of a sizable electorate by reassuring the voters of their own worth and satisfying their need to feel that both governors and governed were in a shared enterprise. These twin aims were achieved by a constant glorification of yeomen virtues, and adherence to a republican ideology that made yeoman righteousness, independence, and military might the principal bulwarks of liberty. In addition, ordinary people were assured that elected and appointed officials had their interests at heart because both the elite and yeomen shared broad similarities of condition—owning property, being white, and devoted to patriarchal household governance. Consequently, people in political authority asserted the interests of white property holders over those people—the propertyless and slaves—who were not part of the political community. Moreover, they promised to protect free men from a potentially menacing central government. The many were prevented from thinking that they themselves could provide protection from threats from below and above just as well as the rich and well-born by participation in feasts and festivals lavishly provided by wealthy men at election time, a type of carnival where the common man was king, where with a curious combination of camaraderie and condescension wealthy men were forced to fraternize with their social inferiors. In short, none questioned the right of wealthy men to rule uncontested as long as there was a pretence of consultation and collaboration between political leaders and freeholders, occasional entertainments for the populace, and a concerted effort to flatter yeomen by effusively praising their character, thus bolstering their already high self-esteem.[27]

Yet ordinary voters were not as easily taken in as this interpretation suggests. Nor were they as happy as wealthy men thought despite the compliments and the carnivals. Ordinary people expected some concrete returns for their votes or for their acquiescence to political appointments. The extent of deference given by nonelite to elite was not without limits. A better way of describing politics in the colonial Chesapeake is to see elected and nonelected officials as facilitators, effectively mediating between the wider Anglo-American world and their own communities. They were expected to provide the necessary services that allowed for an orderly society; they needed to protect free men and their families from harm, either economically and socially, while ensuring both community and individual autonomy; they were meant to continue customary policies and sustain traditional relationships while advancing their constituents' prosperity; and it was hoped that they might pass a little of whatever patronage they had to the residents of their local area. When they did not adequately perform these functions, disaffection was likely.[28]

Undeniably, native-born elite members considerably enhanced their control over the apparatus and direction of government over the course of the eighteenth century. Despite incessant factionalism between competing groups of elite members, elite authority was firmly established both in the organs of provincial government and in the local community. By no means, however, did all members of the community acquiesce at all times to elite authority and ideology. Acceptance of elite authority was always to a greater or lesser degree conditional, depending on the social circumstances of the various inhabitants and on time-specific political events.[29] The classical model of deference was a set of ideal relationships that elite men felt should inform provincial politics but that took place in a far more complex behavioral and ideological matrix than wealthy men imagined. What determined political success was not deference per se (although acceptance that the better sort should govern was widespread at all social levels) but the ability of individuals to pursue commonly agreed political goals combined with natural talent, experience in public affairs, connection with the local community, sense of integrity and the ability to communicate that integrity to neighbors who were well-informed about personal strengths and deficiencies, and the nature and extent of resources that the self-selected group of the politically engaged was able to offer independent electors. The nature of a colony's oligarchical political system was determined by "multidimensional, reciprocal, and developmental relationships among individuals and the existing power structure."[30]

Challenges to elite authority were possible from three directions: from above in the form of executive opposition to legislative desires, from below by social groups not included in political decision-making processes, and from within by competing elite members. At the provincial level, challenges from above were more common and more dangerous than threats from below. The principal political issue of the seventeenth century in Maryland was the extent of executive or proprietary power. It took considerable time for the Maryland legislature to achieve a position of independence with a voice in the government of their province against a proprietary family determined to "keep the province frozen in time like a perpetual palatine of Durham or a subordinate sixteenth century Ireland."[31] Legislative battles with the proprietor continued throughout the eighteenth century with the proprietors and their representatives claiming privileges as part of their prerogatives. The unusual degree of party development in Maryland in this period was the result of such ideological battles over the legitimacy of proprietary political authority.[32] Yet the legislature had won the battle between themselves and the proprietor as early as 1692.[33] Although proprietary powers remained theoretically extensive, in practice the Maryland legislature was successfully able to thwart the proprietor's will in all but the most intractable cases. In Maryland, as in Britain and Ireland, local rulers were able to resist central government's interference in their affairs and significantly enhanced their own independence and the freedom of peripheral power structures from metropolitan dominance.[34]

Accompanying the reduction of proprietary political powers was a concomitant increase in the importance of the Lower House over the Upper House and a change in the composition of the Maryland Assembly to a largely native-born dominated body. Despite complaints from governors that the "Country borne" were "ignorant, and raw in busieness, and naturally proude and obstinate" and that their increasing appointment as legislators and J.P.s was "of ill Consequence" because "they know little of the laws and good Manners they practice less,"[35] Creoles came to dominate politics by the first two decades of the eighteenth century. They posed a more considerable threat to the authority of the governor than their predecessors because they combined large wealth, orthodox Protestantism, and native status with increasing kin links and with longer tenures in office.[36] Taking advantage of the absence of a royal governor between 1709 and 1714, the Lower House steadily advanced its powers at the expense of the Upper House until by the restoration of proprietary government in 1715, the Lower House had achieved a position of dominance as the body most legitimately representing the interests of Maryland freedmen.[37] The Lower House maintained and increased its powers throughout the rest of the century.[38] With minimal patronage to disperse, eighteenth-century governors found it difficult to curb the power of increasingly assertive and independent Creole politicians.[39]

Threats from below troubled the elite less than conflicts between the legislature and the proprietor or the crown because their powers of coercion, especially over slaves, were so great. Consequently, challenges to the established authority of the elite seldom emanated from the lower social ranks. The most dangerous possible challenge, of course, was slave uprisings. Probably as a result of strict supervision over the activities of slaves by whites and, more importantly, because whites outnumbered slaves by more than two to one, slave revolts were rare. Only once in the eighteenth century did the dominant whites face the likelihood of slave revolt. In the winter of 1739–1740 a conspiracy among mainly African-born slaves in Prince George's County was uncovered that demonstrated that slaves had a carefully planned secret design to seize and kill white families in their region. Despite the plot's failure, the white population took strong punitive action against the leaders of the conspiracy. The fear of "being Sacrificed to the rage and fury of merciless and Barbarous Slaves" made whites very wary, and they redoubled their efforts to prevent "Tumultous meetings of Slaves" and the possibility of slave revolt.[40] Yet Maryland was remarkably free of organized racial violence compared to other slave societies in the New World.[41] Crimes of violence committed by blacks and punished by the state were rare. In 1754 and 1755 only ten cases of serious crimes by slaves were reported in the *Maryland Gazette*. In all cases the guilty blacks were hanged and in the three cases in which blacks killed whites, they suffered the further indignity of being hanged in chains. Blacks were also frequently executed for less serious crimes, such as theft: half of all slaves indicted in the county court of Prince George's for theft were hanged.[42] Of course, court indictments of blacks represent only the tip of the iceberg of black criminality (as whites saw it) and black resistance (as slaves understood their actions). Most slaves were punished outside the law, by masters assured of legal protection for almost anything they did to their slaves.

White servants and the propertyless posed more of a threat to elite authority, principally because planters could not discipline servants—whites and Britons—as they could recalcitrant slaves.[43] An analysis of advertisements in the *Maryland Gazette* for two 3-year periods in the mid-eighteenth century shows that of a total of 262 ads for runaways four out of five were for runaway servants.[44] Almost all runaways were men, mostly convicts, sailors, or Irish, social types traditionally believed to be troublemakers. Once they had escaped, servants had more opportunities than slaves did to blend into white society, resist capture, and alarm the populace by engaging in antisocial activities. Sailors were particularly worrisome because they tended to run away from their ships not individually but in gangs of up to seven men. After the travails of a long sea voyage, many sailors fled to experience some of the probably limited vices and amusements that provincial Maryland had to offer.

In 1751, for example, the *Maryland Gazette* reported the activities of a gang of ex-servants and runaways who had become highway robbers.[45] In 1754, John Orrick, an elite member, lost his life when he encountered a runaway servant who stabbed Orrick in the breast and mortally wounded him.[46] Even when a servant remained in the custody of his master, he could prove dangerous, as Jeremiah Chase, a wealthy Baltimore lawyer and legislator, found out. In January 1755, Chase was served poisoned food by William Stratton, one of his servants, immediately took ill, and eventually died.[47] Masters often brought servants to court. George Drew, for instance, brought his servant woman to court in 1733, claiming that she had stolen large amounts of goods from him. She was convicted, whipped, put in the stocks, and made to pay fourfold restitution for the stolen goods.[48] Aquila Paca II presented a servant in 1734 for making a false report about him to the court, with the penalty being a whipping.[49] The traffic was not all one way. Occasionally a servant came to court to complain of ill treatment from his or her master. Thomas Hammond was presented for "suffering his servants to plant tobacco on a Sabbath day" and four elite members from Baltimore County, James Phillips, James Maxwell, Francis Holland, and Skipworth Coale, were all fined for not giving their servants freedom dues.[50]

Servants were all the more difficult to handle because they were white in a society that not only encouraged all whites of whatever station to consider themselves as equals but that was remarkably tolerant about white male aggression. As Isaac notes, a "self-assertive style, and values centering on manly prowess pervaded the interaction of men as equals."[51] Self-assertion, however, was a double-edged sword. Although an emphasis on self-assertion encouraged many of the virtues that Chesapeake gentlemen held most dear, such as manliness, competitiveness, conviviality, and hospitality, it also threatened to return the Chesapeake to the atomistic individualism that characterized the seventeenth century. Violence was never far from the surface. Violence by blacks, of course, was intolerable. Violence was acceptable only between equals, between people who shared common assumptions about the importance of honor. Blacks were excluded from the system of honor, and acts of violence by blacks were followed by savage punishment. Draconian slave codes enforced white refusal to countenance black violence.[52] White violence was more problematic, complicated by the racial ideology that posited all whites as superior to blacks. Colonial Marylanders had little difficulty in perceiving violence by white servants against free whites as illegitimate and deserving of harsh punishment,[53] but because white violence was pervasive and, in certain circumstances, tolerated, such behavior was difficult to police. Gambling and drinking were favorite pastimes of elite and nonelite men alike and were often accompanied by aggressive banter and boastful challenges that often led to brutal brawling. Wealthy Marylanders may not have directly participated in "rough-and-tumble" or "gouging" contests, but they tacitly encouraged such fights, not stopping them when they occurred at taverns and horse races and joining the bystanders who watched and enforced the customary rules of fair play. Violence and activities that could lead to violence (including not only drinking and gambling but cockfighting and quarter racing, great planters' favorite pastimes) might be socially undesirable, especially if engaged in by servants and the poor, but they also drew men from all strata of society together, cutting across but not leveling social distinctions. In many respects, as Isaac argues, "the collective intimacy of collective engagement only served to confirm social ranking," but it could also confuse relationships, especially the increasingly problematic relationships between white men in a racially divided society.[54]

The contrast between difficult elite relations with poor whites and their only infrequently challenged dominion over black slaves needs explanation. In most areas of the eighteenth-century Atlantic world, slaves posed an enormous and real threat to white power. The theoretical threat that slaves posed to white authority was real and blacks' desire to escape slavery and frustrate the ambitions of their master was manifest in many aspects of their day-to-day interaction. Yet the actual threat that blacks posed to whites in Maryland was always very limited, reflecting the intermediate position of the province within British-American slave societies. Slaves never accounted for as much as a third of Maryland's population in the colonial period, peaking at 32 percent in 1770. By contrast, on the eve of the Revolution slaves accounted for 42 percent of the population in Virginia, 61 percent of the population of South

Carolina, and 92 percent of the population of Jamaica. Whites' numerical predominance nullified slave resistance: no white person was killed in a slave rebellion in the colonial Chesapeake. Slavery may not have been as harsh in Maryland as in colonies farther south, but planters' control was more complete. They had a near monopoly on physical force, outnumbered slaves by over two to one, and developed strict legal codes and private understandings that exempted whites from any punishment relating to their private coercion of slaves. White knew that they could treat their slaves with complete impunity. A small planter in Charles County tortured and killed a slave by hanging him from the beams of his house, whipping him over a hundred times, and inflicting severe wounds all over the slave's body. A jury acquitted him of murder.[55] To physical intimidation, they added psychological coercion. In the early eighteenth century, the growing dominance of great planters was accompanied by a systematic and deliberate stripping away from blacks of almost all ties upon which the enslaved persona rested. The Africanization of Chesapeake slavery led to a sharp deterioration in the conditions of slave life, especially between 1700 and 1740, a period that marked the nadir of slave experience in the region. Slaves arrived singly from diverse African origins (two-thirds of African slaves purchased between 1702 and 1721 were sold in parcels of just one or two), were stripped of their names, were kept in cramped sex-segregated barracks, were prevented from moving freely through the countryside, were exposed to harsh physical treatment and even harsher racial condescension, and were made at all times aware of their masters' overweening power. The alienation of Africans was almost complete.[56]

The difficulties slaves faced in resisting master control were compounded by the ease with which slavery was accommodated within the prevailing Anglo-American patriarchal worldview. Slaves were considered part of the household, subject to household discipline rather than state intervention. Patriarchalism rationalized the severity of the slave system. In return for protection, slaves were forced to bow to the master's authority. In practice, the protection offered was minimal, the extent of dominion was close to complete, and the retribution for violations was quick and massive. Indeed, masters' relations with slaves were the least problematic part of the patriarchalist doctrine. In dealing with slaves, planters did not have to face the conflicts involved with simultaneously celebrating male patriarchal independence and requiring subservient males—sons and poorer white male heads of households—to submit to patriarchal discipline. Nor did planters have to concern themselves with pretending that the submission of slaves was voluntary. Planters did not expect their slaves to be voluntarily content or submissive, as they expected their wives and daughters to be. Women had much greater freedom than slaves to openly dissent from their husbands' or fathers' decisions or even flagrantly disobey the authority of the male head of the household. As Amanda Vickery has acutely and wittily noted, "the darling daughter was patriarchy's Achilles heel."[57] Masters' dealings with slaves were seldom attended with the complications that marked their relationships with other dependents. Slaves did resist master dominance, but indirectly rather than directly, repackaging patriacharlism after mid-century into the gentler system of paternalism. But paternalism—marked by greater softness, more reciprocity, and less overt authoritarianism—was no less complete a system of coercive control over slaves than had been patriarchalism. The mutation of patriachalism into paternalism was accompanied by a more constant devaluation of slaves' humanity as scientific racism took hold. Masters could be more indulgent to their slaves the more they came to see slaves as less part of an organic social order and more creatures excluded by race from the ranks of civil society.[58]

The elite could cow slaves into obedience by displays of force and through instituting strict laws to ensure discipline. With more difficulty, they could enforce obedience to authority from poor whites. Firm and even savage reprisals against marginal members of society such as slaves, servants, and the propertyless poor were applauded not just by the elite but by property holders in general, who also feared slaves, the poor, and the destitute. Small and middling freeholders shared with the elite a firm conviction that liberty and the protection of property went hand in hand. In addition, yeomen realized that their best protection against depredation was to line up behind their big neighbor, who had the experience, the resources, and the political clout to defend the land and the liberty of all property owners.[59] But they resisted the application of such coercive measures to themselves. Small to middling planters may have been economically worse off than the elite but they remained fiercely jealous of their independence.

It has been argued that one of the principal means whereby the elite secured the support of small freeholders for their continued hold on political power was the establishment of intricate reciprocal networks of credit between them, indebting the small planter both economically and morally to his larger patron.[60] We have already seen how limited was such reciprocity. Wealthy Marylanders were most comfortable establishing close relationships with those of a familiar cultural background. People in separate social groups—the elite, the yeomen middle, the poor, and slaves—tended to interact mainly with each other, with little association across class lines. Interlocking relationships operated across social lines horizontally rather than vertically. The elite tended, moreover, to deal with tenants, tradesmen, and yeomen through intermediaries rather than by personal contact, except in the artificial surroundings of Election Day. Such lack of personal contact was not conducive to fostering firm patron/client relations in a new land where "only persistent personal attention ... warded off the corrosiveness of a liberating social and physical environment."[61] Neither was yeoman acquiescence obtained by exploiting white fears of black violence, a view that insinuates that only a unified white society under the control of the most dominant slaveholders could prevent bloodshed. The lines between black and white were too clearly demarcated and the "naturalness" of white superiority was so obvious that few poor whites felt constrained because they feared their actions might undermine the basic fabric of race relations in the community. Indeed, slavery exacerbated the lack of deference that poorer men held toward richer men. The presence of black slaves "served as omnipresent reminders to independent men of precisely how valuable their independence was" and was "a powerful preventive to their giving unreserved deference to people and institutions in authority," as well as making men in slave societies especially sensitive to challenges to their own liberty as free men.[62]

Rather, small planters agreed to elite domination of political processes partly because they accepted the authority of the well born as a necessary and inevitable component of a well-functioning hierarchical social order[63] and partly because the goals and political aims the elite enunciated were shared by the majority of property holders, who were all similar insofar as they were masters of their own households with shared commitments to upholding patriarchal authority, white dominance over blacks, and manly independence. Localism was important also. Small planters maintained a narrow perspective on the world and reacted only to the most local of issues. Studies of elections in Virginia show that local conditions had the most influence on results. The provincial and imperial world was less important than the intimacy of rural neighborhoods. Not surprisingly, voters chose, when they could, prominent men from their own neighborhood whom they believed could best represent local interests in the wider world.[64] In addition, small planters, engrossed in backbreaking agricultural toil, were unlikely to have had the leisure to engage in politics and had little interest in the usually minor issues that occupied the attention of colonial politicians. For most colonial British Americans, the pursuit of happiness always resided in the private rather than the public sphere.[65] The effects of elite rule, moreover, were generally beneficial. The level of public services offered in the Chesapeake was low, but so too were taxes. Middling planters may have suffered from a lack of public schools and provincially funded churches, neither of which they showed much interest in having, and their roads were often inadequate and badly maintained. Residents of Massachusetts were much better served in all three areas. But northern colonists, especially the poor and middling, paid for what they received. Per capita taxation in Massachusetts was nearly twice as much as in the Chesapeake. As James Henderson notes, in a slave society where taxes were levied on both free and nonfree, "the nonslaveholding farmer gained the most from the local tax system . . . for it was the slaves who labored and the slave owners who actually paid for the majority of public services received."[66] Low taxation was not only desirable financially but also ideologically: the lower the tax, the less intrusion by government in the affairs of a fiercely independent populace. Thus, not only were the elite concerned to keep taxes low for personal reasons, because they paid the majority of the taxes themselves, but low taxation maintained their own political power by appeasing the lower ranks of taxpayers.[67] Elite rule, with requisite elite self-sacrifice in return for the social and economic rewards of office, satisfied both rulers and ruled.

But when elite aims conflicted with the interests of small planters and artisans, the latter were more than willing to abandon deferential politics in favor of policy-oriented politics and to use the franchise to get their voices heard and their grievances addressed, as in the battles between various factions in Maryland over tobacco legislation in the 1730s and 1740s. Tobacco was essential to the Maryland economy, and attempts to regulate its production and distribution concerned all sections of Maryland society. The Maryland legislature considered regulation of tobacco in order to prevent chronic periodic overproduction. Planters disagreed about what legislative remedies should be employed. Divisions over tobacco regulation mirrored social differences in the province. Large planters who controlled the assemblies observed how successful the Virginia Inspection Act of 1730 had been. That measure had instituted a system of regulation where only tobacco that proved to be "good, sound, well-conditioned and merchantable, and free from trash, sand and clay" could pass for export, with the rest being burned.[68] Because most planters in Maryland grew lower quality tobacco than their Virginia counterparts and because gentlemen and merchants feared massive outbreaks of violence if an inspection act was passed, they delayed enacting suitable legislation until after 1745, when prices dropped to a level at which the price of tobacco did not even recoup the costs of production.[69]

The tobacco act of 1747 passed only after several months of debate in the legislature, in the *Maryland Gazette*, and, presumably, in local taverns. The act provided for a system of inspection of tobacco and a new currency to pay taxes and debts.[70] Arguments for and against the law divided along both regional and class lines. Planters on the lower Eastern Shore opposed the law because they produced little tobacco and what they did produce was of poor quality. Poor planters also opposed the act, arguing that the heavy expense of the system would absorb all gains in tobacco prices and, more importantly, that large planters would benefit at their expense as they would not have sufficient good tobacco to pay expenses after inspectors had relieved them of their trash tobacco.

Small planters were quick to make their feelings known. Their response demonstrated the limits of deference in the Chesapeake. Small planters were willing to have elite gentlemen represent them in the legislature, but these delegates were expected to have some consideration for their views and interests. Even popular representatives could not be assured of indefinite election to the legislature if they did not acquiesce to local opinion. In the elections of 1722 and 1749 small farmers responded to tobacco legislation unfavorable to their interests passed in the preceding assembly by turning out sitting delegates in large numbers.[71] Small planter opposition to the inspection act delayed its introduction until 1747, when it became imperative to large producers to do something before declining prices and overproduction overwhelmed them. Even after the enactment of the act, small planters showed their displeasure by refusing to comply with its provisions. Inspectors, who were elected by vestrymen but who canvassed support for their election from all planters, were under strong pressure to pass as much tobacco as they could, and planters devised a number of strategies for repacking trash and second-quality tobacco to get it passed.[72] Although the act succeeded in reducing overproduction, small planter hostility weakened its effectiveness. The elite could not employ the coercive measures used on blacks and poor whites to prevent dissension among small planters. Rather, they had to yield to opinion to retain small property holders' support.

The limits of small planter allegiance to the elite were not seriously tested in this period. It is therefore easy to assume that there were few limits and that deference to the elite was universal and powerful enough to prevent social and political discontent. Yet limits were there and the elite, if they wished to retain their hold on the reins of power, had to be careful to respect the wishes of small planters. Disputes over the regulation of tobacco indicate that small planters were quite prepared to exert their disapproval through both direct and indirect pressure on the elite to temper their policies. That they did not join together to press the elite harder on issues designed to improve their situation or alter Maryland's political direction was probably because the political rule of the elite and the ideologies they espoused seemed both natural and effective. Indifference as much as deference explains why small planters did not exploit a broad franchise to obtain direct political representation.

Yet small planter indifference was not total, and when they were stirred to oppose elite policies they could present a determined challenge to elite rule. This was particularly evident in the tumults leading up to and persisting throughout the Revolution. A sizable number of Maryland small planters and artisans, especially on the Eastern Shore, did not rally to the patriot cause and were vociferous and intransigent loyalists, unwilling to acquiesce to the authority of their betters. Considerable strife and violence followed. In this case the limits of allegiance were broken, and loyalist small planters achieved not insubstantial political gains at the expense of established political leadership.[73]

The largest problem the elite faced both in the legislature and especially at the local level was the flouting of authority from within the elite itself and elite derelictions of their duty.[74] Elite irresponsibility took three forms. First, elite members often did not perform their tasks as officeholders adequately. Second, wealthy men failed in their personal conduct to conform to community standards. Third, some wealthy Marylanders directly challenged the existing political order either by expressing disapproval of individuals in positions of responsibility or by refusing to acknowledge legitimate political institutions in the colony.

Elite dereliction of duty as officeholders was remarkably common. Elite members in Baltimore County, for instance, were often hauled before the court or even the legislature for neglecting to perform the properly allotted functions of various offices. Occasionally such negligence would lead to the delinquent's appearance before the governor's council, especially in the late seventeenth century. George Ashman and John Hall, for example, were fined by the council in 1694 for refusing to serve as J.P.s. Hall was presented for not collecting a poll tax, as he was required to do as sheriff in 1696.[75] In 1717, for instance, John Stokes was presented to the Baltimore court for not obtaining fines as sheriff, and in 1723 Francis Holland, who succeeded Stokes as sheriff, was fined 200 pounds of tobacco for not attending the court.[76] Of more consequence was the presentation in the same year of Lieutenant Colonel Mark Richardson, a J.P., who officiated at the marriage of elite member Thomas Hedge despite being aware that Hedge already had a wife in England. Richardson denied the matter in such "a scornful and deriding manner" that he was dismissed from all of his offices.[77]

Even more common were personal transgressions against public order. One in six wealthy Marylanders from the Baltimore County elite sample were presented for offenses ranging from claiming of expenses for an old black woman when she was levy free, to allowing servants to plant tobacco on a Sabbath day, to assault, and receiving stolen goods. Assaults by elite members were especially frequent, with eleven elite members and two wives of wealthy men presented for this offense. More often than not, the disputes occasioning the elite member's appearance in the court-room were between men of similar status. Skipworth Coale and Jacob Giles, wealthy planters, got into a fight in 1739 and found themselves in court.[78] In 1738 Aquila Paca I and William Govane were presented for assaults on each other.[79] In 1729 Edward Hall was fined 200 pounds of tobacco and fees for an assault on the chief justice of the Baltimore Court, Roger Matthews. George Drew, a few years later, was convicted of assaulting Henry William, a constable, in the execution of his office.[80]

More serious, at least to those concerned about the mainte-nance of social order, were refusals by elite members to accept as legitimate the authority of other elite members. Seven wealthy Marylanders in Baltimore were convicted for contempt of court. Even John Hall I in 1731, at the age of 73 and after a distin-guished career that culminated in his becoming president of the council in 1733, a man that could have been expected to be care-ful to maintain the dignity of the court, was fined 400 pounds of tobacco for indecent behavior to the court.[81] Three other legisla-tors were presented for making disparaging comments about Bal-timore County justices. Samuel Owings in 1739 was loud in his denunciations of J.P. John Risteau, declaring, in the hearing of many people, "he would Strike" Risteau but he feared that the J.P. "would take the Law of Him." Further, he accused Risteau of making unjust decisions.[82]

Contempt for authority could lead conceivably to elite rebellion against elected officials. The possibility of open revolt was proba-bly illusory because the elite would have too much to lose in a revolt. But the fear of social disorder emanating from elite disobe-dience was always present. It was most apparent in the late seven-teenth and early eighteenth centuries when Jacobitism was a constant danger in Britain and when the Revolution of 1688 was still very fresh in men's memories. Consequently, local officials

were vigilant in locating and silencing possible dissent and in pros-
ecuting delinquent elite members as an example to the rest of the
community. Thus Joseph Hill, an elite merchant-planter and legislator, was presented before the council in 1707 for firing guns in
public despite being asked to desist by the local sheriff. That the
episode was nothing more than drunken exuberance and did not
portend rebellion did not prevent the council from viewing this
episode as an "Affront" to the governor and severely chastising
the still recalcitrant Hill.[83] As the councilors were well aware,
highjinks could lead to more serious troubles, even to treason. Discontented colonists in the 1690s, for example, had gathered
around perennial rebel John Coode and several other prominent
planters from St. Mary's County, especially the firebrand Philip
Clarke. Governor Nicholson found these men particularly aggra-
vating, claiming that the reason they were discontented was
because strong government prevented them from engaging "in
their former athiestical, loose and vitious way of living; and debars
them of that Darling, illegal trade" of smuggling.[84] He proceeded
to have these men arrested on charges of fomenting rebellion and
imprisoned Clarke and fined Coode.[85] Bad examples by the elite,
Nicholson and his successor John Seymour believed, could lead to
insubordination by the populace at large. Indeed, voters refused to
learn the lesson that the governors intended to teach, reelecting
Joseph Hill to the legislature despite his complicity in an alleged
conspiracy and his contempt of government. In addition, freeholders in Talbot returned Thomas Smithson to office in 1708 even
though the governor had angrily dismissed him as an assize justice
just a few months earlier.[86]

Electors continued throughout the colonial period to support
elite members who did not conform to established standards of
behavior. At least two wealthy Marylanders were elected to the
legislature despite personal conduct condemned by the respectable
members of the community. Thomas Tolley, a legislator from Baltimore County for 7 years, continued to live with but not marry
Mary Freeborn, although he was repeatedly admonished for this
by the vestry of St. Paul's Parish, Kent County. William Govane
also managed to attain elected office despite a scandalous personal
life. Govane attained most of his wealth through marrying the
heiress Anne Homewood and by appropriating and mismanaging

for his own benefit her considerable estate. Govane was hardly the perfect husband, abusing his wife both mentally and physically and abandoning her for the charms of the Widow Burle. Govane's behavior to Anne was so flagrant that she successfully managed to gain a separation from her husband after a bitter Chancery Court case in 1750 in which Govane's "Perverse Turbulent and Violent" character and arbitrary behavior were conclusively proven.[87] Govane then proceeded to live with Mary Salisbury, with whom he had two children. The vagaries of his personal conduct were echoed in his public life, where he was presented before the local courts both for assault and for contempt of court. Yet Govane was returned to the legislature for 11 years between 1751 and 1761. Moreover, he attained the highest number of votes in at least one election, the disputed election of 1752.[88]

Thus, even at the height of elite domination in the mid-eighteenth century and at a time when wealthy Marylanders could begin to point with some pride at the Anglicization of their society and the establishment of respectable institutions and the trappings of polite society, reprobates such as Govane could attain both popularity and high social standing. What this continuing phenomenon indicates is, first, considerable tolerance for men of dubious character in politics if they were sufficiently wealthy and of some social status and, second, a lack of control both by individuals and by society as a whole over the activities of those elite men transgressing against social norms. This is not to deny that there had been considerable improvement in the political and personal behavior of the elite over the eighteenth century. Govane's violations of social order pale besides those of Thomas Macnemara, an Irish-born lawyer of the early eighteenth century who attained wealth but also a particularly unsavory reputation. But continuing elite derelictions of duty gave pause to those Marylanders concerned about the likelihood of elite political domination as the Revolution approached. Maryland politics were essentially deferential in style, but there were limits to that deference. The essential characteristic of a deferential society is the voluntary acceptance of a leadership elite by the nonelite. Voluntary acceptance was a fragile basis for political allegiance and could easily be withdrawn. Conservative observers in the Chesapeake were all too aware of how much effort was needed to maintain elite authority in a deferential society, especially by the mid-eighteenth century when prosperity allowed Marylanders to reflect upon their society and its virtues and failings. Increasingly, commentators railed against elite extravagance, addiction to gambling, and other forms of pleasure. They were especially censorious about what seemed to be growing immorality and disregard for the traditional values of industry, thrift, sobriety, and private morality.[89] More importantly, the maturation of Maryland society made Creoles much more aware of local deficiencies. No longer solely devoted to the pursuit of material gain, but interested in pursuing a particular life-style, that of the genteel planter, elite members, or at least a small portion of them, became conscious of their shared identity and more aware of the need to maintain their precarious hold over the sources of power in Maryland.

NOTES

1. Russell R. Menard, "Economy and Society in Early Colonial Maryland," (unpublished Ph.D., University of Iowa, 1975); Aubrey C. Land, *Colonial Maryland* (Millwood, NY: KTO Press, 1981), 33–56; and David W. Jordan, *Foundations of Representative Government in Maryland, 1632–1715* (Cambridge: Cambridge University Press, 1987).
2. Bacon's Rebellion, which tore Virginia apart in 1676, never spread to Maryland.
3. Lois Green Carr and David W. Jordan, *Maryland's Revolution of Government, 1689–1692* (Ithaca, NY: Cornell University Press, 1974), 180–231.
4. Jack P. Greene, *Imperatives, Behaviors, and Identities: Essays in Early American Cultural History* (Charlottesville: University Press of Virginia, 1992), 206.
5. Keith Mason, "Localism, Evangelicalism, and Loyalism: The Sources of Discontent in the Revolutionary Chesapeake," *JSH*, LVI (1990), 29–31; and Michael A. McDonnell, "Popular Mobilization and Political Culture in Revolutionary Virginia: The Failure of the Minutemen and the Revolution from Below," *JAH*, 85 (1998), 946–81.
6. Derived from data in Edward C. Papenfuse et al., *A Biographical Dictionary of the Maryland Legislature*, 2 vols. (Baltimore and London: Johns Hopkins University Press, 1979 and 1985). Unless otherwise stated, details of individual legislative careers all come from this source.
7. Gordon Wood, *The Radicalism of the American Revolution* (New York: Alfred A. Knopf, 1992), 88.
8. J.G.A. Pocock, "The Classical Theory of Deference," *AHR*, 81 (1976), 516–23
9. For the differences between upper class and elite, see Gary J. Kornblith and John M. Murrin, "The Making and Unmaking of an American Ruling Class," in Alfred F. Young, *Beyond the American Revolution* (De Kalb: Northern Illinois University Press, 1993), 29–30.

10. Quote from James Horn, *Adapting to a New World: English Society in the Seventeenth-Century Chesapeake* (Chapel Hill: University of North Carolina Press, 1994), 341–42; James R. Perry, *The Formation of a Society on Virginia's Eastern Shore, 1615–1655* (Chapel Hill: University of North Carolina Press, 1990), 196–99; and Jordan, *Foundations of Representative Government*, 69–80.

11. Nicholson to Board of Trade, March 27, 1697, AM, XXIII, 83.

12. *AM*, XIX, 435–40, 475–82, XX, 561–65; Papenfuse et al., *Biographical Dictionary*, I, 233–4; and Carr and Jordan, *Maryland's Revolution of Government*, 245–48.

13. Ronald Hoffman, " 'Marylando-Hibernus': Charles Carroll the Settler, 1660–1720," *WMQ*, XLV (1988), 212–13.

14. Jordan, *Foundations of Representative Government*, 226, 233.

15. Rates of turnover in the Maryland legislature were especially low in the second quarter of the eighteenth century. Jack P. Greene, "Legislative Turnover in British America, 1696–1775: A Quantitative Analysis," *WMQ*, XXXVIII (1981), 446–47.

16. Trevor Burnard, "A Tangled Cousinry? Associational Networks of the Maryland Elite, 1691–1776," *JSH*, LXI (1995), 18–44.

17. Ronald Hoffman, *Princes of Ireland, Planters of Maryland: A Carroll Saga, 1500–1782* (Chapel Hill: University of North Carolina Press, 2000), 270–75.

18. Aubrey C. Land, *The Dulanys of Maryland: A Biographical Study of Daniel Dulany, the Elder (1685–1753) and Daniel Dulany, the Younger (1722–1797)* (Baltimore: Johns Hopkins University Press, 1955).

19. Since Annapolis had two seats in the Assembly, Anne Arundel in effect had six positions available.

20. Charles Sydnor, *Gentlemen Freeholders: Political Practices in Washington's Virginia* (Chapel Hill: University of North Carolina Press, 1952).

21. Pocock, "The Classical Theory of Deference," 516–23; and J.R. Pole, "Historians and the Problem of Early American Democracy," *AHR*, 67 (1962), 626–46.

22. Pocock, "Classical Theory of Deference," 519.

23. Rhys Isaac, *The Transformation of Virginia, 1740–1790* (Chapel Hill: University of North Carolina Press, 1982), Chapters 2, 4–6.

24. Edmund S. Morgan, *American Slavery—American Freedom: The Ordeal of Colonial Virginia* (New York: W. W. Norton, 1975). See also Allan Kulikoff, *Tobacco and Slaves: The Development of Southern Cultures in the Chesapeake, 1680–1800* (Chapel Hill: University of North Carolina Press, 1986), 44.

25. Stephanie McCurry, *Masters of Small Worlds: Yeoman Households, Gender Relations, & the Political Culture of the Antebellum South Carolina Lowcountry* (New York: Oxford University Press, 1995), 92–93.

26. David Hackett Fischer, *Albion's Seed: Four British Folkways in America* (New York: Oxford University Press, 1989), 410–18.

27. Edmund Morgan, *Inventing the People: The Rise of Popular Sovereignty in England and America* (New York: W. W. Norton, 1988), 167–73, 197–208 (quotation from 169).

28. Mason, "Localism, Evangelicalism, and Loyalism," 27.

29. Jack P. Greene has been the most incisive analyst of the limits of deference in colonial America. See, in particular, *Imperatives, Behaviors, and Identities*, 196–202.

30. Alan Tully, *Forming American Politics: Ideals, Interests and Institutions in Colonial New York and Pennsylvania* (Baltimore: Johns Hopkins University Press, 1994), 373.
31. Jordan, *Foundations of Representative Government*, 233.
32. Adrienne Bell, "Calvert's Colony: Proprietary Politics in Maryland, 1716–1763," (unpublished Ph.D., Johns Hopkins University), 278–90. See also Land, *The Dulanys of Maryland*; David C. Skaggs, *Roots of Maryland Democracy, 1753–1776* (Westport, CT: Greenwood Press, 1973); and Charles A. Barker, *The Background of the Revolution in Maryland* (New Haven, CT: Yale University Press, 1940).
33. Carr and Jordan, *Maryland's Revolution of Government*.
34. Jack P. Greene, *Peripheries and Center: Constitutional Development in the Extended Polities of the British Empire and the United States, 1607–1788* (Athens: University of Georgia Press, 1986), 19–76.
35. Governor John Seymour to the Board of Trade, 1709, *AM*, XXV, 263.
36. Jordan, *Foundations of Representative Government*, 147, 153.
37. Ibid, 141 *passim*. The acting governor of the province was Edward Lloyd, one of the leading examples of a dominant "Country borne" politician. Ibid, 181.
38. Jack P. Greene, *The Quest for Power: The Lower Houses of Assembly in the Southern Royal Colonies, 1689–1763* (Chapel Hill: University of North Carolina Press), 1963.
39. Bernard Bailyn, *The Origins of American Politics* (New York: Alfred A. Knopf, 1968), 72–80.
40. *AM*, XXVII, 190.
41. For the 1739–40 conspiracies see *AM*, XXVIII, 188–190, 230–32, and Stephen Bordley's Letterbook, 1738–1740, MHS; Herbert Aptheker, *American Negro Slave Revolts* (New York: Columbia University Press, 1943), 169–70; and Kulikoff, *Tobacco and Slaves*, 329–30. For New World slave revolts outside North America, see, inter alia, Eugene D. Genovese, *From Rebellion to Revolution: Afro-American Slave Revolts in the Making of the Modern World* (Baton Rouge: Louisiana State University Press, 1979); David Barry Gaspar, *Bondmen and Rebels: A Study of Master Slave Relations in Antigua* (Baltimore: Johns Hopkins University Press, 1985); and Michael Craton, *Testing the Chains: Resistance to Slavery in the British West Indies* (Ithaca, NY: Cornell University Press, 1982).
42. Kulikoff, *Tobacco and Slaves*, 390–91.
43. Morgan, *American Slavery—American Freedom*, 338–62.
44. *Maryland Gazette*, 1745–47, 1751–53.
45. *Maryland Gazette*, 11 July, 1751.
46. Ibid, 28 March, 1754.
47. Stratton was convicted and hanged along with two blacks. Ibid, 15 May 1755.
48. Baltimore County Court Proceedings, HWS 9, 1733, 139, *MHR*.
49. Ibid, HWS 9, 1734, 305.
50. Ibid, ISA, 1709, 41; ISC 3, 1718, 2; ISTW 1, 1722, 173; ISTW 4, 1724, 37; BB B, 1755, 240.
51. Isaac, *Transformation of Virginia*, 95.
52. Philip Schwartz, *Twice Condemned: Slaves and the Criminal Laws of Virginia, 1705–1865* (Baton Rouge: Louisiana State University Press, 1988); and Thomas D. Morris, *Southern Slavery and the Law, 1619–1860* (Chapel Hill: University of North Carolina Press, 1996).

53. Fischer, *Albion's Seed*, 404.
54. Isaac, *Transformation of Virginia*, 94–104 (quotation from 104).
55. Jean B. Lee, *The Price of Nationhood: the American Revolution in Charles County* (New York: W. W. Norton, 1995), 68.
56. Ira Berlin, *Many Thousands Gone; The First Two Centuries of Slavery in North America* (Cambridge, MA: Harvard University Press, 1998), 112–14; Kulikoff, *Tobacco and Slaves*, 324; and Paul Edwards (ed.), *The Life of Olaudah Equiano or Gustavas Vassa, the African* (London: Longman, 1969), 54, 90.
57. Kathleen M. Brown, *Good Wives, Nasty Wenches, and Anxious Patriarchs: Gender, Race, and Power in Colonial Virginia* (Chapel Hill: University of North Carolina Press, 1996), 339; and Amanda Vickery, *The Gentleman's Daughter: Women's Lives in Georgian England* (New Haven, CT: Yale University Press, 1998), 49.
58. This interpretation owes much to Philip D. Morgan, *Slave Counterpoint: Black Culture in the Eighteenth-Century Chesapeake & Lowcountry* (Chapel Hill: University of North Carolina Press, 1998), 258–97; and James Oakes, *Slavery and Freedom: An Interpretation of the Old South* (New York: W. W. Norton, 1990), 57–78.
59. Morgan, *Inventing the People*, 168–69.
60. Kulikoff, *Tobacco and Slaves*, 288.
61. Tully, *Forming American Politics*, 375.
62. Greene, *Imperatives, Behaviors & Identities*, 199, 268–89.
63. Marylanders thought an ideal representative was one who enjoyed "private success" since he "with safety may be trusted with the most important interests of his country, as being under no temptations to betray them." Publius Agricola, *Maryland Gazette*, 16 December 1746.
64. John Gilman Kolp, *Gentlemen and Freeholders: Electoral Politics in Colonial Virginia* (Baltimore: Johns Hopkins University Press, 1998), 195–97.
65. Greene, *Imperatives, Behaviors, and Identities*, 201.
66. H. James Henderson, "Taxation and Political Culture: Massachusetts and Virginia, 1760–1800," *WMQ*, XLVII (1990), 99.
67. Ibid, 101.
68. *Virginia Statutes at Large*, IV, 251.
69. The passage of the Virginia Act in 1732 had seen much violence by small planters both in Virginia and also Maryland. Kulikoff, *Tobacco and Slaves*, 109–113.
70. See letters in the *Maryland Gazette*, April 1, 22; May 13; June 17; August 12; October 28, 1746; April 7, 21, 28; May 5, 12, 19, 26; June 2, 16, 23, 30; July 14, 1747; and *AM*, XXVIII, 308–11, XLIV, 516–17, 595–638. See also Vertrees J. Wycoff, *Tobacco Regulation in Colonial Maryland* (Baltimore: Johns Hopkins University Press, 1936); Kulikoff, *Tobacco and Slaves*, 114–16; Mary McKinney Schweitzer, "Economic Regulation and the Colonial Economy: The Maryland Tobacco Inspection Act of 1747," *JEH*, XL (1980), 551–69; and Barker, *Background to Revolution*, 69–116.
71. Bell, "Calvert's Colony," 85–88.
72. Kulikoff, *Tobacco and Slaves*, 115–16, 291–92.
73. Ronald Hoffman, *A Spirit of Dissension: Economy, Politics, and the Revolution in Maryland* (Baltimore: Johns Hopkins University Press, 1973); and Keith Mason, "A Region in Revolt: The Eastern Shore of Maryland, 1740–1790," (unpublished Ph.D., Johns Hopkins University, 1985). For Virginia, see McDonnell, "Popular Mobilization and Popular Culture."

74. The most notable scandal in the colonial Chesapeake involving an elite dereliction of duty was the discovery in 1766 of how Virginia Treasurer John Robinson had enriched his indebted friends with unauthorized loans from the public purse. David J. Mays, *Edmund Pendleton, 1721–1803: A Biography*, 2 vols. (Cambridge, MA: Harvard University Press, 1952), I: 174–208, 358–85.

75. *AM*, XX, 225, 362.

76. Baltimore County Court Proceedings, GM, 1717, 202; ISTW 2, 1723, 422.

77. Ibid, XX, 507–08.

78. Ibid, HWS & TR, 1739, 41 and 44.

79. Ibid, HWS IA, 1738, 318.

80. Ibid, HWS 6, 1729, 96; HWS 9, 1733, 74.

81. Ibid, HWS 7, 1731, 97.

82. Ibid, HW IA, 1739, 319.

83. *AM*, XXV, 17 July, 1707, 214–15

84. Nicholson to Board of Trade, 20 August, 1698, *AM*, XXIII, 492.

85. Ibid, 435–37, 441–43, 447–55, 471–73, 504–10.

86. Ibid, XXV, 214, 237–38, 245; XXVII, 41–47, 62, 114–18, 121, 125–26. See Jordan, *Foundations of Representative Government*, 223–24.

87. Chancery Court Proceedings, IR #5, 820–945, 986–1033.

88. *Maryland Gazette*, 12 March, 1752.

89. Compare here Richmond County, Virginia, where Gwenda Morgan finds a rising tolerance for violations of social order beginning in the 1740s. Gwenda Morgan, "The Hegemony of the Law: Richmond County, Virginia, 1692–1776," (unpublished Ph.D., Johns Hopkins, 1980).

CHAPTER 7

The Development of Provincial Consciousness

The Formation of Elite Identity

By the mid-eighteenth century wealthy Creoles had replaced immigrant leaders as the people who dominated and gave definition to Maryland society. They fashioned social, economic, and political institutions and articulated the values and cultural imperatives that were to shape these institutions. How they defined themselves and how they were defined by others are therefore very important. What was the process of self-definition by wealthy Creoles? How did Creole consciousness grow over the course of the eighteenth century? What was the worldview of wealthy Marylanders? How did it alter over time?

For the first half-century after Maryland was colonized by white settlers, English immigrants seldom recognized that they had shared common values. Even among substantial planters and provincial legislators little sense of a shared identity existed.[1] Marylanders were concerned with clearing the land, establishing plantations, and attaining wealth. If all went well, as it seldom did, an emigrant could return home to England and become reestablished in a better situation within English society. Social development in the region came about slowly and with a minimum of social design. Not surprisingly, men and women were not much given to introspection. Even though they were not in England, they remained Englishmen, who looked to England both for solutions to their problems and for approved models of behavior. They made little attempt to justify their conduct and their society in response to critical comments from Britain, preferring instead to emphasize those aspects of their new environment that would be most appealing to potential emigrants. The most notable inducements for emigrants, in colonial eyes, were the richness of the land and the grand prospects for prosperity and social mobility this richness offered. English America quickly "lost its allure as a field for social experiments" but instead "acquired a growing reputation as an arena for the pursuit of individual betterment."[2]

In particular, early colonists made little effort to glorify their local leaders and native political and social institutions. Immigrant critiques of the inadequacies of the Chesapeake are revealing insofar as they include no defenses of the area's cultural shortcomings. Nor do they attempt to dissociate elite members from general charges of colonial provincialism, boorishness, and incompetence.[3] Immigrant leaders realized that attempts to equate the Maryland elite with the English gentry would have been treated with scorn not only by Englishmen who considered all Chesapeake colonists to be worthless moneygrubbers but also by other Marylanders aware of the social origins of the province's nascent elite. One in five legislators, for example, had originally arrived in Maryland as an indentured servant.[4] The idea that they were English gentlemen in a strange setting was laughable. Not only were their social origins questionable and their political skills debatable, early members of the political and economic elite did not enjoy a standard of living remotely approaching that of a contemporary English gentleman. Wealthy families lived in very spartan conditions without many luxuries and, indeed, without many seeming necessities.[5]

Only with the emergence of a distinctive social and political elite in the late seventeenth century can we discern the beginnings of any consciousness among Creoles that as Marylanders they were in some ways different from other Britons. Two factors account for the beginnings of elite self-definition. First, an increase in the number of women in the province and a decrease in servant immigration resulted in a largely native-born population in the Chesapeake, even though mortality rates remained high.[6] Moreover, even though the majority of wealthy men were immigrants until the beginnings of the eighteenth century, most were long-term residents. Apart from Edward Boothby, who resided in the colony for 13 years before his death in 1698, all other wealthy men who were both immigrants and legislators lived in Maryland for at least 20 years before their death. Several had lived in Maryland for over 40 years. Men who were either long-term residents or natives could hardly perceive themselves as Englishmen temporarily away from the motherland.

Second, elite identity was shaped by the introduction of chattel slavery into the region. The introduction of slavery concentrated wealth into the hands of those few men able to purchase slaves. Soon the men who owned slaves became a distinctive class in whom most of the province's economic and political power resided. The introduction of slavery gave slave owners the money and the leisure time to transform themselves and their environment into a society more recognizably British. Yet the advent of slavery, while facilitating the restructuring of Chesapeake society along more British lines, made the American South a different place from Britain. Patterns of power and social conditions were radically altered by the importation of an alien race suborned by force to remain subservient. Try as they might, aspiring elite members attempting to ape English manners and English society only imperfectly transformed their society into a replica of England and themselves into English gentlemen because the foundations of their power rested on a system that existed only in rudimentary form in the mother country.[7]

In any case, the leading men of the province in the late seventeenth century hardly attempted to become English gentlemen. Unfortunately, this generation left few written records that reveal their attitudes and ideological orientations. But we can speculate about their motivations from their economic behavior and political actions. First, as ambitious, risk-taking entrepreneurs they were consumed by the desire to accumulate wealth. They used surplus profits to buy new slaves or additional land rather than consumer goods. What is remarkable about the late seventeenth-century Maryland elite is the simplicity of their life-style. Economic prosperity meant that families could afford to buy more and somewhat better basic amenities: plain furniture and simple tableware, a greater variety of cooking utensils, good beds, and decent linens.[8] Few wealthy men in the late seventeenth and early eighteenth centuries acquired many luxuries, even when they could afford to do so. Robert Beverley II, one of the leading planters of Virginia, for example, and one of the first Chesapeake gentlemen "to redefine rusticity from a provincial weakness into an American virtue" had his life-style described thus by a foreigner in 1715: "This man lives well; but though rich, he has nothing but what is necessary. . . . He lives upon the product of his land."[9] The only luxury goods that wealthy men who died before 1708 possessed were books, usually few in number and limited in range. Other luxury items, such as china services, fine furniture, clocks, and even sanitary implements such as chamber pots and close stools, were rare. Wealthy men invested heavily in silver objects or "plate," but such goods were not just items of conspicuous consumption but forms of liquid savings in a society in which money was scarce and there were no banks.[10]

The inventory of John Hammond, major general of the Western Shore and a councilor, illustrates how simply even the most prominent Marylanders lived in this period. Hammond left an estate of £1,920.11 of which 10 percent was personal goods. Hammond lived well but very simply. He owned no china, nor any furniture made from good woods such as walnut or mahogany. He had neither a timepiece, nor jewelery, nor even a chamber pot. The only luxury items he owned were a collection of books, some drinking glasses, ivory handled cutlery, and a small amount of silver plate valued at £31.88. A yeoman visiting his modest house may have been impressed by Hammond's status, access to political power, and ownership of 21 slaves and 2,609 acres of land, but he would not have been overawed by the quality of his possessions. A visitor from England would have been appalled at the rude simplicity in which one of the leading citizens of the colony lived and would have found it difficult to conceive of such a man as a talented and cultivated leader of society, let alone as a colonial variant of the English gentry class. To some extent, the primitive conditions in which even wealthy men lived fuelled doubts about colonial abilities.[11]

Wealthy men in the late seventeenth century seldom displayed the essential qualities of gentlemen. Contrary to contemporary English definitions of gentility that saw gentlemen as people removed from the taint of commerce, wealthy Marylanders gloried in mercantile pursuits.[12] Moreover, many wealthy men failed to act in well-educated, well-mannered ways. Thomas Macnemara, for example, furnished an example of how far from the idealized norm some wealthy men were in the late seventeenth and early eighteenth centuries. He arrived in 1703 as a penniless indentured servant but with training in the law in his native Ireland. He soon blazed a notorious path in Maryland before dying in 1719 with an estate of £1,024.06. His ascent, however, was in the style of Al Capone. He was closely connected with the powerful Carroll interest in Maryland, principally because he had raped and then married the niece of Charles Carroll the Settler. Entering the law, he soon became notorious for a variety of personal offenses, including the rape of a woman in the Calvert County courthouse, indictments for biting off a boy's ear, sodomy, and murder, for all of which he somehow avoided not only the gallows but also imprisonment. He abused judges, defended the most disreputable elements of society, and extorted outrageous fees from his clients. He was the bane of the local establishment and well merited the description that some hand scrawled across his will, "a most Troublesome and Seditious Person." Yet despite assiduous attempts by the more respectable members of the bench, the legislature, and the governor to discipline him, Macnemara managed to escape punishment, continued to prosper in his legal practice, and attained provincial office, being clerk of the Lower House from 1714 to 1716 and naval officer of the Patuxtent from 1717 to 1720. His son became mayor of Annapolis in the mid-eighteenth century.[13]

Every elite has men like Macnemara who deviate from accepted behavior, although a more self-confident and secure elite might have been able to exclude Macnemara from membership in its ranks. But even the more respectable members of the first Creole generation were not like English gentlemen. William Byrd I and William Fitzhugh from Virginia left comparatively abundant records of their attitudes and preoccupations and are good examples of how far removed from the English gentry even the upper ranks of the Chesapeake elite were in the late seventeenth century.[14] Men of middle-class origins, intensely ambitious, they always had an eye on the main chance and succeeded in taking advantage of colonial opportunities. But neither lived in splendor nor, more importantly, displayed in their writings any interest in explaining to themselves or to others what they were trying to do in the Chesapeake. Consumed by the desire to get ahead materially, they made no effort to cultivate genteel graces.

Their generation was the first to challenge British political and cultural dominance in the region. In Maryland, the political challenge came between 1689 and 1692 when the Lower House of Assembly enhanced its power at the expense of the Catholic proprietor. The "revolution of government" was directed not against British authority per se but against an overpowerful executive and against the exclusion of the growing and predominantly Protestant local elite from prominent positions within the government.[15] Conservative men who desired no social changes but who wished to have their increasing wealth and local prominence recognized by the imperial authorities led the "revolution." Henceforth, the provincial Creole elite in Maryland was firmly in control of the local power structures and continually and successfully pressed to increase their powers.[16]

The growth of political consciousness within the Maryland elite during the late seventeenth and early eighteenth centuries was accompanied by the first, tentative replies by Marylanders to English criticisms of their rudimentary institutions and social system. In the main, responses to English criticism took two forms. Many colonials accepted provincial inadequacies with stoical resignation and continued to emphasize the natural advantages that their country provided ambitious immigrants.[17] Other colonists reacted to criticisms of their society defensively and argued that what Englishmen took to be defects were in fact virtues, the "virtues of simplicity" opposed to the luxury and corruption of the mother country.[18]

The most interesting counterattack on English assumptions was made by Ebeneezer Cooke in *The Sotweed Factor*, a satirical poem published in 1708. At first glance, its description of drunken planters, fighting lawyers, and rustic boors in late seventeenth-century Maryland seems to be yet another satirical gibe by an Englishman at colonial pretensions, similar to the scabrous works of the Grub-Street scribbler, Ned Ward.[19] But a closer reading reveals that the poem was a subtle mocking of preconceived English attitudes about the Chesapeake. Like Robert Beverley's

History of Virginia (1705), *The Sotweed Factor* ridicules those Englishmen who assumed that America was a wilderness populated by hostile Indians and barbarous, uncultivated Creoles. Cooke was satirizing the greenhorn, not the colonial, with a tongue-in-cheek laugh at the inability of Englishmen to cope with the Maryland environment and at their preconceived notions about provincial deficiencies. On the contrary, Cooke argued, Maryland was not uncivilized.[20] When he commented that "A reverend Judge, who to the shame of all the Bench, cou'd write his Name" and added, solemnly, that very few J.P.s in Maryland could write or read, Cooke was making a burlesque on the English reader who thought that all Americans were illiterate barbarians. Cooke exaggerates the crudeness of provincial manners to such a degree that it is clear that he is satirizing anyone gullible enough to believe such nonsense. Moreover, by portraying his English antihero as an easily deceived city slicker who cannot appreciate the hospitality of his hosts and who is quickly cheated out of his money by a "Quaker . . . a Pious Conscientious Rogue," Cooke was arguing for the superiority of the American over the supercilious and naive English immigrant.[21]

But for all the posturing by Creoles that they really were not uncultivated, that the Chesapeake was sophisticated and cosmopolitan, and that Maryland society possessed certain advantages, noticeably virtuous simplicity, over metropolitan decadence, elite members remained provincials, painfully aware of "a sense of inferiority" that pervaded their culture.[22] The metropolis may have been decadent but it provided models of behavior and a cultural superiority that provincials could only envy and that the richer colonials attempted to emulate. The thrusting, ambitious, middle-class merchant-planters who rose to prominence in the late seventeenth century may not have been gentlemen themselves but they were anxious that their children would have the advantages of gentility. The next generation, the first or second generation born in the colony, would become assimilated to the model of the English gentry and would be able "to perpetuate in the colonies the way of living, privileges and standards of behavior associated with the British upper classes."[23]

To this end, the richest planters and merchants sent their sons to English public schools and less rich men sent their sons to colonial imitations of such schools. They wanted their sons to acquire the marks of gentlemen, enabling them to fulfill their rightful positions as the leaders of colonial society. The defining qualities of gentility are elusive but certain basic elements can be isolated. To a certain extent, being a gentleman resided in having the material possessions and authority in society that could be seen as the peculiar prerequisites of being a gentleman. In addition, a gentleman needed to have an extensive if not deep education in the classics and in the gentlemanly arts of dancing, fencing, riding, and good conversation. Through such an education, an aspirant to gentlemanly status learned good manners, courteous behavior, and, most importantly, developed habits of moderation, temperance, and self-control, enabling him to keep his passions under control and thus become a worthwhile citizen, wise magistrate, and humane and just master.[24]

Fathers had high expectations for their sons when sending them away from home to achieve gentlemanly graces. Elite sons were placed under terrible psychological burdens in this process.[25] Uprooted at a young age from their families and sent to England where they were perpetually reminded of their colonial status and yet where they were expected to be transformed into perfect English gentlemen, Creoles were beset by cultural contradictions. They were torn between their loyalty to their native land, a land in which much of their identity was formed, and their desire to reject the less appealing and more provincial aspects of that culture and assimilate themselves to English genteel culture—a culture that doubted and ridiculed their claims to legitimacy. Not surprisingly, early eighteenth-century Creoles were deeply ambivalent about both the parent culture and its colonial variants.[26]

The little advice they received from their fathers as to what models of behavior they should adopt increased their cultural ambivalence. The counsel that Thomas Bordley, councilor and attorney general of Maryland, gave to his sons at school in London, is revealing. On the one hand, Bordley urged his sons to cultivate the gentry ideal. They should "improve" themselves and attend to their school exercises "with attention, application and Diligence, that you may receive applause from Others, be a Pleasure to me, and by Heavens Blessing on you, which you are constantly to pray for, become both Good and Great yourself"[27] Because the elder Bordley was far distant, the "applause of others" was of paramount importance. To gain that applause meant becoming English gentlemen and thus rejecting their "barbaric" Maryland inheritance. Yet they were also urged by their father to remain loyal to their colonial roots and not "to forget Your Affection to this your Country, which may, perhaps, in time, want your Endeavours to Support its Rights, as well as it has wanted the Endeavours of others" and by no means to "Suffer your Affections to cool towards this your place of Birth to which you owe a Duty."[28]

Some Creoles may have been able to reconcile these two contradictory duties. Many could not. They were neither comfortable as colonials abroad nor as English gentlemen in a provincial wasteland. As Kenneth Lockridge's portrait of William Byrd reveals, the psychological costs attendant upon the attainment of gentility could be immense. Byrd was as socially secure in Virginia as it was possible to be in the early eighteenth century, assured of high political office and very rich. Yet the lure of the metropolis was overwhelming. His ambitions could be satisfied only by being accepted there as the equal of an English gentleman. He hungered after English political offices and aspired to marry a rich heiress. He failed miserably at each ambition. Despite his wealth, his conventional gentleman's behavior, and his pretensions to literary achievement, England never accepted him. Byrd remained a colonial, and thus by definition an inferior.[29]

If Byrd could not assimilate himself into English society, no one else in the early eighteenth-century Chesapeake could. Yet English rejection of colonial pretensions did not prevent native-born Marylanders and Virginians from attempting to emulate the standards of the metropolitan center. Chesapeake colonists had to some extent always attempted to recreate British political, social, and economic institutions in their own society. But this "mimetic impulse" increased after the turn of the century.[30] Social replication of metropolitan behavior occurred not only in the public sphere but also shaped private life. In particular, newly affluent elite members were no longer content to live in the primitive simplicity of their fathers but hankered after the accoutrements of gentility, such as expensive consumer goods.[31]

Major shifts in the acquisition of material goods occurred for the first time between 1713 and 1720, partly because improved prices for tobacco freed up capital, partly because manufacturers were again plentiful in the province after a period of shortages due to European wars, partly because luxury, nonessential goods started to be in demand, and partly because native-born wealthy men did not need to invest as much as their forebears into capital goods for the development of plantations and thus had more disposable income available for other goods.[32] The increase in the range of consumer goods purchased by elite members can be seen in elite inventories. From the second decade of the eighteenth century, luxury goods such as china, specialized furniture, and items associated with the tea ceremony began to appear. Many of these goods were related to the consumption or presentation of food. The elite used more ceremony when dining, a sure indication that they were adopting genteel manners. Evidence of this is provided by the increasing amount of china and tea ware owned by the elite over time. In the late seventeenth century china and tea services were virtually nonexistent in Maryland. They began to appear in elite inventories in the 1720s, but only a minority of elite members owned them. Between the first two decades of the eighteenth century and the next two decades, the percentage of elite members having a tea service nearly doubled, while the percentage having china pieces increased four and a half-fold.[33]

Still, by English standards, wealthy Marylanders did not live well, and some consumer items were noticeable by their absence in the first half of the eighteenth century. Only 10 elite members dying before 1742 and only Samuel Chew of men dying before 1726 owned a riding chaise or carriage. Few elite members owned an extensive collection of specialized beverage glasses, candelabra, or more than one piece of fine furniture. Nevertheless, the differences between the seventeenth century and the early to mid-eighteenth century in elite life-styles are significant. No longer were elite members content to put up with frontier conditions. They wished to display their growing affluence in visible form. In so doing, the Maryland elite attempted to express their position in colonial society and differentiate themselves from poorer groups.

In addition, the elite strove to emulate an ideal of gentility many of them had scorned less than a generation earlier. They were not only signifying their participation in an Anglo-American cultural system,[34] they were asserting that they were the potential equals of English gentlemen. Hugh Jones's description of Williamsburg in 1720 was indicative of new beliefs about the sophistication of Chesapeake culture. Williamsburg elite families, he stated, "live in the same neat manner, dress after the same modes and behave themselves exactly as the gentry in London. . . . The habits, life, customs, computations, etc, of the Virginians are much the same as about London, which they esteem their home."[35] Like Cooke, Jones was defensive about colonial society but, unlike Cooke, opted to emphasize the similarities in provincial society to implicitly accepted metropolitan standards rather than attempt to make colonial deficiencies into virtues.

Nevertheless, despite attempts by Creole gentlemen to transform themselves and their environment in accordance with English tastes, elite Marylanders remained significantly different from their English counterparts. In particular, they were not leisured English gentlemen but were active managers of plantations, intimately involved in every aspect of the production and marketing of their crops.[36] Many were still involved in merchandising in the first third of the eighteenth century.[37] Their emphasis on individualism and their attitudes to work indicate that the elite had values that later scholars have come to identify as essential components of the American character.[38] Consequently, their imitation of English genteel culture was not completely successful as they retained attitudes developed as part of settlement and creolization processes.[39] Englishmen could not accept Maryland and Virginia gentlemen as being their equals for the simple reason that in fundamental ways they and their society were different from the metropolitan models they were attempting to emulate.

Over time, the Maryland elite came to recognize, partly accept, and even welcome the fact that Maryland and Britain were not alike. Somewhat paradoxically, this development occurred at the very time Maryland was becoming more similar to its mother country. By the mid-eighteenth century, the older parts of the province had been settled for over a century. They were no longer frontier communities but were areas in which all available arable land had been claimed, cleared, and transformed into well-developed plantations. Maryland was an increasingly complex society with an array of both rural and urban services and amenities found also in provincial England. A century of settlement had also led to the elaboration and sophistication of indigenous and imported political, economic, and social institutions. Precedents and rules had become long established in representative assemblies and colonial legislators had successfully adopted English legislative practices and ideology. Socially, Maryland increasingly resembled England in wealth and social stratification. Affordable consumer goods flooded into the colony, especially after 1750, enabling elite Marylanders to achieve a standard of living more closely approximating that of England. The Maryland elite had also matured. By mid-century, many of the leaders of Maryland were third- or fourth-generation Marylanders. Their social position was assured. They were firmly in control of the judicial and legislative power structures of the colony. Yet Maryland remained appreciably different from Britain in appearance, social structure, and character. The most visible difference was the presence of large numbers of black slaves in the Chesapeake. Even apart from slavery, however, contemporaries were aware of considerable disparities between the two societies. This awareness can be seen in comments made both by Englishmen visiting Maryland and also by Marylanders resident in Britain.

Reverend Jonathan Boucher, later an influential loyalist, may be taken as typical of the former. Writing to a fellow minister in 1759, not long after arriving in the province, he praised the "Plenty and Abundance" of the country but expressed dismay at the "Manners and Conversation" of the gentlefolk to whom he was introduced. They were, he asserted, "almost in every Thing ye very opposite to my Taste." Admitting that Creoles were "of a livelier, readier wit than we in England," he bemoaned the fact that this "wit" was not employed in "laudable" pursuits but in "dressing and other Pleasures." Boucher could tolerate these foibles but objected to colonial forwardness and lack of gentlemanly restraint, complaining of "their forward obtrusion w[hich] subjects you to hear obscene Conceits and broad Expressions, and from this, there are times w[hen] no sex, no Rank, no Conduct can exempt you."[40] These complaints were strikingly similar to criticisms voiced earlier in the century and in the seventeenth century, charging colonials with boorish behavior. The increasing sophistication of the colonies had not eradicated provincial backwardness.

Colonials responded to such criticisms in a variety of ways.

Some replied defensively, claiming that America was indeed a civilized place with just cause to be compared to the mother country.[41] An influential minority, including what passed for the local intelligentsia, ignored such criticisms, being more concerned with establishing and refining an indigenous literary tradition than with the burdensome task of proving that Maryland was a cultured place. From mid-century onward, two antithetical tendencies can be discerned in Marylanders' attitudes to metropolitan condescension toward provincial cultural aspirations. On the one hand, Marylanders were especially proud of their British heritage, reveled in their position as members of a great empire, and attempted to imitate British cultural forms. At the same time, a separate process we can call the creolization of culture was gaining acceptance among the more sophisticated members of the Maryland social and cultural elite. The continuing development and refinement of Maryland society allowed them to increasingly accept the idea of the province as a cultivated society. Moreover, the growing population in the region, the increasing respectability of political institutions and native politicians, and the establishment of clubs and taverns where gentlemen could meet and discuss local events and intellectual controversies led to an increased interest in their own society. The founding of the colony's first newspaper, *The Maryland Gazette*, in 1738[42] intensified Creole identification with their native land. Gradually, wealthy Marylanders accepted that Chesapeake elite members were not and were never going to be English gentlemen. Consequently, a new model of behavior, fusing elements of English genteel culture with colonial genteel variations on that English standard, had to be developed as an idealized norm to which colonial elite members could aspire. The mimetic impulses of provincials underwent subtle shifts in the mid-eighteenth century from simple imitation to mostly unconscious but creative selection and adaptation of the metropolitan forms most suited to colonial existence.[43]

The mid-eighteenth-century elite was much more secure about its abilities and genteel pretensions than had been its predecessor half a century earlier. Most elite members had grown up not in the frontier conditions of the seventeenth century but in the much less crude environment of the early eighteenth century. These changing social conditions permitted a much easier internalization of genteel values. The introduction of more elaborate cooking utensils and specialized luxury goods for ceremonial eating during the first third of the eighteenth century familiarized elite members with the highly formalized behavior associated with dining and accustomed them to regularized and cultivated forms of social intercourse that the rituals of genteel dining engendered.[44] The trend toward gentility that began in the early eighteenth century continued throughout the century. Changes both in the demand and the supply of consumer goods expanded the number of products available on the colonial market and extended the ability of consumers to purchase such goods. The shift to a native-born population, many of whom had inherited household goods from their parents, freed resources to acquire more luxury goods. Better communications with England also kept wealthy Marylanders in touch with developments in fashion in Britain. Increasing settlement and adoption of genteel manners encouraged Marylanders to buy goods that emphasized "elegance as well as comfort."[45] Increases in the output and the variety of new consumer goods in England expanded the range of goods available on the colonial market and decreased the prices of merchandise. Finally, craftsmen and merchants arrived in comparatively large numbers to Maryland. Their arrival allowed for the quicker infusion of English tastes and English fashions into the province to be adopted by the genteel and for the development of creolized variants of English fashion. It was not until the arrival of master craftsmen in the province that wealthy Marylanders could build the Georgian structures that became such a prominent feature of the colony's capital, Annapolis.[46]

The result of the flood of consumer products into the Chesapeake after 1730 was that the higher reaches of Maryland society acquired most of the trappings of gentility. The inventories of elite members dying after 1750 contained a wide assortment of consumer goods that had previously been considered luxuries but that were now commonplace in elite households: china, specialized beverage glasses, and fine dining utensils. Most wealthy Marylanders also owned at least one and usually several items of furniture made from expensive woods such as black walnut, oak, or mahogany. In addition, wealthy men commonly owned some items previously confined to the very richest men in Maryland, such as gaming tables and riding chaises.

By the latter half of the eighteenth century, most wealthy Marylanders had acquired all the goods available on a limited colonial market that were needed for a genteel life-style. Moreover, these goods were purchased at lesser cost than had been previously possible, with the percentage of estates tied up in personal goods decreasing from 13 percent to 10 percent between the first two cohorts and the last cohort. At the same time, as has been detailed, wealthy Marylanders increasingly became a landed rather than a mixed landed and mercantile class. As such, they approximated more closely the occupational characteristics of the English landed classes: an agrarian elite with a common identity, a common outlook, and similar concerns and interests.

The mid-eighteenth-century elite lived in some considerable style not only in their private dwellings but also in the public arena. The Chesapeake elite had previously found an outlet for its need to mingle with other members of its class only in constant visits between plantations.[47] As the colony prospered, elite numbers expanded. As Annapolis and then Baltimore developed into sizable urban centers (at least by Chesapeake standards), wealthy Marylanders found new and better ways to socialize. By the 1740s genteel Marylanders could meet with other genteel people with similar interests in local taverns, coffee shops, and literary clubs. Moreover, social activities such as balls and dinners were increasingly popular. The solitude of life on the plantation was alleviated by such activities.

Marylanders took the emergence of environments in which cultivated people could meet and display their wit, grace, and good manners as evidence that Maryland was increasingly a civilized and urbane society. Marylanders of the mid-eighteenth century demonstrated a sophistication to which previous generations only aspired. Visitors to the province were often favorably impressed by the unexpected presence of polite society in the region. William Black, visiting the colony from Scotland, for example, described with gusto and apparent surprise a dinner to which he was invited that had "a Table in the most Splendent manner set out with a Great Variety of Dishes, all served in the most Elegant way," and then a following ball where he noted the "very Splendent Appearance" of Maryland women who were "very Agreeable."[48]

Black's praise would have been especially welcome to Maryland ears because residents of the Chesapeake prided themselves on being a hospitable and sociable people. That hospitality was visibly displayed both in an abundantly provisioned table and in their grace on a dance floor. Their conception of hospitality owed less to Christian notions of charity and selflessness than to secular values of competitive self-display, personal assertion, and mutual friendship among equals. Dinners and dances were ideal venues in which self-confident elite members could confirm their public claims that they were gentlemen through demonstrations of their acquisition of genteel manners and where through public admiration of their expensive victuals at dinner and gaudy clothes at balls they could force acknowledgment of their wealth and status. The devotion of wealthy Marylanders to learning the elaborate household rituals associated with the drinking of tea and the seriousness with which they approached dancing, compelling their children to learn to dance under the direction of professional dancing teachers until it could be boasted that there was not a bad dancer in government, is evidence of their desire to be gentlemen and ladies.[49]

Although some Marylanders regarded with regret the passing of rural simplicity and viewed with alarm the increasing sophistication and luxury in society, other elite Marylanders welcomed the progress Maryland had made over half a century. They had no desire to return to less civilized days and were repelled by evidences of vulgarity and primitivism. The classic expressions of cultivated disdain of frontier society are the histories written by William Byrd II in the 1730s about the history of the dividing line between North Carolina and Virginia[50] but Maryland had a counterpart to Byrd in Alexander Hamilton, an Edinburgh-educated physician and Annapolis resident who was the leading Maryland literary figure of his day.[51]

Like Ebenezer Cooke, Hamilton was an emigrant who quickly acculturated himself to life in the new province. Unlike Cooke, Hamilton emphasized the urbaneness of Maryland, or at least of Annapolis, society and regarded with approbation the growing sophistication of mid-eighteenth-century Marylanders. His satires illustrate his satisfaction with the progress Maryland had made since the turn of the century and mocked, principally for the benefit of cultivated Marylanders, those who worried about the corrupting effects of the conveniences and luxuries of progress.[52]

He signaled his impatience with writers who glorified stoic primitivism and who refused to acknowledge the benefits of "civilization" in all of his works.[53] A principal example is his humorous description in his *Itinerarium* of an "elegant meal" he took with an elderly couple that "desired me to eat with them." Hamilton refused, principally on aesthetic and hygienic grounds because their food "was in a dirty, deep, wooden dish which they evacuated with their hands, cramming down skins, scales and all. They used neither knife, fork, spoon, plate or napkin because, I suppose, they had none to use." Aware of the literary vogue praising pastoral scenes of rural innocence, Hamilton parodied such idealist notions in his "analysis" of the situation in which he found himself. "I looked upon this," he stated, tongue firmly in cheek, "as a picture of that primitive simplicity practised by our forefathers long before the mechanic arts had supplied them with instruments for the luxury and elegance of life."[54] Hamilton found ridiculous any attempts willingly to forego "the luxury and elegance of life." In the old battle between ancients and moderns, he was squarely on the side of the moderns, applauding the modern age against its more primitive predecessors.[55] Further, he was confident enough of his own cultivated persona to write without fearing an attack about the appropriateness of a colonial daring to claim cultural superiority over others. Hamilton did not suffer any of the usual cultural apologetics that colonials customarily had when discussing any of their own or their society's shortcomings.

A lessening of awe toward metropolitan society and values signaled how the Maryland elite had culturally matured. In the early eighteenth century, elite Marylanders were firmly convinced of the superiority of England and of London in all things. Stephen Bordley, for example, remonstrated to his mother when she expressed a desire to see him back in Maryland that he felt he needed to be in England, for only there could he learn his chosen profession of law. "Where," he asked, "can [the law] better be learnt than in this nation? 'tis true, there have been many brot [sic] up to it in Maryland, but what are they to English lawyers? I take Mr Dulany to be the best now remaining there, and he is not to be compared to many here in England."[56] Colonials, clearly, were second-rate.

By mid-century, however, Marylanders resident in England were not so sure whether London society was as wonderful and Englishmen as superior to colonials as they had once believed. Most were still delighted by the quantity and variety of genteel amusements possible and regaled their friends at home with descriptions of concerts and plays and tales of fashionable society.[57] But they were critical of what they conceived of as the vanities of metropolitan life and hankered to return to their homeland. The wife of Charles Carroll, the Barrister, for example, preferred "ye domestic amusements of Maryland to ye vanities of St. James," presumably because, as Charles Carroll of Carrollton pointed out in his reply to the couple, "the dissipation, ambition and vanity of ye great are mortal enemies to sincerity, ye source and basis of friendship."[58] Certainly some Marylanders were irritated by what they perceived as English condescension and ignorance of the civilities the province had achieved. Having seen England, Maryland did not seem as backward to expatriates as they might have thought before departure, and many ex-Marylanders yearned for home. Daniel Dulany, Jr., in disgust, wrote to a friend in Pennsylvania in 1755 at the end of the Seven Years' War that "Perhaps in less than a century, the ministers may know that we inhabit part of a vast continent, and the rural gentry hear that we are not all black, that we live in houses, speak English, wear clothes, and have some faint notions of Christianity."[59] James Anderson from Queen Anne's admitted that he wished to return home, realizing he had "a stronger attachment to the Country than I imagin'd and I should really be uneasy if I had no prospect of ever returning."[60]

All of these sentiments illustrate that the Maryland elite were increasingly more certain of their position in Maryland society and of their genteel status. They turned their attention away from the slavish imitation of English manners toward an examination of what their own society represented and how that society could be improved. In part this development reflected the success of the elite in anglicizing their province. Much elite criticism of their society such as denunciations of luxury and irreligious behavior were not peculiar to themselves but were transatlantic concerns shared by many Englishmen. Yet self-criticism also involved a recognition that Maryland was different from the mother country, and that they needed to deal with the problems of their society themselves.

Not surprisingly, in a period of material affluence, the principal weakness of Maryland society seemed to many to be spiritual. In their headlong pursuit of Mammon, Marylanders appeared to have become morally bankrupt. By the 1750s it was clear to a few Anglican ministers, notably the Reverend Thomas Bacon and the Reverend Thomas Cradock, that the challenge to established religion and to the maintenance of traditional social order was a serious issue. Despite the evident material affluence of the leading citizens within Maryland, the province, Bacon and Cradock believed, faced a spiritual malaise.[61] When they sought explanations for the lack of religious fervor in the country, they blamed neither blacks nor slavery as morally corrupting[62] nor lamented the failings of poor whites and servants, although Cradock did bemoan the "Ignorance and Immorality that prevails among the *meaner* [sort]."[63] Nor did they focus on the challenge posed by Methodism and itinerant preachers. The problems of the Anglican Church lay within the Church itself. It was afflicted by unworthy members of the priesthood, the lack of Episcopal supervision, and, especially, by the indifference and deism of wealthy planters, merchants, and professionals.

In a sermon preached in Annapolis before an audience including most of the prominent politicians in the province, Cradock noted that the real enemies of the Church were to be found in that "set of men" who "are of no Religion at all, and make a jest of the Christian Scheme and Ordinances" and who "laugh at the *Bible* as fit only for the amusement of old Women and Children."[64] Cradock lamented the elite's disillusionment with traditional religion and their dalliances with deism, rationalism, and atheism, as "the Vulgar are influenced most by Example."[65] Thomas Bacon complained to the Secretary of the Society for the Propagation of the Gospel that deism was "rampant" in Maryland. He was concerned that a notable rationalist book such as Mathew Tindal's *Christianity as Old as the Creation* could be found "in most Houses where anybody reads" and deplored the influence of radical Whig tracts such as Trenchard and Gordons' *Independent Whig*.[66] Evidence of the distaste for established religion by the educated in mid-eighteenth-century Maryland can be seen in the acid comment of Henry Callister, a Talbot County factor, that "I shall not endeavor to enforce the necessity of propagating Truth as well as Religion in this Infant Country, for in my opinion they are two distinct things."[67] Callister confirmed his radical credentials in religion so firmly that elite member and fellow deist Robert Morris, the father of the Revolutionary financier, summoned him at his deathbed to read to him from Plato's *Phaedo*.[68]

Dissenters and the evangelical counterculture also posed a challenge to defenders of established religion.[69] Not all dissenters, moreover, came from the lower orders. The moving narrative of James Rigbie, written in the fortieth year of his life, in 1760, reveals why the son of an elite member turned from normal genteel pursuits such as "music, dancing and gambling" and resigned a military commission and the possibility of a promising military career after hearing George Whitfield and New Light Presbyterians preach. It also provides an insight into the reactions of Rigbie's genteel friends to his conversion. Rigbie recalled how soon after his first appearance as a Quaker minister, an old companion, James Hollyday II, a member of one of the wealthiest and most powerful Eastern Shore families, came to visit him to see if, indeed, Rigbie "had become a fool and turned Quaker." Entering his house "with an air of gentility" while a Quaker meeting was taking place, Holliday first expressed amazement that Rigbie had indeed become a Quaker and then, "using vile, extravagant expressions cursed me from head to foot, viewing my plain appearance and behavior."[70]

Although evangelicals recruited most of their adherents from the ranks of poor planters, artisans, and slaves, the occasional convert from the ranks of the elite caused great consternation. Undoubtedly the greatest conquest evangelicals made in the eighteenth-century Chesapeake was Robert Carter of Nomini Hall, the grandson of Robert "King" Carter, the richest Virginian of his generation, and the husband of Frances Ann Tasker, the daughter of Benjamin Tasker, Sr., the president of the council of Maryland. Carter's manumission of his more than 500 slaves justified elite revulsion against wealthy evangelicals. In a social system that depended on the forced subjugation of black slaves, Carter's freeing slaves from one of the largest slaveholdings in the Chesapeake was an act of class betrayal amounting almost to treason. Moreover, it was an attempt to deprive his children of a major part of their inheritance. If evangelicalism could make a man substitute individual interests and aspirations for the responsibilities owed to class and family, it was clearly opposed to most of the values conservatives such as Cradock held dear.

One reason why men such as James Rigbie and Robert Carter left the established Church and sought to find meaning in their lives through revivalism was that they rebelled against the self-indulgence increasingly characteristic of genteel men and women in the eighteenth century Chesapeake, especially among people attracted to new models of elite sociability. Rigbie speaks feelingly of how his initial youthful acceptance of the easy values of his parents led to such "a growing thirst ... in my mind for worldly-pleasure and the gratification of my corrupt passions in gradual advances, so that I became almost proficient in wickedness."[71] Cradock also attacked elite Marylanders for their headlong pursuit of pleasure. To Cradock, such pursuit of pleasure led to moral bankruptcy, to irreligion and deism, and inexorably to the breakdown of the ideal society. Believing in the organicism of the social as well as the natural world, he and other social conservatives argued that in return for the privileges of the world afforded the genteel, the elite needed to fulfill their duties and obligations to the family, the community, and the world at large. In particular, they needed to be an example to the "Vulgar." Yet many of the elite neglected this principal obligation and were not punished for their transgressions. Conspicuous consumption, a predilection for luxury, and excessive gambling on horses and cards were manifestations of elite derelictions of duty. Attacks on luxury, it should be emphasized, were not just a colonial preoccupation but were common on both sides of the Atlantic.[72] The fulminations of Chesapeake commentators against extravagance and consequent indebtedness were another example of colonists' increasing participation in transatlantic ideological debates. The activities of a few conspicuous reprobates such as William Byrd III, who destroyed his handsome inheritance through gambling and extravagance on an hitherto unimagined scale, provided frightening examples of the results of dissolution, indigence, and neglect of duty.[73] Display and liberality were accepted qualities of a gentleman and could legitimately include overt self-assertion but the other guiding principle of genteel behavior, the ideal of moderation, seemed to some to be conspicuously absent in the mid-eighteenth-century Chesapeake.

In Maryland, Cradock was the leading critic of social behavior, both in his sermons and his satirical verse.[74] Cradock utilized the popular literary genre of the Latin pastoral as a medium for social comment. The pastoral poem was usually employed to contrast Arcadian simplicity to urban corruption but Cradock turned this form on its head, describing the countryside and the rural society within which he lived as neither tranquil nor idyllic but a haven for vice and immorality in which blasphemy, cruelty, greed, drunkenness, and contempt for religion and wanton display untempered by moderation flourished unchecked. Cradock's "Maryland Eclogues" were a considerable advance on Cooke's *Sotweed Factor*, at least in illustrating the growing cultural confidence of the province. Whereas Cooke satirized English preconceptions of Maryland for an audience concerned about how the English metropolitan center viewed them and was intent on showing that the colony was not a provincial backwater, Cradock accepted that the province had achieved a certain measure of civilization and decried the spiritual consequences of such civilization.

Cradock's vituperations against Marylanders' excess showed that he realized that Marylanders had a distinct identity that had both admirable and deplorable features. Maryland writers had advanced to the point that they could disagree about the character of colonial society and about the future of Maryland. Although these disagreements mimicked in a provincial center contemporaneous debates in Britain between "moderns" and "ancients," their imitativeness was not their primary significance. The quality of local literature may have been mediocre and competing visions of Maryland's future still rudimentary and tentative, relying on metropolitan models for any cogency they did possess. But that there were competing visions and that the aspiring intellectuals of Maryland society were attempting to create an indigenous culture with local meanings suggest that provincial consciousness had progressed considerably from the empty and imitative bravura of the early eighteenth century.

It would be going too far to claim that by the last tumultuous decade of Maryland's existence as a colony the elite had achieved cultural independence from the mother country. Generally wealthy Marylanders prided themselves on being Britons and evaluated the quality of colonial life on how closely it approximated British standards. But some observers were increasingly willing to judge Maryland society from a provincial rather than from a metropolitan perspective. The quest for gentility—a quest that consumed the attention of wealthy gentlemen after the late seventeenth century—was a key ingredient in these important reformulations of provincial identity. By the middle of the eighteenth century, wealthy Marylanders were reasonably secure in their understanding of themselves as gentlemen who followed the rulings of a genteel ethos and who conducted themselves with propriety and taste. They saw themselves as deserving members of the British gentry and resented metropolitan condescension. They were even secure enough in their gentility for some of the third- or fourth-generation elite members, such as William Byrd III and Robert Wormeley Carter, to display their class position through fast living.[75]

The successful pursuit of gentility by wealthy gentlemen brought its own tensions and contradictions. A love of beautiful things could easily turn into an unhealthy materialism, ostentation, and love of luxury, as with Byrd and Carter. It also did not reduce wealthy Marylanders' dependence on metropolitan authority. Indeed, the pursuit of gentility was a deeply conservative impulse that relied on distant metropolitan arbiters for a definition of what was proper and tasteful. As Rozbicki notes "for most of the eighteenth century, English high culture remained the exclusive consecrating agency of taste and style for the colonial gentry, and conversely, English authors judged provincial culture strictly by the degree to which it conformed to these norms."[76] Nevertheless, by the third quarter of the eighteenth century colonial gentlemen, though still keenly conscious of the need to fit into metropolitan models of taste and propriety, had developed effective mechanisms to counter metropolitan condescension. They were able to follow a strategy employed by British critics of metropolitan moral degradations since the turn of the eighteenth century in turning metropolitan criticism in on itself by claiming for the provinces superior virtues to metropolitan corruption.[77]

Finally, gentility was always problematic because the boundaries between genteel and common were so porous, especially in America where some of the traditional means of demarcating between social ranks—birth and lineage, in particular—were largely absent. Gentility was useful in a socially homogeneous society with a limited cultural and social hierarchy in validating the right of the well bred (if not well-born) to social superiority. But it was extremely difficult to regulate the ranks of the aspiring genteel. Gentility was thus both exclusive—it kept out those whose behavior did not meet approved standards—and also egalitarian— it allowed in anyone, whatever his origin, who behaved as a gentleman ought to behave. In Maryland, gentility rested almost entirely on manners and was closer to respectability—the assertion of a person's moral worth as an individual, demonstrated primarily by his behavior—than to what Europeans recognized gentility to be. Consequently, the boundary between vulgar and refined was constantly being crossed, and the boundary itself had to be constantly redrawn in order to accommodate expanding expectations of what the genteel life should be.[78]

But the disadvantages of gentility as an ethos were not sufficient to detract from its advantages, which Rozbicki considers to be four-fold. First, it gave the elite cultural legitimacy and validated its social power. Second, it provided wealthy Marylanders with a new group identity. Third, it provided stability in a fluid society, allowing the elite to steer a careful course between the Scylla of undue openness to arrivistes, who might diminish elite authority, and the Charbydis of excessive exclusiveness, which might breed resentment among those excluded. Finally, gentility allowed individual elite members a means of improving themselves, gaining politeness, and achieving what Richard Bushman calls beautification, both of person and material environment.[79]

The most successful, and enduring, model of gentility practiced in colonial Maryland was that advanced by Dr. Alexander Hamilton in the club that he helped found, the Tuesday Club, in 1745. Hamilton molded the club into a center of pleasurable companionship for cultivated gentlemen. The club was a place where a self-chosen group of gentlemen refined their genteel skills in a select social environment that excluded coarse and vulgar people. Hamilton's vision of a genteel gathering place was a significantly superior version of gentility than had previously existed in Maryland. It supplanted the social virtue of hospitality with the more flexible concept of sociability.

Hospitality was a deeply rooted set of rituals among wealthy planters firmly linked to developing and deeply held notions of honor. It became by the early eighteenth century a defining characteristic of southern and West Indian planters. But it had manifest disadvantages, as David Shields has acutely pointed out, especially for those people who did not participate in preexisting elite networks. For people such as Hamilton, tied into an increasingly integrated and growingly urbane Atlantic world, hospitality was "a historically retrograde emulation of the customs of traditional hierarchies." Hospitality was a problem because it insisted on the primacy of the host. It forced strangers to enter into a contract of voluntary subordination to the host and did not allow for a sharing of power. Sociability, on the other hand, was a doctrine that "signified the eclipse of the traditional social organizations in which one was bound . . . by neighborhood, congregation, family, and common employment." Instead, men such as the elite Annapolitans in the Tuesday Club, followers of sociability rather than hospitality, based their interactions on friendship, mutual interest, and shared appetite—fraternity, in short, rather than lineage. Sociability suited men dwelling in Atlantic port cities and in London, places of rapid change and places used to receiving strangers who needed to be incorporated into social structures. Men in these places were receptive to modes of genteel behavior that promoted the free and friendly conversation of people meeting in public spaces. Sociable men celebrated rather than rejected commercial values. They associated sociability with "urbanity, egalitarian conviviality, innocence, the arts, table fellowship, and wit." Sociability was a genteel style that synthesized gentility with a competitive individualism and commercial entrepreneurship—a version of gentility that would be appealing to men of commerce or the descendants of men of commerce and was appealing also to those planters wishing to avail themselves of urban pleasures.[80]

By the Revolution, some members of the elite, notably those associated with trade and urban life, were pushing on toward a form of gentility that preserved elite status while accommodating the insistent demand for Republican egalitarianism that emerged during and after the Revolution. The many Marylanders who stuck with older versions of gentility, especially the planters who continued to adopt hospitality as a primary value and who combined it with an increasingly all-embracing paternalism, were to an extent left behind. But older ideas and traditional cultural models of gentility remained important, making it important to see the advance of sociability as neither universal nor uncontested. The Tuesday Club may have been an oasis of culture in a "barbarous and desolate corner of the world"[81] but "provinciality, vanity, and familial competition, and hypocrisy"—attributes that urbane men of commerce often associated with the cult of hospitality—still existed. Indeed, as the elite became increasingly a planting class, such traits might be expected to prevail. The conflict between two competing models of gentility played itself out after the Revolution. Sociability won out, appropriated in the nineteenth century as the public mode of the middle classes and becoming in course of time "respectability."[82] Before this, however, the Maryland elite had participated in a revolution, in which they made manifest their growing Creole consciousness and asserted their claims to gentility on a world stage.

NOTES

1. For a view of the early Chesapeake elite as integrated, culturally dominant, conspicuously self-aware, and immensely influential see David Hackett Fischer, *Albion's Seed: Four British Folkways in America* (New York: Oxford University Press, 1989), 207–25, 256. For a refutation of Fischer, see James Horn, "Cavalier Culture? The Social Development of Colonial Virginia," *WMQ*, 3d. Ser., XLVIII (1991), 238–45. In Maryland, Roman Catholic officeholders attached to the proprietary interest may have had a more pronounced sense of identity, based on deep adherence to a persecuted faith. Ronald Hoffman, "'Marylando-Hibernus': Charles Carroll the Settler, 1660–1720," *WMQ*, 3d. Ser., XLV (1988), 215–16.

2. Clayton Colman Hall (ed.), *Narratives of Early Maryland* (New York: Barnes and Noble, 1910); Jack P. Greene, *The Intellectual Construction of America: Exceptionalism and Identity from 1492 to 1800* (Chapel Hill: University of North Carolina Press, 1993), 61, 68–69.

3. Carole Shammas, "English-Born and Creole Elites in Turn-of-the-Century Virginia," in Thad W. Tate and David S. Ammerman, *The Chesapeake in the Seventeenth Century: Essays on ANglo-American Society* (Chapel Hill: University of North Carolina Press, 1979), 280.

4. David W. Jordan, *Foundations of Representative Government in Maryland 1632–1715* (Cambridge: Cambridge University Press, 1987), 243; and Shammas, "English-Born and Creole Elites," 275–77.

5. Gloria L. Main, *Tobacco Colony: Life in Early Maryland, 1650–1720* (Princeton, NJ: Princeton University Press, 1982), 246; Lois Green Carr and Lorena S. Walsh, "Changing Lifestyles and Colonial Behavior in the Colonial Chesapeake," in Cary Carson et al., *Of Consuming Interests: The Style of Life in the Eighteenth Century* (Charlottesville: University Press of Virginia, 1994), 62–68.

6. Darrett B. and Anita H. Rutman, "Of Agues and Fevers: Malaria in the Early Chesapeake," *WMQ*, 3d. Ser., XXXIII (1976), 31–61; idem, *A Place in Time: Middlesex County, Virginia, 1650–1750* (New York: W.W. Norton, 1984), 76; and Anita H. Rutman, "Still Planting the Seeds of Hope: The Recent Literature of the Early Chesapeake Region," *VMHB*, 95 (1987), 7.

7. Michal J. Rozbicki, "The Curse of Provincialism: Negative Perceptions of Colonial American Gentry," *JSH*, LXIII (1997), 746.

8. Carr and Walsh, "Changing Lifestyles," 62–68; and Main, *Tobacco Colony*, 225–39.

9. Michal J. Rozbicki, *The Complete Colonial Gentleman: Cultural Legitimacy in Plantation America* (Charlottesville: University Press of Virginia, 1998), 107; and John Fontaine, "Diary," in Ann Maury, *Memoirs of a Huguenot Family* (New York: G.P. Putnam, 1852), 265, cited in Main, *Tobacco Colony*, 265.

10. Main, *Tobacco Colony*, 238.

11. Shammas, "English-Born and Creole Elites," 275–87.

12. See Richard Allestree, for example, who stated in a work published in 1676 that "a Gentleman is now supposed to be only a thing of pleasure, a creature sent up into the World, as the Leviathan unto the deep, to take his pastime therein . . . and then 'twill be no wonder if it be ridiculous Soloecism to attempt to define his Calling, whose very Essence is thought to consist in having none." Richard Allestree, *The Gentleman's Calling* (London, 1676), preface. Allestree's definition was contested by the rising English commercial middle class, who attempted to redefine gentility using the new mode of conduct associated with urban England denoted as sociability. Daniel Defoe was a principal inventor of this revised model of gentility. Nevertheless, as Rozbicki insists, in the opposition between a commercial model of gentility that disregarded ancestry in favor of manners or "politeness" and an entrenched model of gentility based on immutable foundations of land and birth, the latter was much more culturally powerful, at least until the nineteenth century. See Rozbicki, *Complete Colonial Gentleman*, 28–75; David S. Shields, *Civil Tongues and Polite Letters in British America* (Chapel Hill: University of North Carolina Press, 1997), 31–38; and Lawrence E. Klein, *Shaftesbury and the Culture of Politeness: Moral Discourse and Cultural Politics in Early Eighteenth-Century England* (Cambridge: Cambridge University Press, 1994).

13. *Testamentary Proceedings*, 24 (1719), 54 MHR; *Provincial Court Judgments*, TL3 (1704), 268–70; PL3 (1710), 231–34, 243, 257, 398–400; JP2 (1712), 495, 586–88; VD1 (1716), 360, 732–36; VD2 (1718), 1, 4–6; *Anne Arundel Court Judgments*, G (1704), 493; TB3 (1710), 100; RC (1717), 31–32; *AM*, XXIII, 142–144; XXXIII, 134–35, 168–69; 189–90; 197; 426–29. For details of Macnemara's career, see Alan F. Day, "A Social Study of Lawyers in Maryland, 1660–1775," (unpublished Ph.D., Johns Hopkins University, 1976), 920–22; and Aubrey C. Land, *Colonial Maryland* (Millwood, NY: KTO Press, 1981), 108–109.

14. See Richard Beale Davis (ed.), *William Fitzhugh and His Chesapeake World, 1676–1701* (Chapel Hill: University of North Carolina Press, 1963); William Byrd I Letterbooks, published in *VMHB*, XXIV-XXVIII (1916–1920); and Marion Tinling, *The Correspondence of the Three*

William Byrds of Westover, Virginia, 1684–1776, 2 vols (Charlottesville: University Press of Virginia, 1977), 3–191.

15. Lois Green Carr and David W. Jordan, *Maryland's Revolution of Government, 1689–1692* (Ithaca, NY: Cornell University Press, 1974), 221.

16. See Jack P. Greene, *The Quest for Power: The Lower Houses of Assembly in the Southern Royal Colonies, 1689–1776* (Chapel Hill: University of North Carolina Press), 1963; Adrienne Bell, "Calvert's Colony: Proprietary Politics in Maryland, 1716–1763" (unpublished Ph.D., Johns Hopkins University, 1986); and Allan Kulikoff, *Tobacco and Slaves: The Development of Southern Cultures in the Chesapeake, 1680–1800* (Chapel Hill: University of North Carolina Press, 1986), 280–99.

17. Hugh Jones, "Maryland in 1699; A Letter from the Reverend Hugh Jones," Michael Kammen (ed.), *JSH,* XXIX (1963), 362–72.

18. Shammas, "English-Born and Creole Elites," 288.

19. Edward Ward, *A Trip to Jamaica* (London, 1698) and *A Trip to New-England* (London, 1699).

20. Ebenezer Cooke, *The Sotweed Factor, A Satyr* (London, 1708). For a similar analysis see J.A. Leo Lemay in *Men of Letters in Colonial Maryland* (Knoxville: University of Tennessee Press), 1972, 77–110; and Robert D. Arner, "Ebenezer Cooke: Satire in the Colonial South," *SLJ,* VII (1975), 105–23. For a contemporaneous poem that went even further than Cooke's in mocking the motives of British enterprise abroad, see Henry Brooke's "The New Metamorphosis," skillfully elucidated in Shields, *Civic Tongues and Polite Letters,* 79–88.

21. Cooke, *The Sotweed Factor,* 14–15, 399–400.

22. John Clive and Bernard Bailyn, "England's Cultural Provinces: Scotland and America," *WMQ,* 3d. Ser., XI (1954), 207–210; and Rozbicki, "The Curse of Provincialism," 727.

23. The quotation is from G.C. Bolton, "The Idea of a Colonial Gentry," *Historical Studies,* 13 (1968), 307–28. See also Louis B. Wright, *The First Gentlemen of Virginia: Intellectual Qualities of the Early Colonial Ruling Class* (San Marino, CA: The Huntington Library, 1940); Clive and Bailyn, "England's Cultural Provinces," 207–10; and Jack P. Greene, "Search for Identity: An Interpretation of the Meaning of Selected Patterns of Social Response in Eighteenth Century America," *JSocH,* 3 (1970), 189–220.

24. Wright, *First Gentlemen of Virginia,* 1–37; Rhys Isaac, *The Transformation of Virginia, 1740–1790* (Chapel Hill: University of North Carolina Press, 1982), 131–32; Kenneth A. Lockridge, *The Diary, and Life, of William Byrd II of Virginia, 1674–1744* (Chapel Hill: University of North Carolina Press, 1987), 20–34, 151–66; and Jack P. Greene (ed.), *The Diary of Colonel Landon Carter of Sabine Hall, 1752–1778* (Charlottesville: University Press of Virginia, 1965), I, 1–31. For a counter-argument that the relentless pursuit of Old World gentility was a powerful cultural resource legitimizing elite identity and social prominence, see Rozbicki, *Complete Colonial Gentleman,* 3–4.

25. Lockridge, *Diary of William Byrd,* 12–25, 154–60; and Kathleen M. Brown, *Good Wives, Nasty Wenches, and Anxious Patriarchs: Gender, Race, and Power in Colonial Virginia* (Chapel Hill: University of North Carolina Press, 1996), 342–48.

26. Ibid, 156.

27. Thomas Bordley to Stephen Bordley, 24 September 1724, in Bordley Papers, Mss. 64, MHS.

28. Ibid, 6 August, 1725 and 30 August 1725.

29. Lockridge, *Diary, and Life, of William Byrd*; and Robert D. Arner, "Westover and the Wilderness: William Byrd's Images of Virginia," *SLJ*, VII (1975), 105–23.

30. Greene, "Search for Identity," 189–220; and idem, "Political Mimesis: A Consideration of the Historical and Cultural Roots of Legislative Behavior in the British Colonies in the Eighteenth Century," *AHR*, LXXV (1969), 337–60.

31. T.H. Breen, "An Empire of Goods: The Anglicization of Colonial America, 1690–1776," *Journal of British Studies*, XXV (1986), 467–99; and idem, " 'Baubles of Britain': The American and Consumer Revolutions of the Eighteenth Century," *Past and Present*, 119 (1988), 73–104.

32. Carr and Walsh, "Changing Lifestyles," 7–8.

33. For the cultural meaning of tea consumption in the Chesapeake, see Ann Smart Martin, "Buying into a World of Goods: Eighteenth-Century Consumerism and the Retail Trade from London to the Virginia Frontier," (unpublished Ph.D., College of William and Mary, 1993), 319–54. Shields sees the tea ceremony as a "critical institution in the assertion of women's presence in the emerging public sphere" and "a reaction to the masculine infatuation with coffee." *Civic Tongues and Polite Letters*, 104, 113.

34. Richard L. Bushman, "American High-Style and Vernacular Cultures," in Jack P. Greene and J.R. Pole (eds.), *Colonial British America* (Baltimore: Johns Hopkins University Press, 1984), 348.

35. Hugh Jones, *The Present State of Virginia*, Richard L. Morton (ed.) (Chapel Hill: University of North Carolina Press, 1956), 71.

36. T.H. Breen, *Tobacco Culture: The Mentality of the Great Tidewater Planters on the Eve of Revolution* (Princeton, NJ: Princeton University Press, 1985), 40–83.

37. For how trade disqualified people from gentility, see Michal J. Rozbicki, *The Complete Colonial Gentleman*, 68–74.

38. Martin H. Quitt, "Immigrant Origins of the Virginia Gentry: A Study of Cultural Transmission and Innovation," *WMQ*, 3d. Ser., XLV (1988), 639, 643.

39. English values were also changing during this period in ways that led to a shift from the collectivity to the individual and to an acceptance of commerce as an inevitable and necessary element in genteel society. Yet these trends were more pronounced in the Chesapeake than in Britain. See J.E. Crowley, *This Sheba, Self: The Conceptualization of Economic Life in Eighteenth Century America* (Baltimore: Johns Hopkins University Press, 1974). For changes in Britain see Lawrence Stone and Jeanne Fawtier Stone, *An Open Elite?: England, 1540–1880* (Oxford University Press, 1984), 402; Joyce Appleby, *Economic Thought and Ideology in Seventeenth Century England* (Princeton, NJ: Princeton University Press, 1978), 37–41, 250–51; and J.G.A. Pocock, *Virtue, Commerce and History: Essays on Political Thought and History, Chiefly in the Eighteenth Century* (Cambridge: Cambridge University Press, 1985).

40. Letter from Rev. Jonathan Boucher to Rev. Mr James, St Bees, Whitehaven, 7 August 1759, in *MdHM*, 7 (1912), 4–5.

41. See, for example, an anonymous correspondent in the Maryland Gazette in 1760:

> Europe, no more sole Arbitress, shall sit
> Or boast the proud Monopoly of Wit;
> Her *youngest Daughter* here with filial Claim
> Asserts her Portion of Maternal Fame.
> Let no nice Sparks despise our humble Scenes,
> Half-buskin'd Monarchs and itin'rant Queens . . .
> Athens from such beginnings mean and low!
> Saw Thespis' Cart a wondrous Structure grow . . .

    Maryland Gazette, 6 March, 1760.

42. William Parkes had begun a newspaper under the same name in 1727 but it quickly folded.

43. Lockridge, *Diary of William Byrd*, 154–65.

44. Isaac, *Transformation of Virginia*, 74–79.

45. William Eddis and Aubrey C. Land (eds.), *Letters from America* (Cambridge, MA: Harvard University Press, 1969), 58.

46. Richard Bushman suggests that the deficiencies of American styles may be attributed as much to delays and imperfections in the transfer of craftsmen as to rusticity in taste. Bushman, "American High-Style and Vernacular Cultures," in Greene and Pole, *Colonial British America*, 365.

47. See Michael Zuckerman, "William Byrd's Family," *Perspectives in American History*, XII (1979), 274–90; and Daniel Blake Smith, *Inside the Great House: Planter Family Life in Eighteenth Century Chesapeake* (Ithaca, NY: Cornell University Press, 1980), 175–230.

48. Journal of William Black, 19 and 21 May 1744, in *Pennsylvania Magazine of History and Biography*, 1 (1877), 126, 130.

49. For the importance of hospitality in the Chesapeake, see Dell Upton, *Holy Things and Profane: Anglican Parish Churches* (Cambridge, MA: Harvard University Press, 1986), 165–68; and Brown, *Good Wives, Nasty Wenches, and Anxious Patriarchs*), 367–72. For dancing, see Fischer, *Albion's Seed*, 313–14.

50. William Byrd II, *Secret History of the Line* and *The History of the Dividing Line*, in Louis B. Wright (ed.), *The Prose Works of William Byrd of Westover: Narrative of a Colonial Virginian* (Cambridge, MA: Harvard University Press, 1966).

51. Robert Micklus (ed.), *The History of the Ancient and Honorable Tuesday Club* (Chapel Hill: University of North Carolina Press, 1990), 3 vols.

52. Cooke wrote as much for an English audience as for local planters and merchants. See Lemay, *Men of Letters in Colonial Maryland*, 77–110.

53. See, for example, two essays for and against luxury in the *Maryland Gazette* in which the arguments used against luxury are deliberately facetious. *Maryland Gazette*, 16 and 23 December 1746.

54. Carl Bridenbaugh (ed.), *A Gentleman's Progress: The Itinerarium of Dr. Alexander Hamilton, 1744* (Chapel Hill: University of North Carolina Press, 1948), 7–8.

55. Robert Micklus, "The History of the Tuesday Club": A Mock-Jeremiad of the Colonial South," *WMQ*, 3d. Ser., XL (1983), 48–49.

56. Stephen Bordley to his mother, 22 January 1728, in Stephen Bordley Letterbooks, Ms 81, MHS.

57. See the letters of John Gibson to Mrs. John Ross, 1740–43, Gibson-Maynadier Papers, 1669–1819, Ms 1142, MHS.

58. Letter from Charles Carroll of Carrollton to Charles Carroll, Barrister, 3 December 1771, *MdHM*, 32 (1937), 209.

59. Letter by Daniel Dulany, Jr., 9 December 1755, *Pennsylvania Magazine of History and Biography*, 2 (1879), 12.

60. James Anderson to James Hollyday II, from Readbourne, England, 31 October 1767, in Hollyday Papers, 1677–1905, Ms 1317, MHS.

61. Ironically, Cradock and Bacon expressed concern about religious weaknesses in Maryland precisely at the period of greatest strength for the Anglican Church in the Chesapeake. Church attendance were high, church building and the sacralization of the landscape was proceeding apace, and the state church tradition was experiencing a vigorous revival. Anglicization and Anglicanization were contemporaneous phenomena. Jon Butler, *Awash in a Sea of Faith, Christianizing the American People* (Cambridge, MA: Harvard University Press, 1990), 98–99; Mechal Sobel, *The World They made Together: Black and White Values in Eighteenth-Century Virginia* (Princeton, NJ: Princeton University Press, 1987), 178–79; and Upton, *Holy Things and Profane.*

62. Bacon's sermons on the need for black obedience expressed a powerful defense of the slave system. [Thomas Bacon], *Two Sermons, Preached to a Congregation of Black Slaves ...* (London, 1749); and idem, *Four Sermons, upon the Great and Indispensable Duty of all Christian Masters and Mistresses to Bring up their Negro Slaves in the Knowledge and Fear of God ...* (London, 1750).

63. David C. Skaggs, "Thomas Cradock's Sermon on the Governance of the Established Church," *WMQ*, 3d. Ser., XXVII (1970), 648.

64. Ibid, 649.

65. Ibid, 648.

66. Cited in William Stevens Perry, *Historical Collections Relating to the American Colonial Church* (Hartford, CT: The Church Press, 1885), IV, 324–26.

67. Henry Callister to William Henderson, Chester/Galloway Papers, Mss. 1994, MHS.

68. Elaine Breslaw, "Dr. Alexander Hamilton and the Enlightenment in Maryland" (unpublished Ph.D., University of Maryland, 1973), 82.

69. Isaac, *Transformation of Virginia*, especially Chapter 8; and idem, "Evangelical Revolt: The Nature of the Baptist's Challenge to the Traditional Order in Virginia, 1765–1775," *WMQ*, 3d. Ser., XXXI (1974), 345–68.

70. Henry Chandler Forman (ed.), "The Narrative of Colonel James Rigbie," *MdHM*, XXXVI (1941), 39–49. Quotations from pp. 43 and 49.

71. "Narrative of Rigbie," 43.

72. John Sekora, *Luxury: The Concept in Western Thought, Eden to Smollett* (Baltimore: Johns Hopkins University Press, 1977).

73. The deleterious effects of gambling also concerned Landon Carter from Virginia, a conservative defender of traditional social relationships. His sons were incessant gamblers, a fact that greatly upset Carter, who angrily expostulated that "the Gaming Table" was a place "where self and gain alone Govern at the Sacrifice of every duty, whether Moral or Religious." Jack P. Greene (ed.), *The Diary of Colonel Landon Carter of Sabine Hall, 1752–1778*, 2 vols. (Charlottesville: University Press of Virginia, 1965), II, 1122. For discussions of the meanings attached to gambling among the Chesapeake elite see T.H. Breen, "Horses and Gentlemen: The Cultural

Significance of Gambling among the Gentry of Virginia," *WMQ*, 3d. Ser., XXXIV (1977), 239–57; and Isaac, *Transformation of Virginia*, 118–19.

74. David C. Skaggs (ed.), *The Poetic Writings of Thomas Cradock, 1718–1770* (East Brunswick, NJ: University of Delaware Press, 1983).

75. Brown, *Good Wives*, 328.

76. Rozbicki, *The Complete Colonial Gentleman*, 141.

77. J.G.A. Pocock, "Machiavelli, Harrington, and English Political Ideologies in the Eighteenth Century," *WMQ*, 3d. Ser., XXII (1965), 549–83; and Jack P. Greene, *Imperatives, Behavior, and Identities: Essays in Early American Cultural History* (Charlottesville: University Press of Virginia, 1992), 208–35.

78. For the distinction between gentility and respectability, see Woodruff D. Smith, "Complications of the Commonplace: Tea, Sugar, and Imperialism," *JIH*, XXIII (1992), 275–77. See also Rozbicki, *The Complete Colonial Gentleman*, 127–71.

79. Ibid, 187; Richard Bushman, *The Refinement of America: Persons, Houses, Cities* (New York: Alfred A. Knopf, 1992), 96–99.

80. Shields, *Civic Tongues and Polite Behavior*, 30–31, 301–07. See also Steven C. Bullock, "The Revolutionary Transformation of American Freemasonry, 1752–1792" *WMQ*, 3d. Ser., XLVII (1990), 347–69; and Quitt, "Immigrant Origins of the Virginia Gentry," 631, 651–55. For Hamilton and the Tuesday Club, see Hamilton, *History of the Tuesday Club*.

81. Alexander Hamilton quoted in Elaine G. Breslaw, ed., *Records of the Tuesday Club of Annapolis, 1745–56* (Urbana and Chicago: University of Illinois Press, 1988), xx.

82. Shields, *Civic Tongues and Polite Behavior*, 301–7, 308–28; Rozbicki, *The Complete Colonial Gentleman*, 172–91; and Bushman, *Refinement of America*.

CHAPTER 8

Conclusion

Toward a History of Elites
in the Eighteenth-Century British Empire

Eighteenth-century men and women were particularly sensitive to where they ranked in society. Their societies were so layered and hierarchically ordered that it seemed possible to line up each man and woman in precise degrees of importance, from the monarch to the vagabond. Wealthy Marylanders judged their position by two standards. First, they evaluated themselves within the multiple circles of Chesapeake society. Thus, they were preeminent within their immediate neighborhood, very important in county society, and significant persons in the whole province. They also judged themselves by their position within the various groups that composed the British Empire.[1]

This second evaluation was the most telling assessment of individual status, especially for the most ambitious elite colonials. Wealthy Marylanders' position in Maryland was relatively secure throughout the late seventeenth and eighteenth centuries. Far richer than the average colonist, the Maryland elite formed a homogeneous group, firmly in control of the colony's political structure and economy, and socially preeminent. Their position within the Empire and especially in relation to the metropolis was less certain. Colonial wealth and power did not necessarily translate into imperial influence. Eager to identify with imparted ideals of gentility, wealthy Marylanders longed for Englishmen to accept them as gentlemen. Englishmen seldom did. Marylanders remained colonials, unappreciated by those whose manners they aped. Consequently, especially from the mid-eighteenth century, they came to identify as much with fellow elites in other colonies as they did with British gentlemen.[2]

Elites were slow to develop in British America, despite most colonization schemes offering considerable inducements for men of quality to remove to the colonies. George Calvert, Lord Baltimore, imaginatively intended the province of Maryland to be similar to the medieval palatine of Durham with a finely graded social order in place from the beginning.[3] But the pressures of eking out a living in frontier communities militated against the development of social institutions and class cleavages similar to those left behind in Britain. Genuine elites, separated by wealth, power, and style of living from the majority of the population, were slow to develop.[4]

Indeed, in most colonies, especially those settled in the seventeenth century, elites did not emerge until 30 or 40 years of settlement had passed. Four conditions appear essential for an elite to emerge. First, a colony had to gain economic viability before some men could differentiate themselves from the mass. Thus, the establishment of sugar in the West Indies, tobacco in the Chesapeake, and rice and indigo in the Lower South preceded and facilitated the emergence of planter classes.[5] Second, mercantilist policies, increased settlement, and growing colonial wealth contributed to a massive expansion after the Restoration of transatlantic commerce between the colonies and the mother country, and between individual colonies themselves.[6] Such commerce allowed planters to amass large profits and provided opportunities for colonial merchants. Not surprisingly, it was not until external trade was well developed that a wealthy merchant class developed in New England or in the Middle Colonies.[7]

A third factor that was important in the plantation colonies was the introduction of slavery. The long-run benefits of chattel slavery soon became apparent and had a significant impact on social structure. Whereas servants were relatively inexpensive, slaves were dear, and only the wealthier planters could afford to buy them. This increased the advantages of the big man over the small producer, an imbalance aggravated when the supply of servants dwindled. The introduction of slavery encouraged aggrandizement and became the basis of elite power and wealth.[8]

Fourth, elites did not develop into tightly organized ruling classes as long as the majority of the leaders of colonial societies were recently arrived immigrants. Certainly, individuals among these immigrants created fortunes and acquired political power. But such men did not form an elite in the sense of an elite as a privileged group with a keen perception of itself and its role in society, a jealousy over its authority, and an eagerness to assert its dominance over—and separateness from—the rest of the population. Immigrants who attained wealth and power remained immigrants, Britons abroad. Believing themselves to be but temporarily absent from the mother country, they exhibited values and behavior that were still essentially British, and displayed relatively little interest in articulating what the character of their new societies were or should become. Consumed by a desire to create a better life for themselves, either economically or religiously, they could hardly conceive of themselves as colonials, as belonging to their new residence.[9]

Their children, however, were different. Born in the New World, and rooted to its soil, they often had little or no direct experience of Britain and, even while emulating metropolitan behavior, could not be unaware that they were no longer emigrants overseas but were a new people, Creoles, with attitudes shaped by a shared colonial experience. Native-born Americans with inherited or acquired wealth and status shared similar backgrounds and common concerns that differentiated them from Europeans and European immigrants. This heritage and experience allowed them to develop self-consciousness and made them eventually ponder what sort of people they were and what sort of society they had been born into. In those areas of British America where native-born elites came to dominate local societies, they coalesced into well-defined governing classes marked by inherited wealth, kinship ties, increasingly more sharply defined governing ideologies, and a shared commitment to genteel values and modes of behavior. Moreover, and probably not accidentally, they tended to have a far more responsible attitude to public life than their pioneer fathers, seeking to establish their right to rule through their cultivation of gentlemanly codes of conduct, rather than just through mere wealth and connections.[10]

Despite considerable social and economic diversity within and between British colonies in the late seventeenth and early eighteenth centuries, the elites that arose displayed striking similarities. A common pattern in elite families was to move from the establisher of a fortune, through one or two generations where the estate was consolidated and enlarged, to a frivolous or unfortunate inheritor who wasted the ancestral fortune. Variations abounded, of course, but it is surprising how often the pattern holds. Some founders of prominent families, like Charles Carroll the Settler of Maryland, James Alexander of New York, William Byrd I of Virginia, and Christopher Codrington I of Barbados, were relatively well-born and with good connections, either in Britain or in the colonies. Others, like Andrew Belcher of Massachusetts, Robert Livingston of New York, Peter Beckford I of Jamaica, and John Carter of Virginia, were men from obscure and humble backgrounds. But all shared certain common characteristics. These included, first, a single-minded devotion to the acquisition of wealth and a corresponding lack of attention to the attainment of social graces; second, considerable involvement in transatlantic commerce that provided them with significant interaction with elites elsewhere in the Empire; and, third, success in the competition for access to the political and economic favors of colonial governors. Ambitious, thrusting, hardheaded men, they accumulated wealth and political influence, both of which they passed on to their sons.[11]

The sons of these crude, boisterous, and self-serving planters and merchants inherited their fathers' wealth and social and political position but seldom their single-minded devotion to getting ahead. Unlike their fathers, they were Creoles who had no need to establish themselves in a new land, but instead hankered to be accepted in the old society of Britain. They sought not only to enhance but also to justify their fortunate inheritances. Some, like Charles Carroll of Annapolis and Robert "King" Carter, concentrated on turning a large inheritance into a major fortune. Most, however, although concerned to increase wealth and benefit from the economic opportunities present in growing economies, put much of their energies into politics and cultural pursuits. By the early decades of the eighteenth century native-born men of inherited wealth were in positions of importance everywhere: William Byrd II in Virginia, Isaac Norris II in Pennsylvania, Peter Beckford II in Jamaica, and Thomas Hutchinson in Massachusetts. The distant goal for the most ambitious of these men was to become not just a colonial member of the British ruling class but an English country gentleman with influence in British politics. Few achieved this aim, except in the West Indies. Jonathan Belcher, Jr., for example, the son of one of the rare North American Creoles who became a colonial governor, failed in his attempt to win a secure place in English society, and returned home a comparative failure, as, earlier, did William Byrd of Virginia. Colonel Daniel Parke, a glamorous Restoration rake and scoundrel, Byrd's father-in-law and a notably unsuccessful governor of Antigua, was perhaps the only man from the mainland colonies to become a truly cosmopolitan English political figure, and even Parke, despite a single-minded obsession with his own advancement, rated as only a very minor figure in Augustan England.[12]

The only colonials who cut any figure in English society were returning East India Company nabobs and West Indian absentee planters.[13] Yet even extremely wealthy and talented Creoles from the Indies who were accepted in English society felt doubts about their status. Born in the colonies but not comfortable there, they were attracted to but never totally assimilated by the metropolis. Even Christopher Codrington II (1668–1710) of Barbados, the most gifted colonial of his day, could not resolve the tensions created by creolization. Autocratic, arrogant, and brilliant, Codrington was an accomplished poet, a friend of Locke and Addison, and a fellow of All Souls. But the Caribbean ever loomed in his thought, being the springboard for his success, a magnet for his talents, and, finally, a trap, in which his finely attuned sensibilities were at odds with New World crudeness. Codrington was a rare case, being affected with a melancholy perhaps peculiar to the Caribbean, but his unease concerning his Creoleness was common among elite men from Massachusetts to the Leeward Islands.[14] To be an elite colonial was to live one's life in the shadows, torn between seeking English legitimation and commitment to one's native land.

Not all members of prominent families were assiduous cultivators of fortunes and ambitious seekers of place and power. Often, usually in the third or fourth generation, a wastrel appeared. William Byrd III was a prime example of a reckless heir whose excessive gambling and lack of attention to business devoured an estate. William Beckford II (1759–1844) was another. Although a creative Romantic novelist, he managed to dissipate the largest of all colonial fortunes, principally by his compulsion for building extravagant Gothic towers and obsessive collecting. In Maryland, the descendants of Charles Carroll of Carrollton diminished a very large estate through incompetence. Few families could continue to produce talented member after talented member, and they seldom used the device of the strict settlement employed by British gentry families to protect estates from irresponsible heirs. Consequently, one heir often destroyed an estate carefully built up over several generations. Few families maintained their influence unabated into the nineteenth century. Moreover, even when heirs were careful and competent, miscalculations, such as being on the wrong side in the American Revolution or being a West Indian slave owner in an abolitionist age, could lead to a family's decline. Thus, in Maryland, the promising career of Daniel Dulany, Jr., came to a halt after 1776, when he chose to remain loyal to the Crown. Similar declines occurred for Thomas Hutchinson in Massachusetts and Joseph Galloway in Pennsylvania. Family oligarchies were difficult to preserve.

Although individuals and families rose and fell, by the mid-eighteenth century native-born elites dominated every British-American colony, even in the British West Indies, where continuing demographic disaster prevented naturally increasing native-born populations.[15] As colonial leaders, they shared a similar status within an imperial framework. But elite wealth, family structure, political power, and relationship to the imperial power structure varied widely from region to region. The Maryland elite needs to be placed into its proper position within these elites. Furthermore, it should be compared to the British gentry, the model to which all colonial elites aspired.

In the northern colonies, the richest and most important elite members were merchants in the port cities of Boston, New York, and Philadelphia. The great landed magnates of the Hudson Valley were the major exceptions to northern mercantile dominance. In the plantation colonies of the South and the Caribbean, planters were prominent. Occupational differences became more pronounced over time. Until the early eighteenth century, ambitious men were usually entrepreneurs, anxious to make money in as many ways as they possibly could. By the middle of the eighteenth century, however, occupational specialization in the southern colonies and the West Indies was increasing. Large merchants were still part of the elite, but even in the major port cities of Kingston, Charleston, Bridgetown, and Savannah fewer elite members combined mercantile and planting activities, and the majority of wealthy people, and the people with the greatest political clout, were planters. Conflict between the two groups was not unknown, but generally planters prevailed, as in Jamaica in the mid-1750s where a grand constitutional conflict between metropolis and colony was complicated by a division between Kingston merchants and wealthy sugar planters. The latter forced the former to acquiesce to their will.[16]

Thomas Doerflinger has argued that occupational differences between north and south had serious repercussions. Specifically, he states that agricultural specialization led to economic stagnation because it hindered entrepreneurship. Planters were competent managers, but their neglect of trade and business limited their economic horizons and bound them to activities that rendered them quite unable to strike out into new enterprises when adversity beckoned.[17] It was true that merchants in the northeastern seaports were dynamic risk takers whose encouragement of innovation and diversification allowed them to take advantage of the economic opportunities offered by the Industrial Revolution. It was also true that southern planters became steadily risk averse and displayed little interest in expanding their incomes after they had reached a comfortable sufficiency. Yet it is much easier to see how the economic attitudes of southern planters fostered decline viewed from the early national or antebellum periods than from the prerevolutionary era. In the mid-eighteenth century, Chesapeake planters managed to adapt to changing markets with ease, as when they introduced grain to complement tobacco in the Chesapeake and indigo to complement rice in the Carolinas and Georgia. Southern planters were eager to exploit new avenues of moneymaking such as large-scale land speculation or iron production. Their decision to remain in agriculture was a rational choice and did not necessarily betoken a loss of innovativeness.

Moreover, to explain the economic success of any region by attributing superior business virtues such as the "spirit of enterprise" to inhabitants seems too glib. If elite tidewater southerners withdrew from trade and avoided commercial risk in the nineteenth century, so too did the proper Philadelphia descendants of Doerflinger's thrusting merchants.[18] Moreover, economic dynamism in the nineteenth century was displayed not just by Yankee industrialists but by cotton planters on the southwestern frontier and by agriculturists in the American Midwest, Australasia, and Argentina. Rapid economic growth, further, was not always accompanied by aggressive entrepreneurship. Russia and England, for example, were controlled by strong aristocratic oligarchies averse to sullying their hands in trade. Yet both experienced remarkable expansion in the eighteenth and nineteenth centuries. And Maryland, as Doerflinger admits, managed to "leap the chasm from plantation agriculture to modern industry" despite having an economic and social structure much like that of declining Virginia.[19] Why Maryland became an "expanding beachhead of commercial enterprise in a staple plantation economy" and Virginia did not cannot be explained merely by reference to economic ideology.[20]

Indeed, Maryland became remarkable during the nineteenth century for containing within its boundaries examples of both northern and southern societies. Baltimore grew from its straggling colonial origins to become a bustling center of commerce and industry. Meanwhile, the once-flourishing tobacco counties of southern and eastern Maryland stagnated. In northern Maryland, slavery and the plantation economy were, at most, tangential: in southern Maryland and on the Eastern Shore, slavery remained fundamental to a continuing plantation culture and the basis of a slave society. As Barbara Fields points out, there were two Marylands in the antebellum period. Yet the line between the two societies was always fluid: slavery unified as much as it divided. The bonds between Baltimore and the slave economy were not just political but were also "the complex ones of friendship, family connection, mutual clientship, and joint endeavor."[21] Accidents of geography and the revolutionary ideology of the Revolution led one section to concentrate on tobacco and the other to supplying the rapidly developing wheat-producing hinterland of western Maryland and southern Pennsylvania. Over time, the nature of a career in commerce rather than in agriculture helped to fashion changes in the cultural meanings attached to enterprise, but this was a result of the shift from agriculture to commerce in Baltimore rather than a fundamental cause of that shift. The rise of the independent merchant coincided with increasing specialization among planters. Both developments were part of the same general trend rather than evidence of growing ideological splits over the meaning of work.[22]

One result of individual economic success was a healthy income. The average incomes of elite Marylanders ranged from around £200 to over £1,000 per annum and made them rich within their own society. In comparison with other elites, however, they were not especially wealthy. As befitted a middle colony, the Maryland elite made middling incomes. They were, in general, wealthier than northern elites and less rich than wealthy men farther south. Northern elites were the proletarians of the Atlantic world in the seventeenth and early eighteenth centuries.[23] Only four estates probated in Philadelphia and Boston between 1684 and 1699 exceeded £2,000.[24] Just two people in New Hampshire probated before 1740 had estates valued at over £3,000.[25] The growth of transatlantic commerce in eighteenth-century port cities lessened the differences between northern and southern wealth, at least at the highest levels. In the decades preceding the American Revolution, a number of northern merchants amassed large fortunes matched by only the very richest Chesapeake planters. Merchants could still live genteelly for less than £500 per annum, but the richest men had much higher incomes. Major merchants, such as Samuel Waldo in Boston, James DeLancey in New York, and Charles Willing, Israel Pemberton, and Samuel Powell in Philadelphia, had fortunes exceeding £20,000 sterling.[26] Landed proprietors in New York may have equaled these fortunes.[27] Nevertheless, such wealth was exceptional. Northern elites remained comparatively poor. The top tenth of decedents in the Middle Colonies and New England in the 1770s owned only a quarter of the physical wealth of their southern counterparts.[28]

The farther south one traveled, the richer the wealthy men. The wealth of colonial Virginians is difficult to ascertain, but Jackson T. Main's analysis of the wealthiest 100 Virginians after the Revolution suggests that Virginian planters were somewhat richer than their Maryland counterparts. South Carolinians were a good deal richer. Between 1736 and 1775, one in five South Carolinians left estates worth more than £1,000. In the 1770s, the average South Carolinian estate was valued at £1,281 sterling, or nearly four times the average estate value of Maryland decedents in the same period.[29]

The West Indies was the place where real colonial fortunes were to be made. The islands of the Caribbean were the jewels in Britain's imperial crown, and planters with large sugar plantations were among the wealthiest of the Crown's subjects. By the late seventeenth century, planters in Barbados were the richest men in English America.[30] Eighteenth-century planters in the Caribbean surpassed these early achievers and their wealth dwarfed that of the Chesapeake. As early as 1720, nearly one-quarter of probated estates in Jamaica were over £1,000. By 1750, a third of men had probated estates over £1,000 in personal wealth. On the eve of the Revolution, average inventoried wealth was £3,188. The wealthiest planters were colossally rich. Peter Beckford died in 1735 with an inventoried estate of £145,749 and total wealth of £264,999 sterling. In 1777, Sir Simon Clarke, the son of a baronet transported for highway robbery, left land and property estimated at £350,120 sterling.[31] The wealth of the West Indian planters was on a scale different from wealth in Maryland. The value of an average sugar plantation was over £19,000, an amount few Marylanders possessed.[32] Such large capital sums enabled West Indian planters to attract large amounts of credit, and, consequently, in many cases, sizable debts.[33] It also enabled some to forsake the colonies and become *rentiers* in England. That they were able to attract such capital points to an essential difference between the West Indian elites and other colonial elites: only West Indian sugar planters with their incomes running into thousands of pounds sterling could compete financially with English gentry. Elite wealth in Maryland hardly compared to metropolitan riches. Even in provincial South Wales an income of £1,000 per annum (the upper limits of Maryland wealth) placed a landlord only on the outer fringes of the gentry. The incomes of peers and London merchant princes far outstripped what all colonials except for West Indian planters could imagine. After 1710, incomes of over £10,000 per annum became common for aristocrats, and London merchants such as Sir Theodore Jannssen in the late seventeenth century and

Sampson Gideon in the mid-eighteenth century left fortunes of over £300,000.[34]

Nor was the Maryland elite a leisured class. Maryland planters and merchants, like elites elsewhere in English America, never acquired that defining characteristic of gentlemen, freedom from work. The Chesapeake elite was a working elite, with planters resident on their plantations and merchants toiling in their shops.[35] Thus, they were easily distinguished from European elites that were *rentier* classes, often long absent from the sources of their wealth and seldom directly concerned in the day-to-day management of their estates. In an important sense, the Maryland elite were from the start bourgeois with bourgeois attitudes toward work and toward capitalism. Therefore, it is not surprising that they easily adapted to and took advantage of an emerging transatlantic economy and that they remained receptive to changes in the marketplace.[36]

Elite members, of course, did not devote themselves solely to the accumulation of riches. A fortune was of limited use if it could not be passed on to future generations. Historians, therefore, have paid much attention to family formation among elites and to the role of inheritance in sustaining elites over several generations. They also have attempted to evaluate the principal social and attitudinal characteristics of elite families. Unfortunately, most studies of the colonial family, especially in the Chesapeake, have been afflicted by demographic determinism. In other words, behavioral patterns in families have been implied from underlying demographic realities such as life expectancy and family size. This reliance on demography to explain the nature of family life has led to considerable historiographical contradictions. Thus, harsh demographic conditions in the seventeenth-century Chesapeake hindered elite development, made for unstable and disorganized households, and weakened patriarchal authority. The chaotic family of the seventeenth century gave way in the early eighteenth century to an emerging patriarchal society as life spans lengthened and as slaves took over most of the drudgery of plantation labor. This stable patriarchy in turn gave way in the late eighteenth century to the sentimental family in which the achievement of domestic tranquility was valued over all else and families became remarkably affectionate, companionate, and child centered.[37] These developments happened in reverse in

New England. There, early immigrants arrived in family groups and lived remarkably long lives. Stable family structures emerged immediately, dominated by authoritarian patriarchs who denied autonomy to their sons. By the mid-eighteenth century, however, a Malthusian crisis existed in which there was both a rapidly increasing population and a steadily declining supply of land per capita. Land scarcity diminished the ability of fathers to act as patriarchs and sons became much more economically independent at earlier ages than previously.[38]

Demographic crises in New England and the Chesapeake thus seemingly produced an increase in sons' autonomy, even though one crisis resulted from too successful family formation and the other from the inability of individuals to create stable family structures. In England, however, a demographic crisis similar to that in the Chesapeake, a failure of families to reproduce, led to the entrenchment of the aristocracy's control over the economic resources of the nation.[39] Too much emphasis, I believe, has been placed on demography as the determinant of family behavior in the early modern period. Historians, accustomed to look for change and to attribute a great amount of significance to the changes that they find, have overemphasized the extent to which family structures altered and the importance that should be attached to those alterations. For example, Chesapeake historians have insisted that the stable society of the eighteenth century developed only after the demographic crisis of the seventeenth century had ended, whereas historians of New England argue that economic problems arose from the continuation of the stable family structures that when formed in the Chesapeake led to prosperity and oligarchical domination. For demography to be such a dramatic agent of historical change, shifts in family structure need to be substantial. Often they were not. In the Chesapeake, demographic change cannot bear the weight of causality commonly attributed to it. In particular, life expectancy did not increase appreciably and early death and orphanhood remained constant, even for the most privileged sectors of society. As the length of settlement increased, kin networks did develop to provide help to families broken by death. But the nuclear household supported by extended family idealized by the twentieth century was seldom realized.

Indeed, the most significant fact about the colonial elite family is that it did not change very much. Certainly, the principal power relationships within families remained unchanged. Husbands remained superior to wives, and parents assumed considerable authority over children. This is not to deny that there were not differences between families from region to region. The self-conscious establishment of a religious, communitarian, traditional society in New England helped give the Puritan family its distinctive character and differentiated it from families found in the Chesapeake and the West Indies, which were fluid societies on the make with weak social institutions and only minimal devotion to religion.[40] The religious orientation of New England Puritans continued to make their families singular and was as least as important as demography in determining family behavior.[41]

But as native-born elites developed throughout the New World, elites who were increasingly alike in background and outlook, the similarities in elite family behavior became as apparent as the differences. One prominent characteristic was an emphasis, if not an insistence, on the priority of individual interests over family imperatives and the early affirmation of the necessity of rearing autonomous individuals who would continually demonstrate that autonomy throughout their lives. Colonial stress on the importance of the individual contrasts strongly with the preoccupation with family continuity evidenced by European elites, especially the English landed class. In colonial families, there was no sense of any analogous identification of interest between family members. Nor was there any desire that the survival of the kin-group was of paramount importance, transcending individual needs.[42] The identity of a family was seldom permanently associated with its senior branch. Consequently, family property was diffused, usually with all sons sharing more or less equally in the division of wealth.[43]

Yet diffusing property widely among family members meant that few children could do more than replicate their fathers' social position. Only a handful could build their inheritances into formidable fortunes. Elite inheritance practices thus narrowed the gap between the wealthy and the moderately well off, weakening potential trends toward oligarchy. By choice, elite members made entry into the elite easier than was possible in England, where strict settlement and primogeniture favored the entrenchment of prominent families from generation to generation.

Inheritance patterns reveal more than just the disposition of property. They were also important indicators of the extent of parental control over children. Wealthy Marylanders were eager to allow their sons considerable freedom, but were reluctant to do so at the expense of their own independence. Therefore, they seldom disinherited themselves in favor of adult sons. Many sons received their inheritances at the time of their father's death rather than at the date of marriage, demonstrating less heavy-handed patriarchalism than an unwillingness to become economically impotent.[44] The desire for individual autonomy lasted until death. In New England, where fathers lived long lives, this reluctance to part with property often led to generational strife between stern fathers and rebellious sons, especially in the eighteenth century when the pressure of population on land was greater. Significantly, when land scarcity forced the issue, the need for sons to be autonomous overcame fathers' wishes to assert paternal authority.[45] In the Chesapeake, however, short life spans and abundant land meant that father–son conflicts seldom arose, at least in this period.

When the independence of fathers was not directly threatened, as in children's marriages, few restrictions were placed on the freedom of sons to do as they pleased, at least within broad limits. Early death, once again, meant that fathers in practice did not have much control over children's marriages, but they seldom attempted to prescribe whom their children should wed even when this was possible. In Maryland, few sons were forced to delay or postpone marriages because of parental disapproval. What limited qualitative evidence survives suggests that love and companionship counted for more than either material benefits or the cementing of ties between families. The most compatible mates were invariably from one's own social circles. Thus, intermarriage between elite members was common, not just in Maryland but throughout the colonies. By the mid-eighteenth century, each colony had a ruling elite whose members were related in far-ranging and complex kin networks, even if kinship remained relatively unimportant in determining relationships. In the main, these networks were locally based with only the very richest colonials marrying into outside elites.

Affection was the guiding principle in family government. Lack of evidence for the seventeenth century makes it difficult to measure the extent of emotion in early elite marriages, but seventeenth-century merchants and planters seem to have had a romantic ideal of companionate marriage. Wills, for example, which were limited indicators of family feeling, do not change in content between the seventeenth and eighteenth centuries. Wives were often appointed executors, a position of considerable trust, and testators were principally concerned to provide for their immediate family. In the eighteenth century, the affectionate nature of the colonial family becomes clear, especially in plantation colonies in which other social institutions that could compete for a person's emotional attachments were weak. Affection particularly marked genteel families, with parents indulging children and encouraging their offspring to be self-assertive and to seek and enjoy pleasure. Love for family was combined increasingly with fostering the graces of polite society and with the imperatives of public duty.[46] Hospitality and, among the more sophisticated and urbane members, sociability became their hallmark, and display their preoccupation and their most prominent vice. Some of elite life was played out in public arenas. But domesticity and the desire for a private and more intimate family life became more important as the century progressed.[47] This type of family life was most typical of families in the plantation colonies in which gentility was perhaps most assiduously pursued, but was also characteristic of genteel families elsewhere. For instance, Thomas Hutchinson, governor of Massachusetts, was extremely close to his family, the intimacy of which was a refuge and a comfort to a very public man.[48] As colonial elites prospered in the eighteenth century, they acquired more of the prescribed English gentlemanly ideals, and their family behavior became both more alike and increasingly assimilated to an urbane metropolitan model. Nevertheless, a gap did develop between genteel practices on the plantation, in which home and hospitality dominated, and urbane gentility, in which taste, style, and gentlemanly behavior were pursued less at home than in distinctive public spheres. During the nineteenth century, this gap between southern planter gentility and northern urban sociability increased, leading to cultural miscomprehensions between both parties.[49]

The tendency for public display was not surprising for colonial elites concerned with politics and public life. A common elite

culture led to an increasingly common political culture, transforming a chaotic variety of political arrangements into remarkably similar political systems.[50] By 1700, distinctive elites,
comprised either of immigrants with excellent transatlantic contacts or Creoles assimilated to the New World, had seized effective
power in most colonies.[51] These elites took advantage of the
opportunities offered in an increasingly integrated English Atlantic
polity to consolidate their power, usually at the expense of the
local executive, and exert their own judicial and political dominance. The interests of colonial elites, insistent on their rights and
on protecting their regions from metropolitan interference, and
those of the imperial government, concerned with centralizing an
increasingly complicated and interdependent political system,
often conflicted.[52] Yet, despite the inherent tensions and contradictions within this relationship and the desire by the imperial government to place limits on elite power, elites everywhere in British
America were firmly in control of important political processes by
the first third of the eighteenth century. In the long run, the rise of
these elites was only partly based on their ability to walk a
tightrope between acquiescence to imperial control and outright
rejection of metropolitan commands. More importantly, the
appearance of indigenous political elites and the rise in importance
of colonial political institutions reflected growing colonial wealth
and increasing involvement in transatlantic commerce.[53] The elite
itself became stronger. Wealthy colonials who had both connections in the parent country and influence in their own region had
important advantages over itinerant governors. Elite members
could act as "brokers" of political, economic, and social power
between their locality and the larger empire, bypassing governors.
Their success in doing so legitimized their rule and gave their
countrymen confidence that they could offer protection against
provincial or imperial tyrannies.[54] The solidification of elite
authority was accompanied by a lessening of popular involvement
in politics. Only in Massachusetts, Connecticut, Rhode Island, and
Virginia did increases in the size of colonial assemblies match population growth, and as representatives sat for longer terms, opportunities for newcomers to enter politics declined.[55] Moreover,
representatives were increasingly distinguished from nonrepresen-
tatives by their wealth and superior social prestige.[56]

The degree to which elite politicians dominated colonial society varied. In wealthy and established colonies such as Virginia and Barbados, powerful and unified elites were firmly in control of political affairs by the end of the seventeenth century. These colonies were decidedly oligarchical with considerable ruling class solidarity.[57] In other colonies, such as Pennsylvania, New Jersey, and Jamaica, considerable dissension between rival groups of elite members existed for lengthy periods before one group achieved dominance.[58] In New York, the elite was nearly always divided and factional politics were endemic.[59] Nevertheless, even where rival segments of the elite competed, elites in most colonies had achieved unquestioned legislative authority by the mid-eighteenth century. North Carolina was the exception and here the reasons for its exceptionalism are instructive. In contrast to political elites elsewhere, North Carolina's assembly members were newcomers to the province without sufficient wealth and education to distinguish themselves from the general population.[60]

Maryland falls midway between oligarchical Virginia and the faction-ridden Middle Colonies. It never quite developed the unity and power of the Virginian elite, in part because the existence of a proprietor in Maryland allowed for a variety of allegiances impossible in Virginia, but it never sank into the factional discord that characterized New York politics. Yet although disputes between "court" and "country" were common, the Maryland elite remained firmly in control. Moreover, despite their differences, colonial rulers in Maryland retained an underlying agreement about common aims. In this respect, Maryland was similar to Pennsylvania, which achieved considerable settledness by the mid-eighteenth century, albeit that the subdued conflict between Quakers and Anglicans that disrupted Pennsylvania politics in the 1750s was wholly absent in Maryland.[61]

The principal problems facing colonial politicians were challenges to their authority from the executive and from less privileged social groups. Executive threats and demands caused most concern. The most characteristic political developments in the colonies in the eighteenth century were the rise of the assembly and the attempts by native-born elites to achieve a measure of political autonomy from Britain.[62] In so striving, assemblies ran up against the conflicting imperatives of a metropolitan government that endeavored to systematize and centralize colonies, and subdue colonial pretensions. When these efforts were intensified after the Seven Years' War, they resulted in revolution for the mainland colonies and dissatisfaction in the Caribbean.

Challenges to elite authority emanating from less advantaged groups in society were less common and less serious. Common folk did not wrest power from elites anywhere in the colonies in the eighteenth century. Even in the tumultuous 1770s, no social revolution from below occurred.[63] On the contrary, elites gathered more power to themselves as the century progressed, and only the transforming event of the American Revolution prevented that development from increasing in importance. Yet lower-class groups were not willing to leave politics altogether in the hands of dominant elites. The rule of the few over the many was considered natural and desirable, but the few were expected to provide for the many, and when they did not the common people found ways to make their complaints heard.

The extent of popular discontent with elite rule varied from colony to colony. Variables included the ability of elites to present themselves as legitimate rulers, the extent to which elites were able to integrate themselves into the local community, their effectiveness in providing political regulations and guidance appropriate to the social and economic characteristics of the region, and, most importantly, the kinds of issues that were presented for public discussion. Elites adopted several strategies to quell possible unrest and were remarkably successful in diminishing the chronic discord of the seventeenth century. One method was to end faction-ridden politics and consciously to promote more responsible government.[64] In this way, elites endeavored to justify their claim to rule by right by appearing as disinterested, public-spirited, and virtuous gentlemen.[65] Deference was most completely achieved in South Carolina, Barbados, and Virginia, in which the elite was most self-confident and most obviously superior to the ordinary populace, and, in general, in rural areas more than in urban centers. As responsible government became more the norm in many colonies and as factions decreased, issues that could cause conflict diminished, and elections became, if not mere formalities, affirmations of the existing social order. In South Carolina, as elite rule solidified, few elections were contested and popular participation in politics declined. In Virginia, one-third of elections were competitive, but even when elections were fiercely contested, the choice was between which elite man would best represent local interests.[66]

Nevertheless, freeholders were as insistent on their independence as the elites and, if Maryland can be taken as an example, were not reliant on elite members alone for credit. Consequently, freeholder acceptance of elite authority can be explained only by a combination that includes the general acceptance of deference, voter indifference, and the apparent satisfaction both with the goals enunciated by the elite and with the methods employed to fulfill those aims. Overt dependency or elite exploitation of racial fears was not as important as satisfying popular rule and aspirations. When elite and lower-class interests conflicted, the common people were ready to abandon deferential politics. For example, economic depression and controversy over paper money led to considerable popular protest in Boston, discord that continued until the Revolution, and disputes over landholding in New Jersey and New York provoked extensive agrarian unrest and violence.[67] Popular protest was more muted in the south, and after 1700 virtually nonexistent in the West Indies, but could emerge, as it did in the Chesapeake in the 1720s and 1730s over tobacco. Limits to lower-class allegiance to elite authority existed, and most elites learned at least to respect if not to follow the wishes of freeholders.[68]

The most frightening form of popular rebellion, of course, was a slave uprising. Elites were therefore determined to control the movement of slaves and, to a lesser extent, servants and to punish severely unfree challenges to order. In the mainland colonies, they effectively cowed blacks into obedience. The major threats to social order emanated instead from footloose ex-servants and the urban poor. In the West Indies, however, a small number of whites brutally dominated a much larger group of blacks and rebellions occurred with some frequency and with a great deal of violence, especially in Jamaica. Although no slave rebellion in the British Caribbean was successful and abortive uprisings were quelled by horrific displays of institutionalized savagery, leaving blacks terrified and powerless, whites feared for their lives to a degree unknown on the mainland.[69] Undoubtedly, this fear affected politics and ensured that the West Indian relationship to the imperial government would be somewhat different from that in the rest of British America.

Another important difference between island and mainland

relationships to the metropolis was the degree of interaction that local elites had with Britain. The parent culture was a constant magnet for wealthy colonials, and they continually tried to turn their colonies into replicas of Britain abroad and themselves into proper English gentlemen. London fashions were quickly copied in the colonies. Metropolitan standards of behavior were the norm by which provincials judged themselves. Yet, wealthy colonials were ambivalent about their relationship to Britain. On the one hand, they desperately wanted to be accepted in English society as the equal to English gentlemen. If they could afford to, they sent their children to English schools, traveled on occasion to London, imported English goods into their homes, and cultivated English genteel graces. But they remained provincials. Metropolitans derided colonial societies as socially deficient and culturally backward and mocked the unwarranted arrogance of local leaders. As William Penn, an authentic English gentleman, noted of Pennsylvania leaders, if they were forced to come to England their insignificance in English crowds would temper their vanity and, at their return, they would be "much more discreet, and tractable, and fit for government."[70]

Colonials responded to metropolitan disdain in various ways and in ways that changed as the length of settlement increased. One response was essentially defensive, to negate British notions of superiority by claiming, first, that the colonies were indeed cultivated places, and, second, that even if they were not Britain's cultural equals, Americans exhibited moral superiority over the effete and corrupt sophisticates of Augustan England. But these counterattacks were only marginally effective. They implicitly conceded that the colonies at best were cultural provinces, and that only the metropolis offered sufficient scope for men of taste and ambitions.

Increasingly, however, provincials ceased to try and live up to metropolitan standards, and by recognizing that their societies were new societies that were different from European societies, attempted instead to define what their own societies were and who they, as Creoles, represented. By the mid-eighteenth century, some members of American elites had embarked upon a process of self-definition, led by men such as Dr. Alexander Hamilton and Benjamin Franklin who were interested in measuring provincial societies less against the unattainable standards of Britain than against their own colonial experience and against ideal notions of what colonial societies should be. This process of self-definition as a cultured colonial proved to be very successful, at least for Franklin, whose ability to pass himself off as a virtuous Arcadian rustic and a true apostle of the Enlightenment led to him being lionized by fashionable Paris. Although proudly British, American colonists were quickly achieving an identity independent of the mother country. Elites were in the forefront of this movement.

Colonial self-definition occurred most significantly while colonies were becoming increasingly anglicized. But it also occurred when elites on mainland America were less connected to Britain than they had been in the seventeenth century. In the late seventeenth century colonial elites were remarkably intertwined with excellent contacts throughout the colonies and in Britain.[71] The early Quaker merchants of Philadelphia with their extensive transatlantic networks exemplify such elites.[72] Creole elites did not maintain their transatlantic contacts. Consequently, by the mid-eighteenth century colonial elites had only limited entry into metropolitan power structures. At the same time as provincial imitation of English behavior made them more like the English ruling class, they lost their connections to that elite.

The only colonial elites to retain and, indeed, to increase their influence within English society and politics were the West Indian elites. Perhaps not surprisingly, the West Indian colonies did not join with the rest of the colonies in revolution in 1776. Wealthy West Indians were able to enter British society as gentlemen because their great wealth permitted them to live as absentee proprietors. They were even able to purchase parliamentary seats and form a formidable interest group. Absenteeism may have had some baneful effects on West Indian politics by drawing away potential leaders,[73] but it gave West Indians a voice in imperial politics denied to other colonies.

West Indian planters, despite creating societies that Richard Dunn calls "disastrous social failures,"[74] were remarkably successful in achieving that principal aim of English colonists: their reincorporation into British society at a higher level than their emigrant ancestors. Sir Ronald Syme, the distinguished historian of imperial Rome, has asserted as a general proposition that empires survive only when they can integrate into metropolitan society the leaders of their provinces.[75] In the first British Empire, only the West Indian planter elites achieved that integration. Other elites, including the Maryland elite, were left to pursue paths that confined them to their own local societies. For them, the interests of local society loomed larger than the concerns of the imperial government. When it came to choose between them, as Britain found out to its cost, they opted to remain loyal to their own societies.

NOTES

1. For theoretical discussions of elites see T.B. Bottomore, *Elites and Society* (New York: Basic Books, 1964); Raymond Aron, "Social Structure and the Ruling Class," *British Journal of Sociology*, 1 (1950), 1–16, 127–43; W.G. Runciman, "Class, Status and Power?," in J.A. Jackson (ed.), *Social Stratification* (Cambridge: Cambridge University Press, 1968), 25–61; and Reinhard Bendix and Seymour Martin Lipset, *Class, Status and Power: Social Stratification in Comparative Perspective*, 2d. ed. (New York: Free Press, 1966), 210–19.
2. Jack P. Greene, *Pursuits of Happiness: The Social Development of Early Modern British Colonies and the Formation of American Culture* (Chapel Hill: University of North Carolina Press, 1988), 171–206.
3. David W. Jordan, *Foundations of Representative Government in Maryland, 1632–1715* (Cambridge: Cambridge University Press, 1987), 1–7; David B. Quinn, "Introduction: Prelude to Maryland," in David B. Quinn (ed.), *Maryland in a Wider World* (Detroit, MI: Wayne State University, 1982), 11–25. For similar attitudes in other colonies, see T.H. Breen, *Puritans and Adventurers: Change and Persistence in Early America* (New York: Oxford University Press, 1980), 16–24, 69–80, 106–26, 164–96; Darrett B. Rutman, *Winthrop's Boston: Portrait of a Puritan Town, 1630–1690* (Chapel Hill: University of North Carolina Press, 1965); Edmund Morgan, "The First American Boom: Virginia, 1618–1630," *WMQ*, 3d. Ser., XXVIII (1971), 169–98; and Jack P. Greene, "Changing Identity in the British Caribbean: Barbados as a Case Study," in Nicholas Canny and Anthony Pagden (eds.), *Colonial Identity in the Atlantic World* (Princeton, NJ: Princeton University Press, 1987), 228–29.
4. For a contrary view, see David Hackett Fischer, *Albion's Seed: Four British Folkways in America* (New York: Oxford University Press, 1989), 207–25.
5. For the rise of a planter class in the West Indies see Richard S. Dunn, *Sugar and Slaves: The Rise of the Planter Class in the English West Indies, 1624–1713* (Chapel Hill: University of North Carolina Press, 1972). For the Lower South, see Richard Waterhouse, "The Responsible Gentry of Colonial Self-Carolina: A Study in Local Government, 1670–1770," in Bruce C. Daniels (ed.), *Town and County: Essays on the Structure of Local Government in the American Colonies* (Middletown, CT: Wesleyan University Press, 1978).
6. Paul G.E. Clemens, *The Atlantic Economy and Colonial Maryland's Eastern Shore* (Ithaca, NY: Cornell University Press, 1980). See also Richard Pares, *Merchants and Planters*, Economic History Review, Supplement 4 (Cambridge, 1960); and Ian K. Steele, *The English Atlantic, 1675–1740: An Exploration of Communication and Community* (New York: Oxford University Press, 1986).

7. For New England merchants see Bernard Bailyn, *The New England Merchants in the Seventeenth Century* (Cambridge, MA: Harvard University Press, 1955); and Richard Pares, *Yankees and Creoles* (Cambridge, MA: Harvard University Press, 1956). For Philadelphia, see Frederick B. Tolles, *Meeting House and Counting House: The Quaker Merchants of Colonial Philadelphia, 1682–1763* (Chapel Hill: University of North Carolina Press, 1948). See also Gary B. Nash, *The Urban Crucible: Social Change, Political Consciousness, and the Origins of the American Revolution* (Cambridge, MA: Harvard University Press, 1979), 20–23. For New York, see Cathy Matson, *Merchants and Empire: Trading in Colonial New York* (Baltimore: Johns Hopkins University Press, 1998).

8. Russell R. Menard, "From Servants to Slaves: The Transformation of the Chesapeake Labor System," *Southern Studies*, XVI (1977), 355–90; David W. Galenson, "Economic Aspects of the Growth of Slavery in the Seventeenth-century Chesapeake," in Barbara L. Solow (ed.), *Slavery and the Rise of the Atlantic System* (Cambridge: Cambridge University Press, 1991), 265–93; Hilary McD. Beckles and Andrew Downes, "The Economics of Transition to the Black Labor System in Barbados, 1630–1680," *JIH*, XVIII (1987), 225–48; Edmund S. Morgan, *American Slavery—American Freedom: The Ordeal of Colonial Virginia* (New York: W.W. Norton, 1975), 295–315; Peter Wood, *Black Majority: Negroes in South Carolina from 1670 through the Stono Rebellion* (New York: Alfred A. Knopf, 1974); and Dunn, *Sugar and Slaves*, 224–62.

9. Such considerations remained paramount in the British Caribbean throughout the eighteenth century. Andrew O'Shaughnessy, *An Empire Divided: The American Revolution and the British Caribbean* (Philadelphia: University of Pennsylvania, 2000), 4; and Michael Craton, "Reluctant Creoles: The Planter's World in the British West Indies," in Bernard Bailyn and Philip D. Morgan (eds.), *Strangers Within the Realm: Cultural Margins of the First British Empire* (Chapel Hill: University of North Carolina Press, 1991), 348–49.

10. Thomas L. Purvis, *Proprietors, Patronage, and Paper Money* (New Brunswick, NJ: Rutgers University Press, 1986), 95–96. David W. Jordan, "Rise of a Native-Born Elite," in Thad W. Tate and David L. Ammerman (eds.), *The Chesapeake in the Seventeenth Century* (Chapel Hill: University of North Carolina Press, 1979), 243–73; Alan Tully, *William Penn's Legacy: Politics and Social Structure in Provincial Pennsylvania, 1726–1755* (Baltimore: Johns Hopkins University Press, 1977), 77; Robert Zemsky, *Merchants, Farmers, and River Gods: An Essay on Eighteenth Century American Politics* (Boston: Gambit, 1970); and Bailyn, *New England Merchants*, 168–97.

11. Bernard Bailyn, "Politics and Social Structure in Virginia," in James Morton Smith (ed.), *Seventeenth Century America* (Chapel Hill: University of North Carolina Press, 1959), 90–115. See also Bailyn, *New England Merchants*, 195–200; Dunn, *Sugar and Slaves*, 57–59, 79–83; Tolles, *Meeting House and Counting House*, 38–44; and Sung Bok Kim, *Landlord and Tenant in Colonial New York: Manorial Society, 1664–1775* (Chapel Hill: University of North Carolina Press, 1978), 1–86.

12. Helen Hill Miller, *Colonel Parke of Virginia: "The Greatest Hector in the Town"* (Chapel Hill: Algonquin Books, 1989).

13. For the East India Company, see Lucy S. Sutherland, *The East India Company in Eighteenth Century Politics* (Oxford: Oxford University Press, 1952); and P.J. Marshall, *East India Fortunes: The British in Bengal in the*

Eighteenth Century (Oxford: Oxford University Press, 1976). For West Indian influence, see Sir Lewis Namier, *The Structure of Politics at the Accession of George III* (London: Macmillan, 1957); and Lillian M. Penson, *The London West Indian Interest in the Eighteenth Century* (London: Macmillan, 1924).

14. Angus Calder, *Revolutionary Empire: The Rise of the English-Speaking Empires from the Fifteenth Century to the 1780s* (London: Macmillan, 1981), 412–13; and Vincent T. Harlow, *Christopher Codrington, 1668–1710* (Oxford: Oxford University Press, 1928).

15. Trevor Burnard, "'The Countrie Continues Sicklie': White Mortality in Jamaica, 1655–1780," *Social History of Medicine*, 12 (1999), 45–72; and Jack P. Greene, *Imperatives,Behaviors, and Identities: Essays in Early American Cultural History* (Charlottesville: University Press of Virginia, 1992), 31–34.

16. George Metcalf, *Royal Government and Political Conflict in Jamaica, 1729–1783* (London: Macmillan, 1965),152–66; Jack P. Greene, "Liberty, Slavery and the Transformation of British Identity in the Eighteenth-Century West Indies," *Slavery and Abolition*, 21 (2000), 1–31.

17. Thomas M. Doerflinger, *A Vigorous Spirit of Enterprise: Merchants and Economic Development in Revolutionary Philadelphia* (Chapel Hill: University of North Carolina Press, 1986), 344–64.

18. E. Digby Baltzell, *Puritan Boston and Quaker Philadelphia: Two Protestant Ethics and the Spirit of Class Authority and Leadership* (New York: Free Press, 1979).

19. Doerflinger, *Vigorous Spirit of Enterprise*, 363–64.

20. Ibid, 364. For later Maryland development see Edward C. Papenfuse, *In Pursuit of Profit: The Annapolis Merchants in the Era of the American Revolution, 1763–1805* (Baltimore: Johns Hopkins University Press, 1975); Charles G. Steffen, *The Mechanics of Baltimore* (Urbana: University of Illinois Press, 1984); Stuart W. Bruchey, *Robert Oliver, Merchant of Baltimore, 1783–1819* (Baltimore: Johns Hopkins University Press, 1956); and Whitman H. Ridgway, *Community Leadership in Maryland, 1790–1840* (Chapel Hill: University of North Carolina Press, 1979).

21. Barbara Fields, *Slavery and Freedom on the Middle Ground: Maryland during the Nineteenth Century Cycle* (New Haven, CT: Yale University Press), 22. See also T. Stephen Whitman, *The Price of Freedom: Slavery and Manumission in Baltimore and Early Maryland* (Lexington: University Press of Kentucky, 1997).

22. Charles G. Steffen, "Gentry and Bourgeois: Patterns of Merchant Investment in Baltimore County, Maryland, 1658–1776," *JSocH*, XX (1987), 530–48; and idem, "The Rise of the Independent Merchant in the Chesapeake: Baltimore County, 1660–1769," *JAH*, 76 (1989), 7–33.

23. Doerflinger, *Vigorous Spirit of Enterprise*, 139.

24. Gary B. Nash, *The Urban Crucible: Social Change, Political Consciousness, and the Origins of the American Revolution* (Cambridge, MA: Harvard University Press, 1979), 20–23.

25. Greene, *Pursuits of Happiness*, 70.

26. Nash, *Urban Crucible*, 257; Doerflinger, *Vigorous Spirit of Enterprise*, 126–36; Robert J.Gough, "Towards a Theory of Class and Social Conflict: A Social History of Wealthy Philadelphians, 1775 and 1800" (unpublished Ph.D., University of Pennsylvania, 1977), 225–29; and Matson, *Merchants and Empire*, 276.

27. Jessica Kross, "'Patronage Most Ardently Sought': The New York Council,

1665–1775," in Bruce C. Daniels (ed.), *Power and Status: Officeholding in Colonial America* (Middletown, CT: Wesleyan University Press, 1986), 216–17; and Sung Bok Kim, *Landlord and Tenant*, 129–63.

28. Alice Hanson Jones, *American Colonial Wealth: Documents and Methods*, 2d. ed. (New York: Columbia University Press, 1977), Vol. III, 2113–15.

29. Jackson T. Main, "The One Hundred," *WMQ*, 3d. Ser., II (1954), 354–84; Richard Waterhouse, "South Carolina's Colonial Elite: A Study in the Social Structure and Political Culture of a Southern Colony, 1670–1760" (unpublished Ph.D., Johns Hopkins, 1973), 161–63; and Joyce Chaplin, *An Anxious Pursuit: Agricultural Innovation and Modernity in the Lower South, 1730–1815* (Chapel Hill: University of North Carolina Press, 1993), 189.

30. Richard S. Dunn, "The Barbados Census of 1680: Profile of the Richest Colony in English America," *WMQ*, 3d. Ser., XXVI (1969), 3–30; idem, *Sugar and Slaves*, 95–96.

31. Trevor Burnard, "Prodigious Riches: The Wealth of Jamaica before the American Revolution," *EHR*, LIV (2001), 505–23.

32. Edward Long, *History of Jamaica*, 3 Vols. (London, 1774), I, 456–63.

33. See, for example, the large amount of debt held by Jamaican sugar magnate Sir Charles Price, who owed at least £75,000 at his death in 1772. Michael Craton and James Walvin, *A Jamaican Plantation: The History of Worthy Park, 1670–1970* (London: University of Toronto Press, 1970), 156–59. Gedney Clarke, a leading merchant in Barbados, went bankrupt for £100–200,000 sterling in 1774. Richard Sheridan, *Sugar and Slavery: An Economic History of the British West Indies, 1623–1775* (Bridgetown, Barb.: Caribbean University Press, 1974), 464.

34. Philip Jenkins, *The Making of a Ruling Class: The Glamorgan Gentry, 1640–1790* (Cambridge: Cambridge University Press, 1983), 49–50; Lawrence Stone and Jeanne Fawtier Stone, *An Open Elite?: England, 1540–1880* (Oxford: Oxford University Press, 1984), 193–210, 221–28, 266–69; W.A Speck, *Stability and Strife: England, 1714–1760* (Cambridge, MA: Harvard University Press, 1977), 42–43; Nicholas Rogers, "Money, Land, and Lineage: the Big Bourgeoisie in Hanoverian London," *JSocH*, 4 (1979), 438–41; and J.V. Beckett, *The Aristocracy in England, 1660–1914* (Oxford: Oxford University Press, 1986), 288–311.

35. See T.H. Breen, *Tobacco Culture: The Mentality of the Great Tidewater Planters on the Eve of Revolution* (Princeton, NJ: Princeton University Press, 1985).

36. Martin H. Quitt, "Immigrant Origins of the Virginia Gentry: A Study of Cultural Transmission and Innovation," *WMQ*, 3d. Ser., XLV (1988), 643.

37. For an essay that attempts to synthesize these contradictory interpretations of the colonial southern family, see Daniel Blake Smith, "In Search of the Family in the Colonial South," in Winthrop D. Jordan and Sheila L. Skemp (eds.), *Race and Family in the Colonial South* (Jackson: University Press of Mississippi, 1987), 21–36.

38. Philip J. Greven, *Four Generations: Population, Land, and Family in Colonial Andover, Massachusetts* (Ithaca, NY: Cornell University Press, 1970).

39. Stones, *Open Elite?*, 55–65; and Peter Roebuck, *Yorkshire Baronets, 1640–1760: Families, Estates, and Fortunes* (Oxford: Oxford University Press, 1980).

40. The classic description of the Puritan family remains Edmund S. Morgan, *The Puritan Family: Religion and Domestic Relations in Seventeenth Century New England* (New York: Harper and Row, 1966). For social

conditions in the early Chesapeake and the West Indies see idem, *American Slavery—American Freedom*; James Horn, *Adapting to a New World: English Society in the Seventeenth-Century Chesapeake* (Chapel Hill: University of North Carolina Press, 1994); Dunn, *Sugar and Slaves*; and Alison Games, *Migration and the Origins of the English Atlantic World* (Cambridge, MA: Harvard University Press, 1999).

41. Philip J. Greven, *The Protestant Temperament: Patterns of Childrearing, Religious Experience, and the Self in Early America* (New York: Alfred A. Knopf, 1977), 21–150.

42. Bernard Bailyn, "The Beekmans of New York: Trade, Politics, and Families: A Review Article," *WMQ*, 3d. Ser., XIV (1957), 607. But see Holly Brewer, "Entailing Aristocracy in Colonial Virginia: 'Ancient Feudal Restraints' and Revolutionary Reform," *WMQ*, 3d. Ser., LIV (1997), 307–46.

43. C. Ray Keim, "Primogeniture and Entail in Colonial Virginia," *WMQ*, 3d. Ser., XXV (1968), 545–86; Lowell J.Ragatz, *The Fall of the Planter Class in the British Caribbean, 1763–1833* (New York: The Century Co., 1928), 43; Bryan Edwards, *The History ... of the British West Indies*, 5th ed., Vol II (London, 1819), 35; and Edward Long, *History of Jamaica*, 2 Vols. (London, 1776), II, 326–27, 332–33.

44. For similar patterns among middling Pennsylvania farmers, see Stephanie G. Wolf, *Urban Village: Population, Community, and Family Structure in Germantown, Pennsylvania, 1683–1800* (Princeton, NJ: Princeton University Press, 1976), 313–15.

45. Greven, *Four Generations*, 251–22; Richard Bushman, *From Puritan to Yankee: Character and the Social Order in Connecticut, 1690–1765* (Cambridge, MA: Harvard University Press, 1967), 20.

46. Greven, *Protestant Temperament*, 265–331

47. Jan Lewis, *The Pursuit of Happiness: Family and Values in Jefferson's Virginia* (New York, 1983); and Rhys Isaac, *The Transformation of Virginia, 1740–1790* (Chapel Hill: University of North Carolina Press, 1982), 301–05.

48. Bernard Bailyn, *The Ordeal of Thomas Hutchinson* (Cambridge, MA: Harvard University Press, 1974), 28–30, 361–65.

49. David S. Shields, *Civic Tongues and Polite Behavior in British America* (Chapel Hill: University of North Carolina Press, 1997), 327–28.

50. John M. Murrin, "Political Development," in Jack P. Greene and J.R. Pole (eds.), *Colonial British America* (Baltimore: Johns Hopkins University Press, 1984), 417–24.

51. Bailyn, *New England Merchants*; idem, "Politics and Structure in Virginia," 90–115; idem, "The Beekmans of New York," 598–608; and Jordan, "Emergence of a Native Elite," 243–73.

52. Steele, *The English Atlantic*, 229, 277–78.

53. Jack P. Greene, *The Quest for Power: The Lower Houses of Assembly in the Southern Royal Colonies, 1689–1776* (Chapel Hill: University of North Carolina Press, 1963), 11.

54. Steele, *English Atlantic*, 277–78.

55. Jack P. Greene, "Legislative Turnover in British America, 1696 to 1775: A Quantitative Analysis," *WMQ*, 3d. Ser., XXXVIII (1981), 442–63.

56. Thomas L. Purvis, " 'High-Born, Long Recorded Families': Social Origins of New Jersey Assemblymen, 1703–1756," *WMQ*, 3d. Ser., XXXVII (1980), 592–615.

57. Isaac, *Transformation of Virginia*, 34–42, 88–135; Allan Kulikoff, *Tobacco and Slaves: The Development of Southern Cultures in the Chesapeake, 1680–1800* (Chapel Hill: University of North Carolina Press, 1986), 280–300; and Dunn, *Sugar and Slaves*, 98–103.
58. Tully, *William Penn's Legacy*; Dunn, *Sugar and Slaves*, 156–62; and Purvis, *Proprietors, Patronage, and Paper Money*.
59. Patricia U. Bonomi, *A Factious People: Politics and Society in Colonial New York* (New York: Columbia University Press, 1971).
60. A. Roger Ekirch, *"Poor Carolina"; Politics and Society in Colonial North Carolina, 1729–1783* (Chapel Hill: University of North Carolina Press, 1981).
61. Alan Tully, *Forming American Politics: Ideals, Interests, and Institutions in Colonial New York and Pennsylvania* (Baltimore: Johns Hopkins University Press, 1994).
62. Greene, *Quest for Power.*
63. Nash, *Urban Crucible*, 383.
64. Purvis, *Proprietors, Patronage, and Paper Money*, 95–97.
65. Greene, *Imperatives, Behaviors, and Identities*, 225–32. Greene notes that over the course of the eighteenth century the private sphere, rather than the public arena, became increasingly more attractive as a field for successful endeavor.
66. Richard Waterhouse, "Merchants, Planters, and Lawyers: Political Leadership in South Carolina, 1721–1775," in Daniels (ed.), *Power and Status*, 151; and John Gilman Kolp, *Gentlemen and Freeholders: Electoral Politics in Colonial Virginia* (Baltimore: Johns Hopkins University Press, 1988), 36–58.
67. Nash, *Urban Crucible*, 76–88, 129–40; Sung Bok Kim, *Landlord and Tenant*, 281–415; Purvis, "Origins and Patterns of Agrarian Unrest in New Jersey, 1735 to 1754," *WMQ*, 3d. Ser., XXXIX (1982), 600–27; and Countryman, " 'Out of the Bounds of the Law': Northern Land Rioters in the Eighteenth Century," in Alfred F. Young (ed.), *The American Revolution: Explorations in the History of American Radicalism* (DeKalb: Northern Illinois University Press, 1976), 41–49.
68. For alternative political cultures to the elite in Virginia, see Albert H. Tillson, Jr., *Gentry and Common Folk: Political Culture on a Virginia Frontier, 1740–1789* (Lexington: University Press of Kentucky, 1991); Woody Holton, *Forced Founders: Indians, Debtors, Slaves, and the Making of the Revolution in Virginia* (Chapel Hill: University of North Carolina Press, 1999); Michael A. McDonnell, "Popular Mobilization and Political Culture in Revolutionary Virginia: The Failure of the Minutemen and the Revolution from Below," *JAH*, 85 (1998), 946–81.
69. David Barry Gaspar, *Bondmen and Rebels: A Study of Master-Slave Relations in Antigua* (Baltimore: Johns Hopkins University Press, 1985); Michael Craton, *Testing the Chains: Resistance to Slavery in the British West Indies* (Ithaca, NY: Cornell University Press, 1982); Hilary M. Beckles, *Black Rebellion in Barbados: The Struggle Against Slavery, 1627–1838* (Bridgetown, Barbados: Antilles Press, 1984); and O'Shaugnessy, *An Empire Divided*, 34–57.
70. William Wistar Comfort, *William Penn and Our Liberties* (Philadelphia: Penn Mutual Life Insurance Co., 1947), 150–51. For ambivalent relations between metropolis and provinces, see Kenneth Lockridge, "Colonial Self-fashioning: Paradoxes and Pathologies in the Construction of Genteel

Identity in Eighteenth-Century America," in Ronald Hoffman et al. (eds.), *Through a Glass Darkly: Reflections on Personal Identity in Early America* (Chapel Hill: University of North Carolina Press, 1997), 274–339; and Michal J. Rozbicki, "The Curse of Provincialism: Negative Perceptions of Colonial American Gentry," *JSH*, LXIII (1997), 727–52.

71. Emphasized by Bernard Bailyn in *New England Merchants*, 168–97; idem, "Politics and Structure in Virginia," 90–115; and idem, "Beekmans of New York," 598–608.

72. Tolles, *Meeting House and Counting House*, 90–100; and Jacob M. Price, *Overseas Trade and Traders: Essays on Some Commercial, Financial and Political Challenges Facing British Atlantic Merchants, 1660–1775* (Aldershot: Variorum, 1996), Chapters 3 and 4.

73. Richard Sheridan, *The Development of the Plantations to 1750* (Kingston: Caribbean University Press, 1970), 104; and O'Shaugnessy, *An Empire Divided*, 2–4.

74. Dunn, *Sugar and Slaves*, 340. For a counter view, see Greene, "Changing Identity in the British Caribbean."

75. Ronald Syme, *Colonial Elites: Rome, Spain, and the Americas* (London: Oxford University Press, 1958).

The Creation of the Elite Sample of Wealthy Marylanders

This study concerns a sample of 461 men in four Maryland counties who died between 1691 and 1776 (in other words, between the Glorious Revolution and the American Revolution). Each man left inventoried personal estates of at least £650, with pounds held constant at 1700 values.[1] Wealth, rather than birth or the attainment of political office, has been selected as the principal criterion for entry into the elite because wealth was the major, but not the sole, determinant of status in the colonial Chesapeake. Without requisite wealth, it was difficult to establish, let alone maintain, genteel status. The achievement of gentility required expenditure—investment in slaves, on luxury possessions, on imposing brick houses, on education, and on largess to keep social inferiors quiescent. No precise amount of wealth signified that a man was elite, but £650 is close to a minimum sum for the mid-eighteenth century. Somewhat less money may have been required for gentility earlier in the century and considerably less in the seventeenth century, but in both of those periods gentility was far less common among wealthy Marylanders and elite status was more debatable. By mid-century, almost all officeholders possessed at least £650. Just two of the twenty-four legislators from the four counties under study who died before 1776 and who served in the Assembly between 1742 and 1751 and whose wealth at death is known left less than £650 at death. By mid-century, near £650 was required to buy the imported luxury goods that flooded into the Chesapeake from the second quarter of the eighteenth century. Few men managed to acquire that amount of wealth: £650 in nonlanded assets placed a man well within the top 10 percent wealth range of the total population of inventoried white adult males.

No elite sample for this period can answer all methodological objections, in part because it so difficult to determine precisely who was or was not of elite status and in part because the records do not allow clear answers to who deserved membership as elite. The boundary between varying categories of Maryland men was especially porous, especially as elite status was based so much on that elusive concept of gentility.[2] Wealthy Marylanders were not like European aristocrats who could be distinguished from everyone else by their title and by their distinguished lineage. They were not even like the British gentry who could be differentiated from their social inferiors because they owned a house recognized to be a county seat.[3] Wealthy Marylanders in this elite sample were not fundamentally different, except for the fact of having more personal wealth, than men with slightly lesser wealth. Social divisions within colonial Maryland society did exist but these were of a different order to the fuzzy boundaries between the leading men and the not-quite leading men of Maryland. The major divisions were between the landed and the non-landed, slave owners and non-slave owners, male and female, and, especially, between free and nonfree. In several important respects—the ability to participate in political matters, the assumption of independent authority within a household, the right to exercise that authority over dependents—the members of the elite sample defined in this work were the same as the rest of the white adult male propertied population.

Yet within this group of independent male householders, differences of degree distinguished some independent male householders as more obviously elite or more obviously genteel than others. It is difficult to define precisely an elite but by the eighteenth century an elite class of gentlemen was in control of public affairs in the province. I have used wealth as the principal criterion for defining this elite because it seems more satisfying and less tautological than other measures such as attainment of political office. If a sociologically inclined commentator on eighteenth-century Maryland had been moved to describe the "worthies" of the province, he or she would have begun with a discussion of the outward manifestation of these worthies' status—the large gangs of slaves, the fine houses, the genteel possessions—before proceeding to describe and analyze their high positions within provincial politics. Although political involvement could shore up wealth, wealth was essential before political office could be obtained from the late seventeenth century onward. Choosing wealth as the criterion for elite membership also allows a flexibility and range that using the attainment of political office as the chief determinant of elite status does not. Not all wealthy men were in political positions, although most politicians were wealthy. Thus, a sample based on wealth can illustrate the degree to which provincial politicians formed a distinct subset of the wealthy.

Nevertheless, even if wealth was the major determinant of status in colonial Maryland, selecting an elite sample solely on the basis of a single high wealth figure is not entirely satisfactory. First, the figure of £650 as a minimum entry standard is not based on any functional difference between estates worth that much and estates worth slightly less. It is merely an arbitrary figure selected to make the size of the elite group under study analytically manageable and a figure that seems to fit in with contemporary understandings of what constituted appreciable wealth (it is equivalent to approximately £1,000 in Maryland currency in 1770). Several planters, merchants, officeholders, and professionals who had estates smaller than necessary for inclusion in this sample would have been recognized by their contemporaries as being gentlemen of elite status, especially in the late seventeenth and early eighteenth centuries. Alternatively, some elite members, especially among those dying in the last decades before the Revolution, were wealthy but not genteel enough to qualify for elite status. Having £650 in personal effects did not entail an abrupt break in life-style or social status from having just £500 or even £400 in personal effects. I have not attempted (I believe it is impossible) to determine the precise moment when a man was not sufficiently wealthy to be classed as part of the elite. When "the elite" is used in this work, it should not be understood as comprising an actual and distinct class but as being shorthand for the behavior and values held by men of considerable wealth and usually high social status in eighteenth-century Maryland.

Then, why choose the admittedly arbitrary figure of £650 as the minimum qualification for entry into this nebulous and ill-defined elite? The two other obvious measures of elite status are achievement of political office or ownership of a minimum number of slaves. Thus, the Maryland elite could be defined as all men who achieved provincial office during 1691 or 1776 or could be delineated as all men who owned twenty or more slaves. Becoming a provincial legislator or a substantial slaveholder were both measures of achievement that contemporaries would have recognized. Nevertheless, men became large slaveholders or aspiring politicians only if they had acquired suitable levels of wealth. The only common denominator among all the members of the broad category of gentry was that they were wealthy. As the dissenter satirist James Reid of Virginia noted of local gentlemen, "There is no matter whether he can read or not, such a thing has nothing in the composition. He has money, land and Negroes, that's enough. These things procure him every honour, every favour, every title of respect."[4]

In the late seventeenth century the levels of wealth needed to strut upon the public stage were smaller than they were to be 75 years later. If my focus had been on establishing the characteristics of the first generation of ambitious merchant-planters, I would have chosen a lower entry level for the elite. Lois Green Carr, Russell Menard, and Lorena Walsh, scholars involved with projects associated with Historic St. Mary's City, who have done so much to establish working procedures for evaluating Chesapeake wealth, have done just that. In their many works, they have chosen £225 as the lower limit of their upper wealth division. This low upper limit works well in the seventeenth century and in some poorer counties throughout the eighteenth century, when relatively few people had acquired much wealth. In the last half of the seventeenth century, only 13 percent of inventoried estates in St. Mary's were greater than £225. A man with £300 or £400 could properly think of himself as among the wealthier citizens of the county. But by the mid-eighteenth century, £225 was moderate rather than considerable wealth. In St. Mary's County, one-third of all estates inventoried between 1768 and 1777, containing over 80 percent of all wealth, were valued at over £225. The percentage is actually higher than this, as they have excluded from their calculations bonded labor and financial assets. When all assets are included, the average household wealth in St. Mary's in 1774 can be calculated at £317.48.[5] In the four counties studied here, between 1760 and 1776, 31 percent of all estates containing 83 percent of total wealth were valued at over £225. A man leaving £200–300 in the decade immediately preceding the Revolution could no longer consider himself rich. Indeed, he might struggle to support an average household on what was less than the mean estate value of £332.79. Setting the lower limit of elite wealth at £650, on the other hand, separates out the 7–10 percent of wealthiest men dying in the second and third quarters of the eighteenth century, men who could conceivably think of themselves as wealthy.

Another way of determining elite status would be to study the top 5 or 10 percent of inventory holders over time. I have rejected this approach for three reasons. First, I wish to emphasize the extent to which growing wealth over time in Maryland expanded elite ranks and allowed more people to acquire the material trappings of gentility. Second, using a fixed level of wealth for entry into the sample allows us to consider the elite as a provincial elite rather than four separate county elites. Unlike other social strata, wealthy Marylanders operated across county lines and saw themselves as important players in provincial politics and society. One aim of this study is to highlight differences between wealthy men in various parts of the colony. A telling difference was the number of wealthy men who lived in a county. That 202 men from wealthy Anne Arundel died with estates over £650 compared to 61 men from Somerset tells us something important about wealth and power in these two areas. Finally, using a fixed level of wealth allows for direct comparisons to be made about wealth, family behavior, political participation, and Creole identity between men with similar resources.

NOTES

1. All values noted in this book have been deflated to 1700 levels unless specifically noted. Raw values have been deflated using model deflators for the colonial period developed by Russell Menard, Lois Green Carr, et al. for the St. Mary's City Commission. These deflators are based on a consumer price index for the period, taking into account rates of exchange. I

am grateful to Lois Green Carr for the use of these deflators. The index is explained in P.G. Harris, "Inflation and Deflation in Early America, 1634–1860: Patterns of Change in the British-American Economy," *Social Science History*, 20 (1996), 469–505. Female estates over £650 have been excluded, partly because this is a study confined to gentlemen and partly because the majority of such estates were composed of property bequeathed to widows by deceased husbands, most of whom were already included in the elite sample.

2. See Trevor Burnard, "A Tangled Cousinry? Associational Networks of the Maryland Elite, 1691–1776," *JSH*, LXI (1995), 36–37.
3. Lawrence Stone and Jeanne C. Fawtier Stone, *An Open Elite?: England, 1540–1880* (Oxford: Oxford University Press, 1980), 10–16.
4. James Reid, "The Religion of the Bible and Religion of K[ing] W[illiam] County Compared," in Richard Beale Davis (ed.), *The Colonial Virginian Satirist: Mid-Eighteenth-Century Commentaries on Politics, Religion, and Society* (Philadelphia: American Philosophical Society, 1967), 56.
5. For the latest summary of these scholars' work, see Lois Green Carr and Russell R. Menard, "Wealth and Welfare in Early Maryland: Evidence from St. Mary's County," *WMQ*, LVI (1999), 95–120.

INDEX

Accomack County, Virginia, 72
Addison, John, 176
administration accounts, 64–7, 83
affection, 106, 129–31, 247–51
Africans, 37–8, 42
Alexander, James, 240
Allen, Benjamin, 80
American Revolution, 88, 168,
  195, 229, 254
Anderson, James, 222
anglicization, 3, 199, 205–30
Annapolis, 4, 6–7, 29, 42, 47, 71,
  178, 209, 217
Anne Arundel County, 5–6, 45,
  71, 73, 116, 269
Ashman, George, 196
Assembly, Maryland, 160,
  168–79, 185–6, 194, 210, 215,
  265

Bacon, Rev. Thomas, 223
Baltimore, 4, 7, 14–5, 22, 29, 52,
  159, 244
Baltimore County, 6, 45, 66, 71,
  91–2, 95, 116, 188, 196–97
Baltimore Iron Company, 47
Barbados, 43, 246, 254
Beale family, 117
Beale, John, 71, 81
Beckford, Peter I, 240
Beckford, Peter II, 43, 240, 246
Beckford, William II, 242

Belcher, Andrew, 240
Bennett, Henrietta Maria, 146
Bennett, Richard, 81, 142, 146
Berlin, Ira, 37
Beverley, Robert II, 208, 210
Beveridge, Andrew, 64
Black, William, 219–20
Bladen, William, 80
Boothby, Edward, 206
Bordley, John Beale, 72, 132
Bordley, Stephen, 47, 51, 132, 221
Bordley, Thomas, 46–7, 81, 179,
  212
Bordley, William, 51
Boucher, Rev. Jonathan, 216
Breen, T.H., 45, 84, 94
Brooke, John, 172
Brown, Kathleen M., 130, 155
Browne, David, 178
Buchanan, George, 80
Burgess, William, 111
Burle, Widow, 199
Burwell family, 42
Byrd, William I, 209–10, 240
Byrd, William II, 69, 155, 213,
  220, 240–2
Byrd, William III, 65, 225, 227,
  241

Callister, Henry, 223
Calvert, Benedict Leonard, 45,
  144, 176

Calvert, George, first Lord Balti-
more, 238
Calvert County, 209
capitalism, 52–53
Carr, Lois Green, 7, 49, 76, 268
Carroll, Dr. Charles, 65, 130, 177
Carroll, Charles of Annapolis,
47–8, 50, 63, 84, 90, 93–4,
129, 131, 177, 241
Carroll, Charles, Barrister, 65,
130, 222
Carroll, Charles of Carrollton, 84,
129, 131, 162, 222, 242
Carroll, Charles the Settler, 34,
65, 72, 80, 170, 209, 240
Carroll family, 30, 47
Carroll, John Henry, 130
Carter, John, 240
Carter, Landon, 131, 155
Carter, Robert "King," 241
Carter, Robert of Nomini Hall,
224–5
Carter, Robert Wormeley, 227
Cary, Robert & Co., 85
Ceded Islands, 86–7
Chamberlaine family, 116, 118
Chamberlaine, James Lloyd, 121
Chamberlaine, Samuel I, 11, 172,
174, 176–77
Chamberlaine, Samuel II, 121
Chamberlaine, Thomas, 147, 155,
160
Chappell, John, 144
charity, 159
Charles County, 110, 115, 190
Chase, Jeremiah, 188
Chew, Bennet, 72
Chew, Dr. Samuel, 147
Chew family, 117
Chew, John, 25
Chew, Samuel I, 111, 214
Chew, Samuel II, 121
childbirth, 123–5
childlessness, 121–2
china pieces, 214
Clarke, Philip, 198

Clarke, Sir Simon, 246
Clemens, Paul, 22, 39, 116
Coale, Skipworth, 188, 197
cockfighting, 189
Codrington, Christopher I, 240
Codrington, Christopher II, 241
Cole, William, 159
Commissary-General, 65–6
competency, 51–3, 59
Connecticut, 252
consumption, 49–50, 76–7, 86,
88, 207–8, 213–4, 218, 225,
266
convicts, 42, 44
Coode, Col. John, 169–70, 198
Cooke, Ebenezeer, 210–1, 220,
226
Cooke, Thomas, 172
Corbin, Richard, 69
Council, Maryland, 172–7
Courts, John, 172
Cowman, Joseph, 34
Cradock, Rev. Thomas, 223–5
Creagh, Patrick, 82
credit, 46, 61–96, 182
creole consciousness, 205–30,
256–8
Cressy, David, 157
Cromwell, John, 151
Cromwell, Richard, 154
Crowley, John, 159

dancing, 219–20
Daniels, Christine, 42
Darnall, Henry, 114
Davis, Hannah, 145
Davis, Tamerlaine, 145
debt, 61–96, 225
and occupation, 73–4
and small planters, 76
as ideological statements, 83–4,
88, 95–6
networks, 77, 91–6
Virginian, 97–8
deference, 16, 168–9, 181–5,
192–6, 199–200, 255–6

deism, 223–5
De Lancey, James, 245
Delaware, 14
Denton, Vachel, 80, 145
Devonshire, Duke of, 50
Dick, James, 29
Dilling, James, 89
dining, 214, 217, 219–21
diversification, 43–5, 52
Doerflinger, Thomas, 32, 243–4
domesticity, 157, 251
Dorsey, Basil, 81
Dorsey, Caleb I, 26, 117, 151
Dorsey, Edward, 26–7, 40–1, 81
Dorsey, Henry I, 82, 114
Dorsey family, 26, 29, 30
Dorsey, John, 26–7, 29
Dorsey, Joshua, 26
Dorsey, Nicholas, 114
Drew, George, 188, 197
drinking, 189
Dulany, Daniel, Jr., 72, 118, 176,
    222, 242
Dulany, Daniel, Sr., 33, 36, 46–7,
    72, 81, 94, 115, 118, 174,
    176–7, 179, 221
Dulany, Walter of Annapolis, 130
Duvall, Mareen, 12
dynastic aggrandizement, 162–3

Eastern Shore, 52, 168, 194, 244
East India Company, 87
East India nabobs, 51, 241
Edmundson, John, 111
education, 160, 211–2
egalitarianism, 4, 228–9
elections, 192–5, 199, 254–5
elites
    attitude to capitalism, 14, 23,
        223
    authority, 168–9, 182–5,
        196–7, 199–200, 228, 250–6
    creditors, 90
    demography, 103–4, 106, 121,
        122–6, 155, 247–8
    dereliction of duty, 196, 209

disputes with proprietor, 185–6,
    210
entry into elite, 11–2, 249
ethnicity, 12
family, 103–33, 240–2, 247–51
immigrants, 11, 25–6, 28, 32,
    34 173, 239–41
income, 50–1
justification of sample, 265–9
native-born, 5, 10–1, 173–5
politics, 110–1, 167–200, 210,
    216, 251–5, 267–8
reproduction, 29
relationship to England, 205–6,
    210–12, 215, 221–2, 226–7,
    237, 242, 256–8, 266
relationship to poor whites,
    160, 189–96, 223, 254–5
relationship to slavery, 13,
    40–4, 52, 131, 182–3, 192,
    223, 268
religion, 12
rise of, 5, 110, 206–7, 239–40,
    249, 252
wealth, 21–53, 245–7, 265–9
English gentry, 50–1, 108–9,
    113–4, 122, 126, 149, 153, 160,
    162, 206–9, 215, 218, 246–7
Ensor, John, 119
entail, 160–1, 165
entrepreneurship, 22–4, 207, 229,
    242–44, 247
executors, 140–2

family, 103–33, 158
fertility, 124–5
Fields, Barbara, 51, 244
Fitzhugh, William, 209–10
Franklin, Benjamin, 256
fraternity, 229
Frederick County, 7
free blacks, 44
Freeborn, Mary, 198
free labor, 42, 44
Free School, Annapolis, 144
friends, 141–2

Gale, Levin, 72–4, 179–80
Galloway, Joseph, 242
Galloway, Samuel, 82
gambling, 189, 225
Garrett, Amos, 33, 47, 66, 91,
    142–3
Gassaway, Nicholas, 11
Gassaway, Thomas, 156
Geist, Christian, 12
gentility, 14–5, 24, 30, 49, 127,
    158, 181, 206–8, 212, 214,
    217–8, 222, 227–30, 251,
    265–6, 269
Georgia, 243
Gideon, Sampson, 247
Giles, Jacob, 197
Gist, Richard, 95
Goldsborough family, 116, 171
Goldsborough, William, 172
Gordon, Robert, 178
Govane, William, 94, 197–9
Grafton, Mary, 130
Grafton, Richard, 130
grain growing, 6, 44–6, 244
Greenfield, Thomas, 173
Greenfield, Thomas Trueman,
    173, 175
Grenada, 87
Gresham, John, 39, 42
Grundy, Anne, 150
Grundy, Deborah, 150
Grundy, Robert, 150

Hall, Edward, 197
Hall, Col. John, 92, 95–6, 174–5,
    197
Hall, John, 92, 196
Hall, William, 92
Hamilton, Alexander, 127, 220–1,
    228–9, 256
Hamilton, Rev. John, 159
Hammond, Ann, 145
Hammond, John I, 25, 208
Hammond, John II, 116, 121
Hammond, Mordecai, 82
Hammond, Nathan, 119

Hammond, Philip, 145
Hammond, Thomas, 188
Hammond, Thomas John, 121
Hammond, William, 119
Hancock, David, 86
Harford County, 92
Hawkins, Matthew, 119, 150
Hayward family, 118
Heath, James, 71, 73
Hedge, Thomas, 196
heiresses, 126, 149–50, 177, 213
Henderson, James, 193
Henry, Rev. John, 115, 146
Hill, Henry I, 154
Hill family, 117
Hill, Joseph, 143, 198
Hill, Moses, 82
Holland, Francis, 92, 188, 196
Holland, William, 144, 173
Hollyday family, 118
Hollyday, James II, 130, 224
Holtzinger, Barnet, 12, 154
Homewood, Anne, 198–9
honor, 53, 188
Hopkins, Gerard, 34, 115, 144
Hopkins, Samuel, 177
Horn, James, 128
hospitality, 53, 181, 220, 228–9,
    251
Hutchinson, Thomas, 240, 242,
    251

identity, colonial, 205–30
imitation, cultural, 215
Inch, John, 74
independence, 75, 84, 90, 132,
    139, 163–4, 183, 255, 266
indigo, 238
individualism, 229, 249, 259
inequality, 35, 55–6, 183
inheritance, 34, 39, 115, 139–64
    community, 157, 159–60
    daughters, 148–53
    executorship, 140–2, 251
    friends, 158
    kinship, 143–4, 157–9

land, 147–8, 154
marriage, 150–3
partible, 153, 161, 249
sons, 142, 149, 153–7, 161–3, 250
wives, 143–8
interest rates, 91
inventories, 7–10, 265–9
Irving, George, 79
Isaac, Rhys, 125–6, 182, 189

Jacobitism, 197
Jamaica, 14, 41, 43, 45, 50, 108, 190, 243, 246, 253, 255
Janssen, Sir Thomas, 246
Jefferson, Thomas, 62, 89–90
Jenings, Edmund, 174
Jenkins, Col. Francis, 115, 146, 172, 178
Jobson, Thomas, 80
Johns, Kensey, 82
Johnson, Robert, 35
Jones, Hugh, 3
Jones, Richard, 80
Jordan, David, 110
Jordan, John Morton, 82
justices of the peace, 157, 178–81, 186, 196

Keech, James, 172
Kent County, 39, 42, 198
Key, Edmund, 127
King, Nehemiah, 41, 159
King, Robert, 159, 178
kinship, 104, 114, 116–7, 119, 126–9, 157–9, 163, 171–8, 248–50
Klepp, Susan, 124
Kulikoff, Allan, 75, 93–4, 118, 124

Land, Aubrey, 22–3
land prices, 34–5, 55
law, 46, 221
Lee, Corbin, 92
Leeward Islands, 241

Lewis, Jan, 129, 157
Liberality, 225
life expectancy, 104, 106–12, 122, 134–5
Lillingston, Rev. John, 119
Livingston, Robert, 240
Lloyd, Edward I, 111
Lloyd, Edward II, 111, 144, 179
Lloyd, Edward III, 33, 72, 142, 171–2, 176, 179–80
Lloyd, Edward IV, 33, 121, 162
Lloyd family, 116, 129, 146, 171
Lloyd, Henrietta Maria, 178
Lloyd, James I, 81, 150
Lloyd, James II, 154
Lloyd, Philemon, 111, 146, 177
localism, 193, 258
Lockridge, Kenneth, 213
London, 221–2
Long, Jeffrey, 152
Lower South, 238, 242–3
Lux, Darby, 34, 81
luxury, 50, 76, 88, 208, 210, 217, 220–1, 225, 227

Macceney, Jacob, 161
Mackall, Benjamin, Jr., 176
Mackall, John, 175, 178
Macnemara, Thomas, 66, 199, 209
Main, Gloria, 23
Main, Jackson T., 245
maleness, 127, 188
Marks, Bayly, 7
marriage, 104, 106, 112–21, 150–53
    age of first marriage, 113–4, 124
    cousin, 118–9, 136
    elite intermarriage, 115–8, 250
    length, 123
    sibling exchange, 119
    sons delaying, 120–1
Maryland Gazette, 187–8, 194, 217
Matthews, Roger, 197

Maxwell, James, 188
McCulloch, David, 28–30
McCulloch, James, 30
McCurry, Stephanie, 182
Menard, Russell R., 109, 268
merchandizing, 24, 28, 30–3, 47, 52, 209, 243
mercantilism, 85, 238
merchants
  British, 62, 78–89, 94
  merchant-planters, 28, 33
  native-born, 28
  northern, 14, 243
meritocracy, 181
Merryman, Nicholas, 119
Middle Colonies, 108, 238, 245, 253
Middlemore, Dr. Josias, 92, 94–6
militia, 157, 180–1
mimetic impulse, 213–4, 217, 226
Moale, Richard, 82
moderation, 225
moneylending, 47, 63, 74, 90–1
Morgan, Edmund S., 125–6, 182
Morgan, Philip D., 38
Morris, Richard, 44
Morris, Robert, 224
mortality, 104, 106–12, 123, 126, 163, 250

Navigation Acts, 85
New England, 108, 113–4, 121–2, 154–6, 193, 238, 241, 248–50, 252
New Hampshire, 245
New Jersey, 108, 253, 255
New York, 43, 108, 242, 245, 253, 255
Nicholls family, 116, 118
Nicholson family, 117
Nicholson, Gov. Francis, 169–70, 198
Nicholson, William II, 71, 73, 81–2
Norris, Isaac II, 240
North Carolina, 220, 253

Oakes, James, 23
occupational specialization, 49, 243–4
occupational versatility, 24
Ogle, Gov. Samuel, 176
old age, 134
Oldham, Edward, 150, 172
Onion, Stephen, 146
Orrick, John, 188
Owings, Samuel, 197

Paca, Aquilla I, 116, 197
Paca, Aquilla II, 34, 188
Paris, Peace of, 86
Parke, Col. Daniel, 241
paternalism, 191, 229
patriarchy, 103–5, 121, 128–31, 182–83, 190, 247
patronage, 169
Peele, Samuel, 80–1
Peele, William, 82
Pemberton, Isaac, 245
Pemberton, John, 144, 150
Pennsylvania, 14–5, 118, 222, 253
Philadelphia, 6, 29, 32, 242, 244–5, 257
Phillips, James, 116, 188
Planner, William, 143
planters, antebellum, 23–4, 51, 243
planters, small, 16–7, 92–3, 168, 182–4, 191–6
Plater, George, 176–7
Pocock, J.G.A., 169
politics, 47, 168–80
Powell, Samuel, 245
Price, Jacob, 27–8
Prince George's County, 187
primitivism, 220–1
primogeniture, 160–1
propertyless, 183, 187, 191
provincialism, 2–3, 205–30, 256–8
public sphere, expansion of, 157

Quakers, 12–3, 159, 178, 224
Queen Anne's County, 160, 222

racing, 189
Raitt, John, 35, 199
reciprocity, 93
Reid, James, 268
religion, 12, 159, 223–5, 253
remarriage, 104, 112–3, 124
republicanism, 183
respectability, 53, 127, 158, 228, 230
Rhode Island, 252
rice, 89, 238
Richardson, Col. Mark, 196
Richardson, Joseph, 114
Richardson, William, 111, 114
Ridgely, Charles, 151
Ridgely, Charles of Hampton, 30
Ridgely family, 30, 47, 118
Ridgely, John, 151, 155
Rigbie, James, 224–5
Ringrose, Moses, 94
Risteau, John, 197
Robins family, 116
Robins, George, 118, 151
Robins, Stanley, 143
Robins, Thomas, 130
Robins, William, 143
Robotham, George, 144
Rogers, Nicholas, 33, 92
Rolle, Feddeman, 147
Rousby, John, 175–6
Rozbicki, Michal, 227–8
Ruff, Richard, 94
Rutman, Anita, 109–10
Rutman, Darrett B., 110

sailors, 187
St. Anne's Vestry, 144
St. Mary's County, 7, 49, 127, 172, 198, 268–9
Salisbury, Mary, 199
Schumpeter, Joseph, 24
Scottish factors, 76, 86, 92–4
servants, 42, 44, 187–8, 191, 206, 223, 238
Seymour, Gov. John, 198
Shammas, Carole, 154

Sharpe, Gov. Horatio, 46
Sheilds, David, 229
sheriffs, 65, 179
simplicity, 207–11, 220
slavery, 34–8, 151–2, 216
  criminality, 187
  introduction, 5, 36–7, 207, 238
  marginality in Maryland, 43, 45
  population, 38, 40–1
  rates of return, 39, 40, 42
  resistance, 186–91, 255
  size of slaveholdings, 38–9, 43
  violence, 188–9
slave trade, 37, 43, 87, 89
Smith, Daniel Blake, 110, 129
Smith, Philip, 66
Smith, Robert, 127, 150
Smith, Walter, 173
Smithson, Thomas, 144, 173, 198
Snowden, Richard III, 33, 152
sociability, 104, 118–9, 219, 225, 228, 229–30, 251
soil exhaustion, 35
Somerset County, 6, 45, 72, 74, 79, 146, 159, 170, 178, 269
South Carolina, 14, 43, 45, 50, 86–7, 89, 159, 189–90, 245–6, 254
Sprigg, Col. Edward, 114
Steffen, Charles, 28, 34
Stewart, Vincent, 94
Stockett, Thomas, 50
Stokes, George, 82
Stokes, John, 66, 196
Stratton, William, 188
Street, Francis, 95
Stuart & Campbell, 81
sugar, 87, 89, 238, 246
Sydenham & Hodgson, 81
Syme, Sir Ronald, 257–8
Sydnor, Charles, 181

Talbot County, 6, 35, 46, 116, 142, 144, 146, 150, 171–2, 177–9, 198
Talbot, Edward, 151
Talbott, Thomas, 92

Tasker, Benjamin, Sr., 47, 118, 174, 176, 224
Tasker, Frances Ann, 224
taxation, 193
tea ceremony, 214, 220
tenants, 44
Thomas, Philip, 47
Thomas, Sarah, 114
Tilghman, Andrew, 129
Tilghman family, 116, 129, 171
Tilghman, Richard, 129, 174
Tindal, Matthew, 223
tobacco, 4, 44–6, 52, 58, 86, 88, 194, 238
tobacco regulation, 17, 194–5, 225
Todd family, 118
Tolley, Thomas, 198
transatlantic context, 2–3, 14, 23–4, 33, 74, 86–8, 214, 225, 229, 237–58
transport, 46
Trippe, Henry, 172
Tuesday Club, 127, 228–9

Ungle, Robert, 177
urbanization, 46

vestrymen, 157
Vickery, Amanda, 191
violence, 188–9
Virginia, 14, 37, 43, 45, 76, 89, 111, 131, 157, 160, 167, 189, 193, 220, 244–5, 252, 254
Virginia Inspection Act, 194

Waggaman, Henry, 147
Waldo, Samuel, 245
Walsh, Lorena S., 7, 40, 42–3, 49, 76, 110, 268
Ward, Edward "Ned," 210
Washington, George, 84–5
Wayles, John, 62, 76
wealth distribution, 7–10, 50–1
Weber, Max, 24, 52
Welsh, John, 115
Western Shore, 71, 91
West Indies, 6, 14, 51, 86–9, 238, 241–2, 246, 249, 255, 257–8
wheat, 44–5
Whitfield, George, 224
widows, 112, 114–5, 140, 144–8
William, Henry, 197
Willing, Charles, 245
Wills, 66, 139–64, 251
wives, 144–8
women, 13–4, 106, 113, 123–5, 140–2, 191, 206, 219
Woodward, Amos, 143
Woodward family, 117
Woodward, Henry, 143
Worthington family, 117
Worthington, John I, 73, 80
Worthington, John II, 73
Worthington, Thomas, 73
Worthington, William, 73
Wright, Nathaniel, 176

yeomen, 182–3
York County, Virginia, 41, 110